THE SEA GETS BLUER

The Sea Gets Bluer

SOME SMALL BOAT WANDERERS
AND THEIR WRITINGS

PETER HEATON

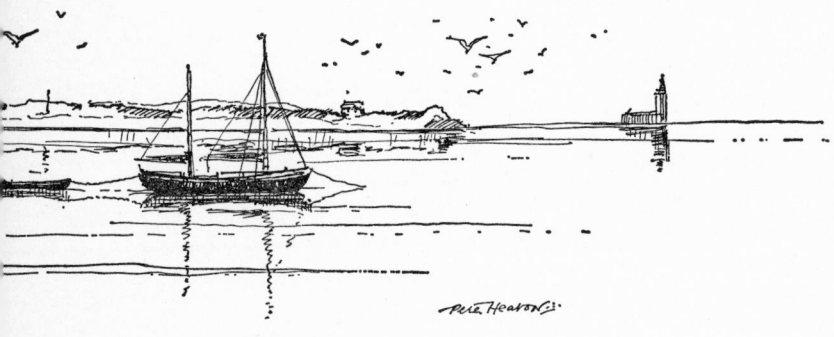

DUELL, SLOAN & PEARCE · NEW YORK

DUELL, SLOAN & PEARCE
AFFILIATE OF
MEREDITH PRESS

TO
MARK

PRINTED IN ENGLAND BY
W. & J. MACKAY & CO LTD, CHATHAM

CONTENTS

ILLUSTRATIONS

Acknowledgements: Sidgwick & Jackson Ltd. for permission to quote from *The Riddle of the Sands* by Erskine Childers; Jonathan Cape Ltd: *The Cruise of the Teddy* by Erling Tambs and *Deep Water and Shoal* by William Robinson; Messrs. Christy & Moore Ltd.: *The Fight of the Firecrest* by Alain Gerbault; A. M. Heath & Co. Ltd.: *Desperate Voyage* by John Caldwell; Oxford University Press and Mr. Eric Hiscock for quotations from the latter's two books *Around the World in Wanderer III* and *Beyond the West Horizon*; Adlard Coles Ltd.: *Trekka Round the World* by John Guzzwell; The Bodley Head Ltd.: *The Venturesome Voyages of Captain Voss*; Meredith Press of New York: *Around the World Single-Handed* by Harry Pidgeon; Mr Frank Carr for permission to quote from his book *A Yachtsman's Log* and Mr Francis Chichester for permission to quote from the latter's book *The Lonely Sea and the Sky*; Messrs. Rupert Hart-Davis Ltd.: *The Falcon on the Baltic* by E. F. Knight and *The Cruise of the Amaryllis* by George Mulhauser; Methuen & Co. Ltd.: *The Wind in the Willows* by Kenneth Grahame; Mrs. George Bambridge for allowing me to quote two verses of *The Long Trail* by her father Mr. Rudyard Kipling; George Philip & Son Ltd. for the World Charts: My thanks are due to the Editor of the *Helmsman* magazine for permission to include certain extracts from articles which have appeared in that magazine; Miss Ann Drummond for typing the manuscript except for 21,000 words which was typed by Miss Rita Wilson to whom I also acknowledge my gratitude, and finally a collective acknowledgement to all who gave advice and encouragement—though last on this list by no means least in the extent to which I stand in their debt.

THE LONG TRAIL

O the mutter overside, when the port-fog holds us tied,
   And the sirens hoot their dread,
When foot by foot we creep o'er the hueless, viewless deep
To the sob of the questing lead!
   It's down by the Lower Hope, dear lass,
   With the Gunfleet Sands in view,
   Till the Mouse swings green on the old trail, our own
      trail, the out trail,
   And the Gull Light lifts on the Long Trail—the trail
      that is always new.

Fly forward, O my heart, from the Foreland to the Start—
   We're steaming all too slow,
And it's twenty thousand mile to our little lazy isle
   Where the trumpet-orchids blow!
     You have heard the call of the off-shore wind
     And the voice of the deep-sea rain;
     You have heard the song—how long?—how long
     Pull out on the trail again!

RUDYARD KIPLING

THE SEA GETS BLUER

"The sea was bluer than any I had seen before." These words, quoted from Harry Pidgeon's book "Around the World Single-handed", express with eloquent simplicity the surprise and delight that everyone who has travelled will recognize. One knows perhaps that in the Mediterranean the sea will be blue, but how very much bluer is the reality not only than that of our imagination but of our memory. There is a dormant wanderbug in all of us. The enormous increase in foreign travel today does not stem from a distaste of one's own country; it exists because more people can afford it.

Yet there are some people for whom the aeroplane, the train and the motor-car, capable as they are of whisking us swiftly to places whose very names are of the magic of wanderlust, are not satisfactory.

The very swiftness of the whisking is to them a disadvantage—so, too, are all the tedious formalities of customs, tickets, queues and the presence of hundreds of other travellers.

These people choose a different way to see the far places of the world; they sail there, in small boats. Sometimes, like E. F. Knight, just as far as the cool fresh Baltic sea; sometimes, like Joshua Slocum or Bill Robinson, right round this boisterous world of ours; sometimes, like Eric and Susan Hiscock, twice round.

These people are not by any means all expert sailors. Harry Pidgeon built his own boat and taught himself navigation by a postal course. Some, like Slocum and Voss, are seamen of long experience. But they all have two things in common: a desire to see as much of the world as they can and see it from the deck of a small boat—and guts. There is no mistake about the latter. Many a projected circumnavigator has turned back in his first real gale at sea.

But there is another attribute which some of these people have, and it is this attribute that provides the inspiration for this book. They can write and tell us what it was like.

This is almost the most wonderful thing about it—we can, in an arm-chair by a winter fire, travel with them, and be whisked, far more quickly than by noisy jet plane, from the cold rainy purlieus of a manufacturing town to sparkling water lapping the white-hot sand of a remote Fijian Island. Moreover, a book does it better than photographs or a film. Anyone who has seen the film of the book knows it is frequently a disappointment. These books let us read between the lines and see and feel something of the exhilaration and triumph as that far-distant landfall is made after weeks at sea. They also let us feel something of the frustrations, setbacks and the disappointments and the fear.

For it is this mixture of good and bad, of frustration and achievement, that gives small-boat voyaging its unique appeal. To arrive in a port no matter how attractive by steamer, is—merely arriving—but to arrive at the same place after a passage in a yacht produces a magical feeling that can turn even a north-east English coaling port into a place of fascination. This mixture of good and bad stands out vividly from the pages of the works discussed in this book.

To start with I have described certain voyages that for one reason or another were not pleasant. This is to give an idea of the hardship involved in such sailing. I then set the scene by a brief description of the wind systems and currents of the world that play so important a part in any long voyage at sea under sail. Then the books themselves; all are true, even, as will be seen, the sea basis for "The Riddle of the Sands". My selection is not comprehensive—there just is not room to include every book of this sort that has been written—neither are all the cruises circumnavigations.

To all those who love the sea and adventure and are not insensible to the lure of distant places this book is dedicated. But especially to the legion of arm-chair sailors who for many a reason can only cruise through the written word.

It is my hope that one of the effects of this book will be to stimulate the reader to go out and buy some, if not all, of the works discussed. I hope I have shown enough to arouse interest not only in the adventures of these men, but in the men themselves and in their writing. But the best result of all would be if but one man were to decide one day that the 8.15 train could leave without him and turn from an arm-chair voyager into a voyager in fact. One has not such a long period of activity on this earth of ours and catching the 8.15 every morning speeds the passing of the days as quickly as anything I know. But even if one cannot sack the boss, and most of us have responsibilities that anchor us to our daily chores, one can still voyage through the wonderful writings of the men in this book.

SOME OF THE HAZARDS
AND AN ACCOUNT OF A SINKING

There are few more violent and awe-inspiring storms at sea than those recounted before a warm winter's fire on shore. By the same token, a yachtsman will plan during the restrictive winter months many a bold cruise which as often as not tends to wilt under the impact of the first gale of the spring equinox.

Of all the winter planners none are more engrossed and full of future prospects than those whose aim is to make a protracted cruise, and especially a circumnavigation. So many hopeful circumnavigators have left the shores of England to the accompaniment of cheering friends and some newspaper publicity, only to end their dreams in some small port not so very many leagues to the west or south-west, that it seemed advisable, before introducing the reader to the romantic water-wanderings of the men in this book, to let in a little light on the dangerous side of such adventures.

Sailormen like Slocum, Voss and others, while holding our interest, nevertheless minimize the dangers of their exploits, because to them there *was* probably no great danger, so experienced were they in the ways of the sea. Anyone who has been caught in very bad weather at sea, however, will read between the lines of their deceptively simple descriptions and will appreciate them so very much more. And so, to give readers without such experience more idea of what it is like when "things go wrong", I have selected some writers who, having "gone through it", were able to write about it, and tell us what it was like.

My first example is a book which recounts a voyage from Panama to Australia —a distance of about 8,500 miles. It is a story by a young man who set off on this voyage who not only did not know the mysteries of navigation but did not even know how to sail. He had only been in a small yacht once before in his life!

Such an undertaking could only be contemplated by someone who was not only young but either desperate or doing it as a publicity stunt. The latter was not the case. The book is well titled—it is called "Desperate Voyage".

The reason for the desperate voyage was the best of all reasons—love. John Caldwell, a young Texan, stuck after the war in 1946 in Panama, wanted so much to get to his bride he had left in Australia a year before that, having tried everything he knew to get a ship, and finding simply that ". . . there wasn't any shipping", just ". . . . bought a small boat".

This book is good entertaining reading for anybody. Caldwell writes simply and engagingly and his attractive personality reveals itself at the outset, but to anyone who has sailed in small boats his departure from Panama is almost unbelievable. He starts with engine, then having lashed the helm goes forward to clear up the tangle of anchor chain on the foredeck. He then falls overboard, holding on to the anchor! He drops the anchor and swims to the surface, to see the yacht, whose name was *Pagan*, about 30 feet away, the engine still running and, with the anchor chain rushing out through the hawse-pipe, about to impale herself on some moored yachts. Caldwell's description of how he swims after his boat is enough to make anyone sweat. He manages to get back on board, not before the yacht has "bumped" her way around several buoys and other yachts, and then with the anchor still dragging, and his engine still running, almost unbelievably, he hoists the sails!

But this is not a man to be trifled with! He manages to get his anchor aboard somehow and heads for the sand bar on the edge of the channel; with sails hoisted, and sheeted, he is, it would seem, safely on his way, when ". . . suddenly . . . *Pagan* eased to a noiseless halt". He had run aground. He is almost resigning himself to the undignified prospect of his "ocean voyager" being high and dry at the start of the passage—in full view of the local Yacht Club, when the wash from a passing steamer lifts *Pagan* clear and she sails free under her engine.

This is the first intimation of the luck that came, time and again, to Caldwell's rescue. It has been said that it is better to be born lucky than to be born clever or rich, but Caldwell was no fool; as each day passed he learnt something new. Nevertheless, his lack of experience in handling a small sailing boat resulted in some hair-raising adventures at the start. But when it comes to describing the most awe-inspiring event of his voyage, then it is indeed fortunate for us that he can write. His description of being in the centre of a hurricane is more than just authentic; it is graphic.

Pagan met the hurricane about 6,500 miles west of Panama, well over halfway to her objective, but before Caldwell had got anywhere near as far as that he had suffered almost every trial that an ocean-going sailor might, in his more pessimistic moments, expect to meet. He was, fortunately for him, extraordinarily quick to learn, and what is more he enjoyed learning. As he himself puts it: "I wondered if I would have begun this trip had I known of the actual uncertainties to be facing me, as I was seeing them now. Yes, I would, I concluded . . . despite the danger, I loved it."

He freely admits his ignorance of navigation, but he could not (or would not) spare the time to attend a navigation school, even for a fortnight's course.

He sailed with a sextant, a watch, a small compass, a lead line, a book called

"The Offshore Navigator" (costing $1.50), various nautical publications, a protractor and a ruler, charts of the island groups likely to be met with on the way and sailing directions and light lists for the waters he was to cross. The cost of his entire navigational equipment was $8.90, and he managed very well with it, teaching himself to plot his position by using the sextant as he went along. He taught himself well. By the time he got to Caroline Atoll, between the Marquesas Group and Samoa, he was able to sight land where he expected it.

The day of the hurricane was a Thursday, the date 5 September 1946. It dawned with a light breeze blowing from the south. By 9 a.m. it was calm and the ship was rolling around in a sultry atmosphere. Soon a swell was observable from the north. This being an unusual direction, Caldwell was at first surprised, then interested, and he looked up sailing directions, charts and weather information. As he considered, so his apprehension grew.

By noon the northerly swell had reached large dimensions, and the little vessel was beginning to be thrown around, and her gear slatted and rattled and creaked. The sky was all the time growing darker. The swells gathered momentum and came more frequently. In the direction of north a noise he describes as a "soughing" could be heard.

Caldwell now took action. Everything that could be lashed he lashed. He cleared his decks and battened down ports and hatches. He rigged lines to lash himself into his bunk if need be. Then he sat on top of *Pagan*'s little cabin . . . "and waited".

He had, of course, strong suspicions that it was a hurricane in the offing to the northward. The time of year, direction and area argued as much. He lamented not having provided himself with a barometer, since without one he could not tell from which precise direction the hurricane might be approaching, or at what rate. However, there was nothing now he could do to avoid it and it was not long in making its appearance.

For those readers who, although they have heard the term used loosely often enough, are not exactly sure what is meant by a hurricane, it may be of interest to define it, without going too deeply into the technicalities of meteorology.

A hurricane is one of several names given to a revolving storm. It is called a revolving storm because the wind revolves round an area of low pressure in the centre of it. Different names are given to revolving storms in different parts of the world. The term hurricane is mainly used in the West Indies and the South Pacific Ocean. In the China Seas the storms are called typhoons, while in the Arabian Sea, Bay of Bengal and Indian Ocean they are known as cyclones. The wind revolves in an anti-clockwise direction in the Northern Hemisphere and clockwise in the Southern. But it does not simply blow round the centre, but towards it in a spiral. The hurricane encountered by Caldwell had thus a clockwise movement.

These storms are not stationary, but move in the tropics as a rule from east to west, then curve towards the nearest pole and afterwards progress from west back to east. This is called the path of the storm, and it is in plotting this path that weather men can be so useful in predicting the probable areas of devastation, so that at least some precautionary measures can be taken.

Sailors and others are further helped by certain laws which govern these storms, but this subject is better suited to Chapter 3 of this book, where we set the stage for our ocean voyagers.

Caldwell, it appears, was aware of at least some of these laws, and he knew enough to know that of all places in a hurricane the worst place to be is in the centre, and this was exactly where he found himself!

He went through a mightily uncomfortable time first, of course, and his description of this is masterly, but although sick, exhausted and battered, he did not feel really scared until he got into the centre. He had fallen asleep from sheer fatigue, having managed to drag himself back on board after being washed over the side; and in that sea! He fell asleep to the sound of shrieking wind and with the yacht pitching and rolling violently. This is his description of what he found on waking:

"I didn't waken because I had slept enough, or because the daylight had caught my eye. Not forty-eight hours of sleep would have been enough. Not a searchlight could have disturbed my profound sleep. I wakened because of *Pagan*'s sudden change in behaviour. Her pitching and rolling became suddenly beyond what I had ever felt before. She inclined to flatness on both beams; and pitched so high that it seemed incredible she didn't jerk her keel off.

"I thought at first my boat must be turning over and over. But I could see the deckhead remain near where the deckhead should be—and I tried to explain to myself what was happening.

"Most perplexing was the absence of the storm's noises. I had passed out with the hurricane shrieking in the rigging. Now, aside from the wash of water in the bilge, a pounding on deck, and an occasional swish of sea, there was little else . . . strange.

"The combination of quiet and violence scared me.

"Unbinding my lashings, I wavered to the hatchway, barely able to keep off the plunging bulkheads. I opened the hatch doors a foot and pushed my eyes above the cabin. I saw a vast circle of foam upshot with rearing cones of water . . . but not a breath of air stirred. There were no rollers or combers as such, only peaks of water shooting up or falling away flatly.

"Instantly I knew I was in the lull of the hurricane; which is to say, the airless central circle around which revolve the cyclonic winds. Pushed into this diabolic arena were thousands of wind-churned seas from countless directions to collide and intercollide.

"I don't know how to explain it, unless I suggest that you visualize yourself on a crag, surrounded by numberless other such, then, at a given signal, they resolve themselves to liquid and each sets upon the others as hunger-crazed beasts.

"As far as I could see, great pyramids of water bolted masthead high from the sea surface. Here and there great cross seas crashed into them, dispersed, reformed, and crashed again. *Pagan* lay to her scuppers beneath a constant deck of water. Her sea anchor was helpless; she danced to all points of the compass, her mast scoring the water on either side. Suddenly she was high and suddenly she was low.

"Nausea assailed me. The sickening surge of the boat, and the unstable watery sight set me to vomiting. I couldn't hold myself up longer.

"I stumbled to the bunk and lashed myself down. I realized that I should get up and pump the bilges; also plug the broken porthole—but I was too dead sick to move. I couldn't even brace myself against the lurch; I just lay there, rolling against my lashings.

"All morning my head spun as the jaunty craft threatened to fall apart. Not once could I sleep, even fitfully. I lay there listening to the noises. I was nervous to distraction as to what could happen to my boat in this constant, violent rough-and-tumble."

*   *   *

Later in this book I shall be discussing a remarkable circumnavigation by a young man called John Guzzwell. He sailed the world in a boat called *Trekka*—the smallest yacht so far to have done so. While he was in the process of doing this he took some time off to make a trip with two friends he had made, a married couple called Smeeton. They had a yacht called *Tzu Hang*. Although the Smeetons had only taken up sailing in 1951 (which was when they bought *Tzu Hang*), they had, by the time that Guzzwell met them (which was in the late summer of 1955), done a lot of sailing, including taking their boat from England to Salt Spring Island near Victoria, B.C., by way of the Panama Canal.

During his voyage Guzzwell laid *Trekka* up temporarily in New Zealand, while he arranged to help his friends the Smeetons sail *Tzu Hang* from Australia (Melbourne) to the Falkland Islands. This was quite an ambitious undertaking, as not only were the Falkland Islands about 6,600 miles away, but it involved sailing round Cape Horn. They duly set sail on 26 December 1956!

The reason for mentioning them here in this context of "danger" is that while on this passage the yacht was struck by a very large following sea while running before the wind and dismasted. This accident has also been described in Miles Smeeton's own book entitled "Once is Enough", and I can warmly recommend it as well as Guzzwell's book. Guzzwell analyses the acident in an appendix to his book and the conclusions he reaches are interesting. He states that he used to believe that a small yacht, if properly designed and handled, could take anything at sea in the way of bad weather, but that his opinions have now altered. He says he does not see how a small yacht—he mentions anything less than 50 feet overall could . . . "avoid being capsized in the extreme conditions it is possible to experience in the wastes of the Southern Ocean".

To get some idea of the enormous destructive force of a big sea, one has only to read the description of what *Tzu Hang* looked like after being hit by that first big sea (she was hit by another, seconds later).

Both masts had been smashed into short lengths and were floating alongside in the water. They looked as if they . . . "had exploded apart". The doghouse had been sheared off clean at the level of the deck. Skylights were smashed and both dinghies were nowhere to be seen! The fact that the Smeetons and Guzzwell were able to save the ship and sail under makeshift rig to the coast of South America is a tribute to their skill and toughness, and both accounts, Guzzwell's and Smeeton's, make exciting reading.

Yes, there are many dangers in ocean voyaging, and the fact that people do seem to sail quite calmly round the world should not blind us to the preparation, the knowledge and the powers of endurance, all of which are necessary if the voyage is to be concluded successfully.

It is in the surmounting of these dangers that a great deal of the excitement and feeling of final achievement lies. This challenge has probably almost as potent an appeal as has the wanderlust aspect—the craving for distant places, not easy of access.

One does not have to sail round Cape Horn to court disaster at sea, however. Mistakes and ignorance can bring tragedy only a few sea miles from one's home port. The following account of the loss of his ship by Frank G. G. Carr, quoted from his fine book "A Yachtsman's Log", is as good a piece of descriptive writing to finish off our "danger" chapter as one could ask for:

"I now come to what was perhaps the saddest event in my sailing career—the shipwreck and total loss of my much-loved *Quickstep II*.

"On the morning of Sunday, August 17th, 1924, my father, my young brother and I sailed from Harwich at crack o' dawn bound for Dover. It was our intention to make for the Scilly Isles by easy stages down Channel, and this day marked our first setting forth on a summer holiday.

"There was a light to moderate nor'-westerly breeze and we left at half-ebb, intending to go out by the Medusa Channel and round the end of the Sunk Sand to the Black Deep, up which we should be helped by the flood. We aimed at crossing the Long Sand about high water by way of the unbuoyed Fisherman's Gat, and so getting off the Foreland at half-ebb, when we should carry a fair tide through to Dover. The glass had been steady, although low, for the past few days. A moderate nor'-westerly breeze would give us a fair wind all the way and although a peculiarly ugly high dawn, with lurid streaks of vivid colour, should have warned us what to expect, and did in fact make my father advise waiting for another day, I was impatient to be off, and we put to sea.

"By the time we had crossed the end of the Sunk Sand, the wind had backed to about west, and with the hot spring tide running up under us, there was quite a nasty popple in the Black Deep. We had to work her to windward, a long leg and a short, and when the wind freshened, we had to heave down a reef. We were now taking a good deal of water aboard, and had to use the pump to free her. After a few strokes, it jammed, and we found a choked suction pipe which we had to take down and clear. We discovered that match-ends and rubbish had been swept into the bilge, possibly when she was away on charter earlier in the season, and these were getting sucked into the pump and sticking in the valves. We tried to rig strainers with dish-cloths, but the matches went endways through everything and after clearing the pump many times we had to abandon it as useless and rely on bailing with a bucket. This was a slow business, for the bucket had to be handed a long way up from the bailing well, and with the violent movement of the ship when the sea got worse, more water was spilt back aboard than went over the side.

"By the time we had got where we believed the Fisherman's Gat to be, we had to heave down our second reef. We then set her at it, and sounding carefully with the lead, we 'felt our way', as I thought through the Gat. From what I remember now of the soundings, I believe we must actually have sailed right over the sand, though I knew no better then. The wind was piping up hard, and there was a really vicious shoal-water turmoil, with every sea steep and breaking. As soon as we deepened the water, we hove-to again and pulled down our third and last reef. The wind had freshened till it was blowing half a gale, and had backed into the sou'west, so that we had a long beat to the shelter of the Kentish shore, with the ebb now running strongly out of the Thames and setting us down upon the Kentish Knock. We must clear that at all costs, so kept punching away on the starboard tack, although the ship was overpowered even with close-reefed canvas. The seas here were really bad, short, ugly, curling and spiteful, and one of them, breaking under the yacht, fell upon the dinghy. Two stout new painters snapped like rotten sail twine, the dinghy did a double somersault and we left her, crushed flat and bottom-up, astern.

"When we thought we were sufficiently far clear to the south'ard of the Knock, we hove-to, for it was obvious that the ship could not stand being driven to windward any more. We soon had so much wind, however, that, even close-reefed as we were, and partially becalmed in the troughs, we were laid almost on our beam-ends on the crest of each breaking sea, and I was afraid that the ballast would shift. We therefore bent our sea anchor, big enough for a consider-, ably larger ship, on to the end of our kedge warp, which we then paid out over the weather bow. This done we stowed sail (the jib flying into ribbons before we could roll it up), and awaited results.

"For a short while, the ship lay comfortably enough, until suddenly a sea, more vicious than the rest, broke on the bluff of the bow and threw her broadside into the trough. There she lay and rolled. She rolled with incredible violence, and I expected the mast to be flung out of her and her framework wrung apart, if she were not actually rolled right over. I believe now that, had we left her there, she would have come to no harm. I believe that Voss is right, and a boat allowed to wallow in the trough will be quite safe, if uncomfortable. But at the time I was convinced that somehow she must be made to face up more to the sea. Hoisting the peak of the mainsail as a riding sail and trying to sweep the stern round with a dinghy oar having proved quite ineffective, I decided to pass the end of the sea anchor warp through the iron traveller on the bowsprit, which I would then haul out to the bowsprit end to get the greater leverage of the spar.

"In trying to do this, I let the end of the warp slip through my hands and overboard! For eleven years I have kept this fact a closely guarded secret! Even my fellow voyagers did not know it had happened thus. I was too ashamed to tell the truth, and in an account I wrote of this adventure in the 'Yachting Monthly' in 1928, I repeated the story that I had told at the time. I said that the warp, not having been protected against chafe, was parted by the iron ring. It was not so, and my father and brother will learn the true facts for the first time when they read of them in this book. I have given myself away because it is such an excellent example of what may happen from neglect of the simple precaution 'always to make fast securely some distance from the end any rope under strain before shifting the end to belay it elsewhere'. I did not realize the sudden pull that every sea put upon the warp, which tautened and slackened alternately. The sudden strain jerked it from my hands, and warp and sea anchor were lost. This loss directly contributed to the loss of the ship, for had it not happened, I believe we would have ridden out the gale where we lay.

"After we had lost the sea anchor, in a desperate effort to get the ship to face up to the sea, we let go the main anchor, hoping its drag would be sufficient to effect our purpose; but it made not the slightest difference, and she continued rolling in the trough in the same alarming way. I now decided that the only thing we could do was to run before it, and hope that in the evening the weather would moderate and that we should get some shelter from a weather shore past Orfordness, which would enable us to get into Yarmouth, the entrance to which port I already knew.

"We had a hard struggle to get our anchor, for having no windlass, we could only gain a few inches when she pitched, seizing a quick turn round the bitts each time to secure what we had won. At last, however, we had the anchor aboard, and under a reefed foresail we ran before the gale, paying out the end of the main sheet astern to steady the ship in running. The drag had a wonderful effect, we ran dryly, with no tendency to broach-to, and the rope divided the seas and made them break astern of the yacht before they reached her, so that the broken water creamed harmlessly away under our counter.

"The sun now shone in a clear sky, and although it was blowing a gale of wind, our spirits rose. I find I can stand any amount of wind if the sun is shining, and I have sea-room. But let the lowering rain clouds scud across a dismal sky, the horizon dark and cheerless bounding a toneless angry sea, with far less wind I feel an inward shiver, and sometimes in the bottom of my heart I have known a nameless fear. Thus it was that in the evening, when the sky was again overcast and darkness would soon have fallen, we came to realize once more that we were not out of danger. I had reached the northern limit of my charts, and of the waters ahead all we knew was that dangerous shoals lay in our way. The weather showed no sign of an improvement, and when the flood made and ran against the wind the sea would at once get worse. According to our dead-reckoning position, the Shipwash Lightship should be five miles N.W. of us, but of her there was no sign. Finally, with the most northerly course we could steer under foresail alone, we should miss the land off Lowestoft by five to ten miles.

"It was then that a tramp steamer appeared astern on a course that brought her near our own. She was obviously bound north from the Channel, having come by the back of the Goodwins. Reluctantly, for it was an admission of failure, I hoisted a signal of distress. One may not mind very much about drowning oneself, but to drown one's father and only brother is a different matter.

"The ship proved to be the *Borgela*, a Norwegian of 2,500 tons, belonging to Fred Olsen's Line, in ballast, and towering high out of the water. She saw our signal, and with engines stopped drove slowly past us to loo'ard. She confirmed our position, which was correct, and agreed to give us the benefit of her lee, and a tow from the end of her bridge in the shelter of her hull, promising to drop us off Yarmouth. I feared a heavy salvage claim, and wanted to fix upon some figure, but the skipper, splendid fellow, would have none of it. 'It will cost you not'ing,' he roared and prepared to take us in tow.

"It semed that our difficulties would soon be over, and so indeed they were, but not in the way that we expected; for it was now that I made the fatal mistake compared with which all other mistakes paled into insignificance. *Borgela* lay motionless to loo'ard and on our port bow. I had only to run on past her, so that she could overtake us on our weather side, throwing a line from her bridge as she steamed slowly by, with which we would haul aboard a warp to secure our bitts. Yet, fool that I was, I ran round her stern and into the shelter of her hull where immediately we lay becalmed. A stout line came instantly hurtling down from aloft; which we as instantly secured. Yet before anything more could be done the end was upon us. *Borgela*, a ballast ship, was drifting broadside through the water at a rate of knots, rolling heavily with no forward way upon her. The suction round her bow and stern drew us at once into her propeller aperture where we lay held like a stock across a sluice, rising and falling some ten feet as every sea broke round her stern. From that moment *Quickstep II* was doomed. In spite of every effort, she could not be drawn ahead, nor could she be dropped astern clear, while *Borgela* could not be moved without her screw cutting us to pieces when it started to revolve. It needed only the first direct blow on the propeller's projecting blade to sink us. We were already making water fast. The time had come to abandon ship if we would save our lives. First my young brother, then my father, after an argument, climbed the Jacob's ladder that had been lowered, and reached safety. My father realized that I wanted to leave the ship last, and knew that the only way to get me out of her quickly was to leave himself, which he did on my promising to follow immediately. I did not do so, for a sea came which threw *Quickstep II* back so that she balanced on *Borgela*'s rudder, and I thought there was still a chance of dropping her astern clear.

"I remember my father shouting, 'Don't be a fool—come up. I'll buy you another ship, I can't buy another son.' A moment later the yacht fell back into the old position, and then suddenly got the first direct blow from the blade of the propeller. With her $3\frac{1}{2}$ tons of iron ballast and her port side sheered in two from the garboard to the deck, *Quickstep II* disappeared like a loaded cane, leaving me clinging to the bottom of the ladder with the North Sea round my legs. As she sank, she bade me farewell, and left a mark I shall carry to my grave. Her topmast shroud, sliding down the rope ladder, caught my thumb as I clung there, tearing it half off so that it hung by the muscle alone. The ladder was hauled up with me clinging to the end of it, and I was dragged over the rail to safety.

"I have never forgotten my father's first words. 'Never mind, son,' he said. 'I'll buy you another ship.' That he kept his word, *Cariad*[1] is the present proof.

"No one could have been kinder to us than our Norwegian hosts, and for Captain Kjoje and his crew, not forgetting his pretty daughter, no praise could be too high. They fed us right royally, and refused to let us pay even the expenses of our passage; the Captain, waving all such suggestions aside with the words. 'Oh, no, I could not. It is the way of the sea—your turn today; my turn perhaps tomorrow!' To the steward's efficient first aid I owe my thumb, for without it amputation would afterwards almost certainly have been necessary. So did our cruise come to an end, and on the Tuesday morning we were landed at North Shields. The wrecked *Quickstep II* lies ten fathoms down five miles south-east of the Shipwash Light, resting her poor wounded side upon the sandy bottom of the North Sea, with nothing but the wheeling gulls above to mark her grave. But some day I mean to sail above the spot where she is lying and cast a wreath upon the waters to show her that her master has not forgotten her.

"I have now only to conclude this long chapter of accidents with a 'Post Mortem' and the first thing I am anxious to emphasize is that *Quickstep II* should never have been lost. The weather was extremely bad at the time, and *Borgela*'s log showed that, in spite of the wind's being aft, she had logged a whole gale half an hour before sighting us. Nevertheless, it was not weather but incompetence that caused the loss of the ship.

"In the first place, we should never have been caught out where we were when the bad weather overtook us. Of the two routes to Dover most generally used, that outside all the sands and eastward of the Knock should only be used by really small craft in settled fine weather and with a fair wind. The route we chose, up the Black Deep and through the Fisherman's Gat, an unbuoyed channel out of sight of land, with no leading marks, was one offering no advantages in point of distance, tides or anything else. It had nothing whatever to commend it. We had a small craft, ill equipped with sails, and with a large open well leading direct into the cabin. We were very inexperienced amateurs, and we should not have hazarded our ship by taking the unprotected route we chose. Smaller craft have sailed round the world, but in the hands of men of infinitely more experience. The experienced yachtsman knows enough to be able to handle his small ship if caught out badly, and for him these warnings do not apply. Small craft, moreover, that make long ocean passages should be properly equipped for them, and should not have a large open cockpit which may be a death-trap in bad weather."

This concludes my list of risks and accidents. I have given these examples to

[1] Frank Carr's Bristol Channel Pilot cutter.

show that one must expect to meet some "stormy ol' weather", as the shanty says, when sea voyaging, and I hope to give an insight into the hazards of the sea that the writers in this book understate with the modesty natural to men of their type.

Enough of disaster! Let us now have a look at the stage on which these dramas are enacted—the ocean itself—and consider how it helps, how it hinders and perhaps get nearer to understanding why it holds such fascination.

3

THE STAGE—
THE WORLD OF WATER

It is fortunate for the sailor that there are, and have been since time immemorial, certain constant systems of winds and ocean currents. It is possible, by using these, to sail wherever you wish to within reason, and the old square-riggers were able to make surprisingly fast passages using this knowledge. Before any sailor-man ventures on the sea, he must understand and know it, its currents, streams and drifts and the winds that blow above it. Without this knowledge he will not only be very seriously handicapped, his enjoyment will also greatly suffer. For this reason I have thought it not out of place to set down here something of the great world of water, before embarking on it, in the chapter that follows, so that we can enjoy that much more the adventures of the writers discussed and also more thoroughly comprehend their difficulties.

The Wind System

Let us consider the remarkable system of winds. Look at the map of the world on page 25. Winds have been classified by meteorologists into five categories; these are as follows: (i) Permanent Winds—like the trade winds; (ii) Prevailing Winds—the westerlies blowing between latitude 35° and 60° both north and south of the Equator; (iii) Variable Winds—like those which blow between the trade winds (i) and the westerlies (ii); (iv) Seasonal Winds—like the monsoons; and (v) Diurnal Winds—the land and sea breezes produced by local conditions.

The permanent and prevailing winds are caused, like any wind, by the natural movement of air from an area of high pressure to one of low pressure. Blow up a balloon, release the air, and it will flow quickly from the high pressure inside the balloon to the relatively low pressure outside. However, although there are permanent areas of high pressure round about latitude 30° north and south, the winds do not blow as might be expected directly from these areas to the Equator or the poles. They do not blow directly north and south, in fact, but at an angle. This is because of the shape and revolving motion of the Earth. In the Northern Hemisphere, winds blowing from mid-Atlantic south towards the Equator are deflected to the west, that is to say they appear to blow from a north-easterly direction and so are called the north-east trades. (Winds are termed by the direction *from* which they blow, *not* by the direction *to* which they are blowing.)

The ocean voyager can, and probably will, experience all of these at one time and another. He will also probably experience areas of calm, where almost no winds blow, like the "doldrums" that lie between the trade winds and the Equator. In these areas of calm the evaporation and resultant humidity is often unbearably high. They were renowned in the old days of the great sailing ships as being places to avoid. But this was not always possible. A sailing vessel making a passage south from England round the Cape of Good Hope would have to sail through the north-east trades and then through the doldrums until she met the south-east trades to rescue her.

The Currents

Look now at the map on page 27. There we see the prevailing currents of the world. These form a pattern of loops which turn with the clock in the Northern Hemisphere and against it in the Southern, and they correspond roughly with the wind system. The first effect of a wind upon water is to make waves. In doing this some of the wind's energy is transferred to the water in the form of a current, but very little in proportion. It follows that currents therefore can be caused by the action of prevailing winds, but because the force causing them is very weak, the effect of the rotating Earth must be taken into consideration, just as in the case of permanent and prevailing winds. In other words a current caused by the wind does not flow in the same direction as that wind but slightly away from it. In point of fact, it flows to the right in the Northern Hemisphere and to the left in the Southern.

But there is also another effect on the sea produced by winds, and this comes from the masses of water moving ahead of them meeting obstacles in the form of contrary currents or land masses. This all helps to complicate the pattern of currents, and, of course, produces many variations within the basic framework. A study of the map will give a good idea of the help which an ocean voyager could, with luck, expect to receive from ocean currents.

The actual rate of these currents is not very much. Over most of the ocean they seldom rise above half a knot. But the more definite and constant currents can rise to 2 knots, while some currents, like the Gulf Stream, can attain a rate of 4 or 5 knots. To get an idea of the advantage of a 4-knot current, picture yourself in a small yacht sailing at 4 knots. If you were sailing for only, say, 6 hours against such a current, you would, to all intents and purposes, not have moved. If you had been sailing with it, you would have progressed a useful 48 miles! Of course, this is much of a generalization, but it serves to show how important it is to make natural forces your friend and not your enemy.

That these great current systems have been used by seamen for hundreds

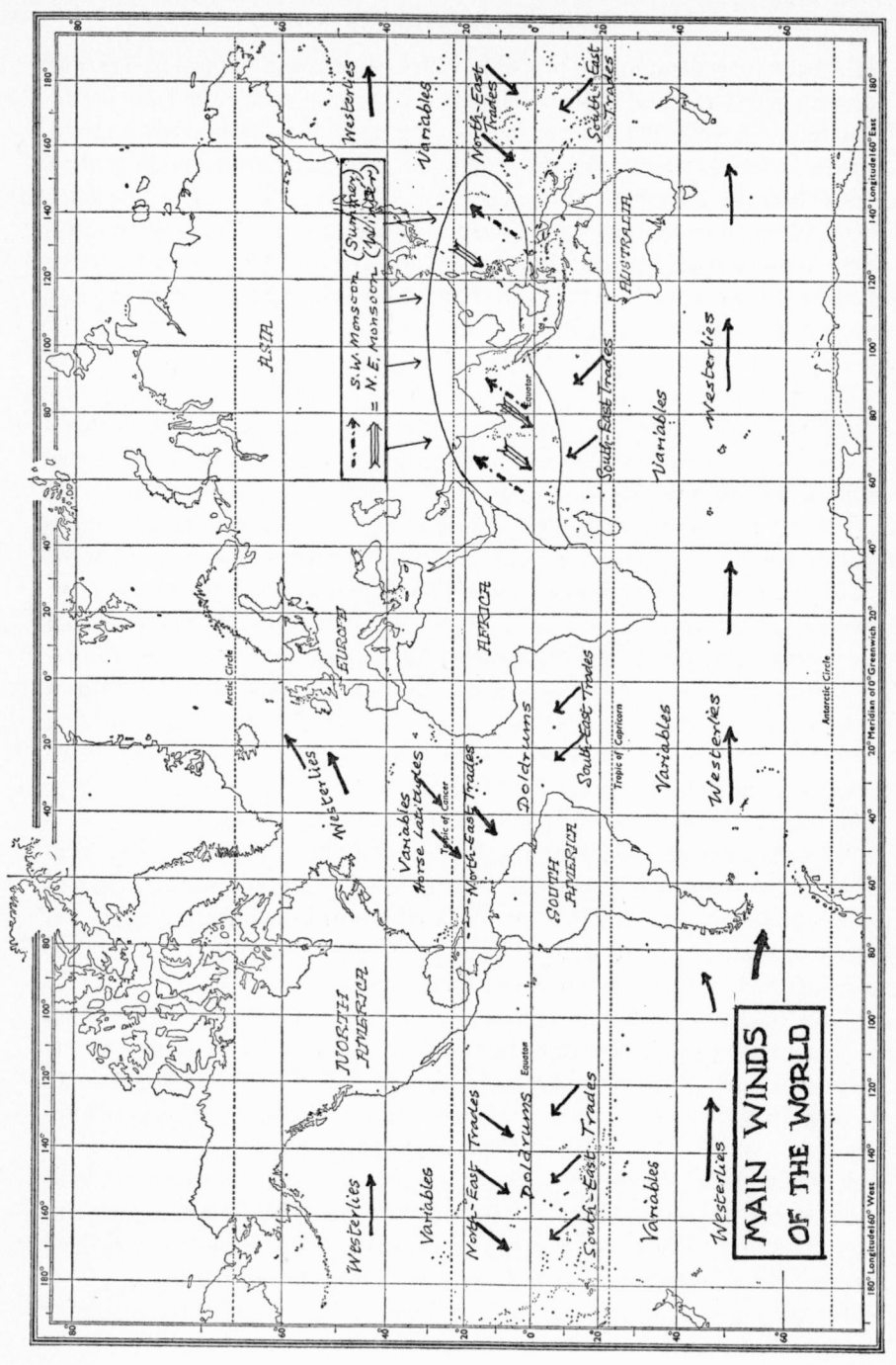

MAIN WINDS
OF THE WORLD

and hundreds of years is indisputable. Thor Heyerdahl and his five companions sailed a wooden raft from the west coast of South America to the Polynesian Islands in 1947. They sailed 4,300 miles in 103 days, thus adding tremendous weight to the fascinating theory that these Pacific Islands were originally populated by prehistoric South Americans! Heyerdahl's book "Kon Tiki" (the name of the raft) was published in 1950 by Messrs George Allen & Unwin, and became deservedly a "best seller".

Where a current has a high rate it will be found to be in deep water. Most currents are not very deep, which is one reason for their slowness of rate. Where you find deep water, like, for example, in certain parts of the Atlantic over which the Gulf Stream flows, the rate in question can be quite high (4–5 knots). Some idea of the collective force of the Gulf Stream may be gauged from the fact that it has been calculated that the volume of water it moves in a given time is by comparison more than a thousand times that of the River Mississippi.

We have, of course, been considering surface currents, because it is these that help the sailor. For the sake of completeness, however, it should be pointed out that there are numerous "deep" currents, The study of the "deep" currents has been made possible relatively recently by the use of scientific instruments, and today oceanographers have a good knowledge of the deep-water circulation of the globe.

Tides

Tides vary greatly from place to place. At the head of the Bay of Fundy, which is between New Brunswick and Nova Scotia, the range of the tide between the lowest low water and the highest high water can be as much as 50 feet, whereas not 100 miles away along the coast the same range is only 2 or 3 feet.

Most people know that it is the Moon, and to a lesser extent the Sun, acting on the water which cause the tides. A tide is, in fact, a vertical undulation of the sea, the rhythm of the motion being connected with the relative position of the Earth, Moon and Sun. This up and down movement is converted into a horizontal movement as the tidal wave is affected by land masses. These horizontal movements are called tidal streams. It is these which play a prominent part in navigation as the ship nears the coast, where they now begin to make themselves felt. Not only must the sailor calculate the rate of the tidal stream in knots, but also its direction, for both will continually be changing, but also the depth of water under his keel, so that he shall not strike outlying shoals or run on sand bars. Apart from these considerations, a knowledge of what the tide is doing can be of invaluable assistance in choosing the best time to round a headland or avoid a race.

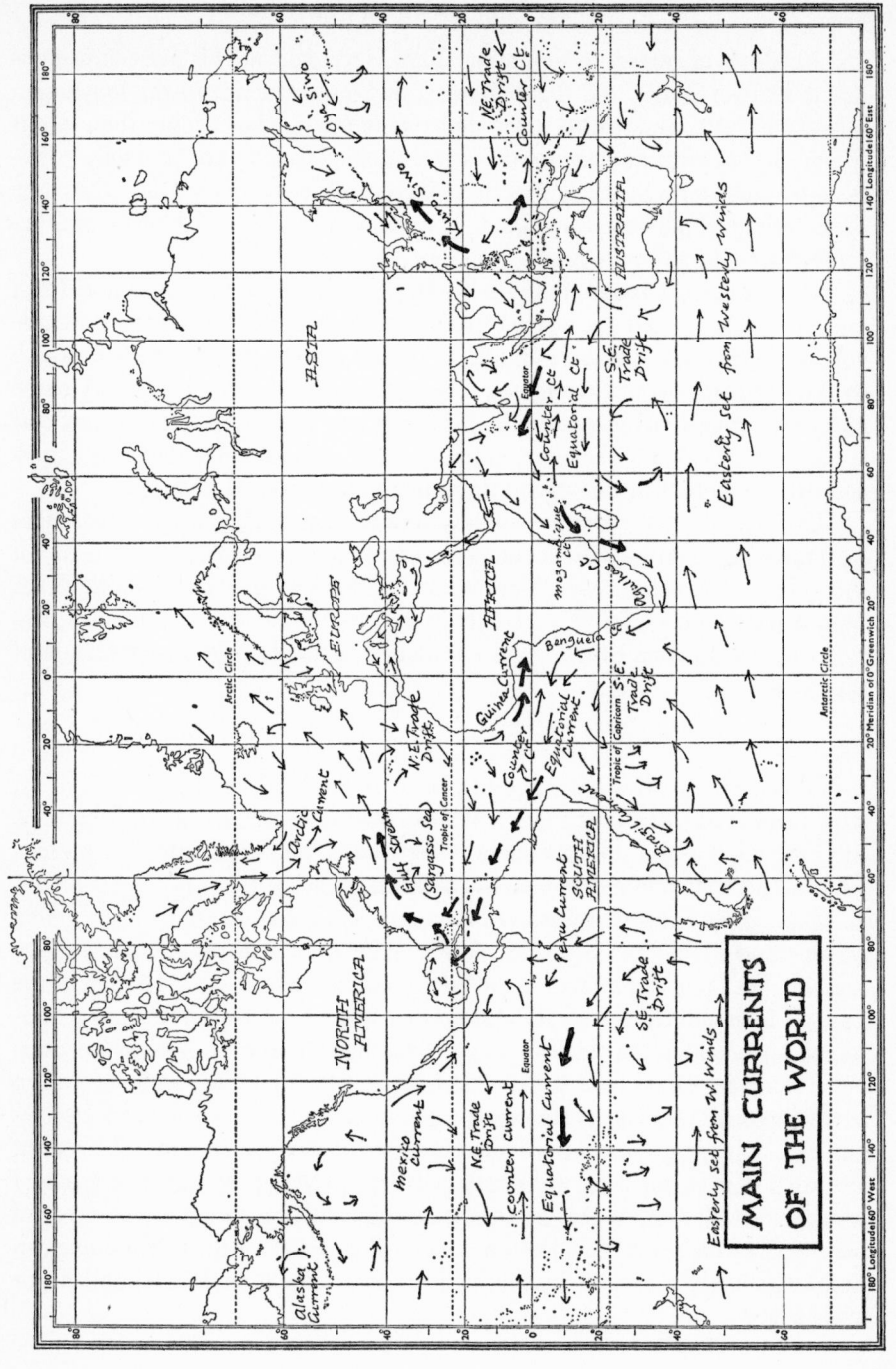

MAIN CURRENTS
OF THE WORLD

The streams, drifts and winds of the world for centuries enabled the old seamen to traverse its waters, and nowadays the sailing yachtsman can make just as good use of this knowledge. The old compass that the sailors of the Mediterranean used had most of its points called after the winds of that sea, and we find the same principle elsewhere. All of which serves to underline how the sailorman's life is dependent on the winds.

The pattern of winds has not changed for thousands of years. In the English Channel, for example, we can be fairly certain that in the early winter, say from October to December, we will get strong westerly winds. Then, through the early spring to about May, we can expect easterly winds. June and July are notable for calms and light variables, while in August we get the south-westerlies that bring the rain and spoil so many peoples' holidays. September by contrast is frequently a fine month with easterly winds attending. So even in the matter of selecting a holiday knowledge of the wind and weather systems can be helpful to those who can choose when they go on holiday. How much more helpful is it in the planning and conduct of a cruise at sea!

Storms

In Chapter 2, I mentioned the tropical revolving storms that the ocean-going sailor will be almost bound to meet at one time or another. Without being too complex, there are certain interesting laws governing the behaviour of these hurricanes, cyclones, typhoons—the name varies with locality—that are relevant to this chapter.

As we saw in Chapter 2, the track along which the storm passes is called its path. The part of the storm area which lies to the right of this path is called the right-hand semicircle and vice versa. From this comes a rule. To a relatively stationary observer the wind will always shift to the right in the right-hand semicircle and to the left in the left-hand semicircle. To continue this—imagine a ship under these storm conditions. If her course, before the wind, will cross the path of an advancing storm she will be in the dangerous semicircle. In the Northern Hemisphere this will always be the right-hand semicircle and vice versa.

Therefore if the sailor thinks he is in the direct path of the storm he should run with the wind on his starboard quarter in the Northern Hemisphere or port quarter in the Southern. Let us assume he is in the Southern Hemisphere. If he is in the left-hand semicircle, he should "heave-to" and endeavour to lie as quietly as possible on the starboard tack, but if in the right-hand semicircle then he should run before the wind on the starboard quarter. In other words, if he is likely to be in the dangerous semicircle, he must "heave-to", which simply means so arrange the sails and helm that the vessel lies as quietly as can be arranged without making any appreciable way through the water.

Now, John Caldwell found himself in the path of what he correctly diagnosed as a hurricane. He had no barometer, but he could observe the increasingly threatening appearance of the sky and the increasing swell. By facing the wind and taking its bearing he would have been able to tell in due course whether it was shifting to the right or left. If it shifted to either side, he could tell which semicircle he was in. If the wind continued to blow from the same direction, he would know he was in the path of the storm, as it turned out he was. When the centre of a tropical revolving storm passes over a vessel the wind, after blowing furiously from one quarter, ceases for a time and then blows equally furiously from the opposite direction. In the windless centre of the storm are to be found the huge confused pyramidal seas, which are particularly dangerous.

Caldwell's description of what it is like to be in a small ship under these conditions is masterly. It is difficult even so to picture quite what it is like to have to tie yourself into your bunk to prevent yourself being killed by being literally flung about the cabin in the nightmare conditions of no wind blowing at all!

These tropical storms are caused by intense heat, which makes the air rise, so forming a partial vacuum into which denser air rushes with a circular movement. When they start they are usually quite small in diameter, but they grow to great sizes of 200 to 300 miles across and move at anything from 8 to 15 miles per hour. They travel in a curve, first westwards and away from the Equator to the pole of the hemisphere in which they start. They follow a curve travelling towards the pole to a point called the vertex or "cod", when they continue to curve back towards the east, where as higher latitudes are reached they eventually dissipate their energy. It is at the vertex of the curve that they are at their most dangerous.

For a wonderful account of a revolving storm, one cannot do better than read the classic description in Joseph Conrad's "Typhoon". But this, magnificent reading as it makes, is described from the point of view of a steamship—Caldwell's description is from the deck of a small yacht. As he himself put it ". . . the hurricane is supreme master; you are its trifle—a cork in a tempest".

Coral Islands

Although coral islands play only a small part in the whole vast itinerary of the circumnavigator, yet there is something fascinating about them that has universal appeal quite out of proportion to the voyage as a whole. They seem to represent the ultimate in escapism. The soft swaying palms, the gently breaking surf, the sighing wind above which may be heard the magical singing of native voices. As you hear in imagination those melancholy harmonies and picture against the sunset the undulating figures of Polynesian girls you can almost smell the scent of the Tiare Tahiti, the flower that once smelt is said always to call you back again across no matter how many countless miles of ocean.

And, again, the Pacific is so vast, it takes a great deal of effort to reach these islands, and their remoteness is surely part of their magic. The fact that runways are even now being built to take the largest jet-liners I will pass over. There are islands *without* runways! And anyway I do not believe you can kill their romance as easily as that. Be that as it may, let us look for a minute at how such islands are formed.

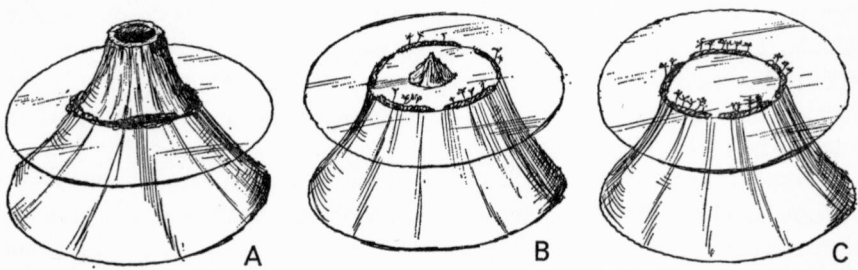

A   B   C

The best way to describe the formation of a coral island is by using drawings. Figure A represents a section of the sea bed upon which volcanic action has thrown up a sea mount, and a volcanic island has been built up so that it projects above the sea-level. The extra weight caused by lava and ash from the erupting volcano solidifying as it runs down the slopes of the volcano eventually becomes so great that it causes the "island" to "sink" into the crust of the Earth (see Figure B). Meanwhile coral has been growing on the fringes of the island, and as the island sinks this builds up, forming a protective barrier reef. We now have the familiar effect of the central volcanic island set in a lagoon, encircled by a coral reef. Coral is a pink-white hard substance which is secreted by a number of types of marine polyps (or low organisms) upon which the latter live and build up, secreting more coral. If the island continues to sink, and sinks faster than the coral builds up, the latter is dragged down into the water and stops growing. In the case of some islands the original volcanic peak has disappeared and only the atoll remains, containing its lagoon (see Figure C). When the mass of the volcanic island is supported by the underwater surface material that has been displaced by its sinking, it stands to reason that it will sink no farther. This may leave the surface just below the sea, or well below it.

Distances

We have spoken of the immensity of the Pacific Ocean in connection with the remoteness of the Polynesian islands, and there are other vast distances to be covered by anyone who would sail round the world. The distance from Balboa, at the southern end of the Panama Canal, to the Marquesas Islands in the South Pacific (it may be useful here to look at any one of the world maps) is just under 4,000 miles. If, say, you started from England, from the Solent, you would have to sail just about 1,800 miles to reach the Canary Isles, and then be just about half-way to the West Indies on the other side of the Atlantic. (This assuming that you took the usual route south and west, using the trade winds.) The distance between the Pacific islands appear misleading. For example, looking at the map, one can appreciate that it is a very long way from Balboa in Panama to the Marquesas, but it is less easy to realize that from the Society Islands, Tahiti, Moorea, or Bora Bora farther west, it is over 1,000 miles to Samoa. Although this is little by comparison with that first great step in the Pacific, yet there must seem an awful lot of mileage to put under the keel before reaching Newfoundland or Australia.

Another long passage is that from the northern tip of Australia, somewhere perhaps like Thursday Island in the Torres Strait, across the Indian Ocean via Christmas Island, the Cocos Islands and Mauritius to South Africa. From Thursday Island to Christmas Island is just over 2,000 miles. From Christmas Island to Mauritius it is about 2,900 miles, and from there to Durban direct it is about 1,700 miles—the total distance being some 6,600 miles of sailing!

Given sufficient wind, the speed of a small yacht depends upon her waterline length. In a small boat of about 25 feet on the load waterline you would expect to average a little over 5 knots, but, of course, the time that it took you to sail from any given port to another would depend on the wind's force and direction.

Bill Robinson, in *Svaap*, made one passage of 1,282 miles in 9 days, an average of over 142 per 24 hours, his fastest passage being 190 miles in 24 hours. He himself says in his book that he often did over 175 miles in 24 hours. *Svaap*'s waterline length was 27 feet 6 inches. One hundred and twenty-five miles in 24 hours means that she was averaging over 7 knots. This is really moving in a small yacht, but Robinson admits that he drove his vessel to her utmost.

On Eric and Susan Hiscock's first circumnavigation in *Wanderer III*, a vessel of 26 feet 4¾ inches on the load waterline, their best day's run was 157 sea miles, so they were not loitering either. It is to some extent a matter of luck with the weather, but most long-distance sailors would probably agree that if you sail far enough and for long enough things will "average out". The average circumnavigation covers 32,000 miles (e.g. Robinson 32,000 miles; the Hiscocks 32,433 miles).

When Rudyard Kipling wrote:

"And it's twenty thousand mile to our little lazy isle
Where the trumpet orchids blow!"

one can only assume that he was envisaging a journey from England (he mentioned "the Foreland" and "the Start") east about round the Cape of Good Hope. In the days of the great sailing ships this was the easiest though longest route, avoiding Cape Horn. It was the route taken by the ill-fated H.M.S. *Bounty*, after battling vainly against the Horn. It was, as most people know, in Tahiti that the crew of the *Bounty* first tasted the delights of the Polynesian islands and the magic that has drawn man across these great tracts of water ever since.

Having considered something of the system of winds, currents and tides of the world and also something of the nature of tropical storms, we have touched on coral islands and finally paused to consider the immense distances involved in ocean cruising. This brief survey completes the oceanic and climatic part of our stage setting, but before letting the reader embark on the first of our circumnavigations I think that it would add to his or her appreciation of what follows if I set down here a brief description of some of the places which our circumnavigators tend, in the order of things, to visit. Not that they do not describe such places: they do, and far better than my pen does, but they give in the main a personal impression of people met and situations dealt with against a certain amount of descriptive background. It is my intention to supplement this with some facts about history, situation, climate, politics—each place will be treated differently and, so as not to prolong this section unduly, sparingly. It will, in the nature of things, contain mainly descriptions of islands, headlands, canals and strategic (from a circumnavigator's point of view) harbours.

I would like to make it clear that the impatient reader can easily skip from here and get aboard the *Spray* with Joshua Slocum in Chapter 4; but I think that he who continues with me in this chapter will find his appreciation of what follows enhanced. I have decided to tackle the problem by postulating an imaginary world voyage, starting from England. It is not comprehensive, nor is it meant to be, but it does contain many of the places that the world navigators in this book have touched at. The various world chart spread throughout the book may be used for reference.

THE BAY OF BISCAY

Let us assume, then, that having started from a port in the south-west of England we have rounded the island of Ushant (or Ouessant) and have entered the waters of the Bay of Biscay. It is our intention to sail across the Bay of

Biscay, sail down the Spanish and Portuguese coasts to the island of Madeira, thence to the Canary Islands, and from there to cross the broad Atlantic, hoping for a landfall at Barbados. Before Madeira, however, a word about the Bay of Biscay. This bay has with most people a bad reputation. People who have never been nearer the sea than a brief summer bathing holiday have heard how "seasick" one can be in "the Bay". If you were to see the fishing boats in the gay colours on the sparkling waters of the Bay in midsummer, you would find the stories hard to believe. But they are not in fact, unfounded. With a westerly gale blowing the picture is very different. The reason is as follows:

The Bay of Biscay is undefended and open to the full sweep of westerly Atlantic gales. The waves may have been building up over hundreds and hundreds of miles. As they approach the Bay they run upon the Continental shelf. This is like a plateau that extends underwater some 50 miles westwards, roughly following the shape of the French coast; although at the southern end it extends very much less. It is remarkably flat this plateau, its depths varying from 50 to 100 fathoms.

As the seas reach the western edge of the shelf they break, and it does not need much imagination to picture the scene. The long barren coastline of Bordeaux is only relieved by the harbours of the Loire and Garonne. In the days of sail a ship caught in the Bay in a westerly gale would often have nothing but rocks and almost certain destruction under her lee.

Even in calm weather there is a slight continuous swell in the Bay. The tidal range is as large as almost anywhere in the world, measuring up to 40 feet. Small wonder, then, with all these factors, that, as will be seen, many a young circumnavigation has had its first real test in "the Bay".

MADEIRA AND THE CANARY ISLANDS

Madeira, our first port of call on this imaginary voyage, can be seen from afar at sea in good visibility, as it is of volcanic origin and has several mountains; the highest point, Pico Ruivo, rises to over 6,000 feet. Many people who can afford it go and stay in Madeira during the winter months, but to most folk it is known for the drink that bears its name. Indeed, today almost the whole of those parts of the island that are not built on is given to viniculture. These vineyards climb the mountains, terrace by terrace, and no piece of cultivatable land is wasted. The island, which measures in length some 30 miles (roughly speaking half as long again as the Isle of Wight), is popularly supposed to have been discovered by Robert Machin, an Englishman, eloping to France with his bride. Their ship was driven ashore on Madeira by a gale, thus setting a persistent fashion for honeymooners. If they were sailing from England to France (as the legend has it), they must have encountered a northerly gale of some violence. Northerly winds of gale force in winter and early spring are often accompanied by severe snowstorms in the western entrance to the English Channel and the Bay of Biscay. No doubt Machin and his bride could not choose their time of sailing and met with just such weather, but wise circumnavigators (like, for example, Eric and Susan Hiscock) choose the more civilized month of July to cross the Bay!

From Madeira we sail now to the group of islands, relatively near by, called the Canaries. If the highest peak in Madeira can be seen from afar, how much more so is the case of Pico de Teide, the high point of Tenerife, which rises to over twice the height of the other mountain. And here we meet with one of our first wonderful surprises. The scenic effects of the Canary Islands are so beautiful, and at the same time so dramatic, that they surpass anything we may have imagined. The contrasts are vivid. On their eastern side the islands are almost desert, while the Atlantic seaboard flowers with subtropical brilliance with gardens and vineyards in profusion.

The islands have a fascinating history. Phoenician, Greek and Roman ships knew them. In the fifteenth century a French expedition, sailing from La Rochelle, invaded and took possession of some of the smaller islands, but it was the Spanish who shortly afterwards annexed Canaria and Palma. In spite of a number of invasion attempts by British, French and Dutch fleets, the Canaries have been in Spanish hands for some five centuries. Las Palmas in Gran Canaria saw the start across the Atlantic of that famous voyage in 1492, when Christopher Columbus sailed his ships westwards to a New World, and what more fitting place for our own departure, trusting in the trade winds to carry us across some 2,660 miles to Barbados, the most easterly islands in the lesser Antilles, in the West Indies.

THE ATLANTIC OCEAN

This huge expanse of water which, on our imaginary cruise, we must now cross is named after the legendary "lost continent" Atlantis. It is shaped roughly like the letter S and covers an area of some 32,000,000 square miles. To east and west it divides the continents of Europe and Africa from the Americas, and to north and south the Arctic from the Antarctic Sea, being limited at these two extremities by the polar pack ice. We have already had a look at the wind and current systems of this great ocean, and how they can be used to the advantage of the mariner.

Although on maps it is convenient to divide the Atlantic Ocean into two halves, a "north" Atlantic and a "south", this is more than *just* a convenience, for the two halves are vastly different in character. The north touches the coasts of the greatest variety of countries in the world, and it contains many islands, ranging from those covered with ice and snow to those in the tropics with lush vegetation and humid climates. The southern Atlantic by contrast has only a few islands in it, and there is far less variety in the character of its coastlines.

The deepest part of the Atlantic lies off the island of Puerto Rico in the West Indies (and is called the Puerto Rico Deep). In it the ocean bed lies 30,249 feet below. The area of the Sargasso Sea, which lies to the north and east of the West Indies, is the largest area of deep water in the Atlantic. The Sargasso Sea (which extends roughly from the West Indies to the Azores) is a calm region in which patches of weed float about. This has given rise to some very far-fetched stories of vessels being gripped in a dense mass of weed from which they could not escape! In reality there are large areas of clear water between the patches of drifting weed. It is not known from where the weed (Sargassum) comes, but the name came from the Portuguese sailors who thought the air-filled bladders of the weed resembled grapes—"Salgazos" in Portuguese. A good many theories have been advanced about it, but there is still much uncertainty. The weeds reproduce themselves by budding. They are strong and vigorous, and in them live all manner of small fish, Octopuses, crabs and sea slugs, many of them curiously resembling the weed upon which they live. It is a strange place the Sargasso; it has a desolate air about it. It is very calm and sweaty hot an uncomfortable, rather sinister part of the ocean, created by the winds and currents. It is a place, really, to avoid, and a study of the charts in this book of the courses of the various circumnavigators and others reveals that they, too, avoided it.

THE SPANISH MAIN

Barbados is so named because the first European settlers, the Portuguese, called it after the local fig trees, which sport beards! The climate is pleasant. There are cooling breezes from the north-east trades and there is less humidity here in the summer months than in other islands of the West Indies—but it must be remembered that we are now in the hurricane danger zone!

Bridgetown is the capital. It is, as one might expect, colourful and busy, but it has an "old world" atmosphere about it that is attractive. On the Atlantic coast is an area known as Scotland, and if one can imagine the Highlands of that country with the addition of tropical flowers, the comparison is apt. Perhaps the chief difference is the presence overhead day after day of a hot, glaring sun.

Before sailing westward to Cristobal and the Panama Canal, many circumnavigators have been tempted to explore further the fascinating islands of the West Indies, so let us take a quick look at some of them.

Who has not heard of Martinique! It was here that the artist Paul Gaugin first tried capturing tropical hues and tones on canvas, before moving on to Tahiti. Martinique is the typical romantic adventure novel island of the Carribbean Islands. It is exotic and colourful. It is the home of Creole women who wear the hibiscus flower in their hair and charm visitors with their beauty. It is also the home of the fer-de-lance, one of the most deadly snakes in the world, said to have been imported by French slave-owners to make the undergrowth too dangerous for the slaves to attempt an escape. Humidity is high in Martinique and it has a very heavy rainfall. It is consequently not a place where most Europeans feel at ease during the hot months. Its history has been violent from the time when it was first discovered by Christopher Columbus. Everything about Martinique is violent. It has had over thirty hurricanes and been swept by more than ten tidal waves in the past quarter-century.

South of Barbados, and off the coast of Venezuela, lies Trinidad, visited by Captain Joshua Slocum on his historic voyage. Another of Columbus's discoveries, Trinidad was a Spanish possession until captured by the English towards the end of the eighteenth century. Like Martinique, Trinidad has had an exotic history. Originally one of the most famous haunts of the pirates of the "Spanish Main", it has now a very mixed population of negroes, Chinese, Spanish, Portuguese, French and English. It is the home of the steel band, and the calypso, and although nowadays modern shops and offices have largely replaced the lovely Spanish architecture of the old buildings, yet there is a wonderful atmosphere of gaiety about the place. On the debit side, and since the trade winds do not blow as far as Trinidad, humidity is high in the summer and the heat at times wellnigh stifling.

Perhaps it may seem a little obvious to include Jamaica in our itinerary, but surely one cannot leave it out while in these waters. In 1494 Columbus discovered this island, but it was not until 1507 that the first Spanish settlers came. The British cast their acquisitive eyes on the island about ninety years later, but on this occasion and also on the occasion of another attack in 1643 they were defeated. It was left to Admiral Sir William Penn and General Robert Venables to secure the island for Oliver Cromwell and England in the year 1655.

To most people Jamaica means a place for a fabulous holiday, a place where they make rum, sing calypsos, and the home of pirates, ranging from the notorious Sir Henry Morgan to contemporary villains setting their wits against Mr James Bond and other similar "agents"; and this, although ridiculously over-simplified, does convey an idea of the place. Jamaica is just under 150 miles in length and just over 50 miles wide. It has mountains, the highest peak of which is the Blue Mountain, touching 7,400 feet. It has arid lands where live only cacti and small leathery shrubs. It has grazing land and farmland, where grows a fantastic variety ranging from sugar cane to bananas, and from rice to breadfruit. It has bauxite, an earthly compound containing alumina, the basis of aluminium, and it has Montego Bay, with its great hotels and sweeping beaches. Like all West Indian islands, it is a place of contrasts, of surf-riding and tidal waves, of calypso songs and hurricanes, of want and of great riches, but of the Arawak Indians, the original inhabitants before the coming of Spanish ships, there are no survivors.

ENTRY TO THE PACIFIC

Having got some idea by now of the West Indian Islands let us head west-south-westwards for Cristobal and the Panama Canal. Although there are many others islands, such as, for example, the delightful French island of Guadeloupe, there is a certain similarity and I do not wish to weary the reader with repetition. Most people are familiar with the epic story of the Panama Canal; of how the great builder of the Suez Canal, M. Ferdinand de Lesseps, presided over an international congress in 1879 to consider the project of cutting a way through from the Atlantic to the Pacific; of how in 1881 work was begun under de Lesseps and of how, because of graft and treacherous dealing, thousands of people who had put their money into the project lost it. The story of how de Lesseps fell from being a hero to an object of hatred has been told many times. Most people are also familiar with the American attempt in 1904, when yellow fever killed so many of those working on the site, and of how this handicap was finally overcome by Colonel Goethals and how the work was completed by 1914. What is perhaps not generally known is that in 1955 Panama signed a new treaty with the U.S.A. under which, amongst other things, the latter agreed to give to the Republic of Panama certain land and railway installations and to build a bridge over the Pacific entrance to the Canal. The Canal Zone is administered by the U.S.A., and it will be seen that in postwar years the latter has extended a "helping hand" in, literally, no "mean" way. Only 40 miles separate the Atlantic end of the Panama Canal from the Pacific. The tide range at the Atlantic end is about 2 feet, while at the Pacific end the range is some 14 feet. There are twelve locks arranged in pairs. At the Atlantic end there are three. There is one at Pedro Miguel, and then at the Pacific at Miraflores come two more. The locks measure 1,000 feet by 110 feet. The third (Atlantic end) lock, that is Gatun lock, leads into the Gatun lake, 85 feet above sea-level. The Canal is being modernized and vast sums are being expended on improvement programmes on what, by any standards, is a remarkable feat of engineering.

On entering the Pacific Ocean we become aware of enormous distances. It is true that one can, so to speak, "break the journey" to the Marquesas and Society Islands by a call at the Galápagos Islands, a mere 1,050 miles or so as compared with the stupefying distance of the 4,000-odd miles to the Marquesas! Circumnavigators have varied. Slocum, of course, went round the Horn. In his day the Canal was not built. Bill Robinson "took in" the Galápagos on his way to Tahiti, and so did the Hiscocks on their second circumnavigation. The first time round they sailed direct from Balboa to the Marquesas, a distance which they logged as 3,972 miles, and which kept them at sea for just under 37 days! Let us consider then this vast, unsuitably named expanse of water, the "Pacific" Ocean.

THE PACIFIC OCEAN

If you measure the width of the Pacific at the Equator, you will find that it is roughly 11,000 miles wide. It is not only the largest of the oceans, it contains the greatest recorded depths, the deepest being the 30,000 feet of what is called the Marianas Trench, which lies, west of the Philippine Islands and north of New Guinea. The 180th degree of longitude runs up through it, as may be seen from any world map. A seaman crossing this finds a difference of 24 hours in time. Sir Francis Drake, in his world circumnavigation in the *Golden Hind* from 1577 to 1580, was the first Englishman to sail across the Pacific, but not the first man to sight it. This was the Spaniard, Vasco Nunez De Balboa, in 1513. Neither was Drake the first to enter the Pacific, this honour belonging to the Portuguese Fernão de Magalhaes, known to us as Magellan. Sailing under Spanish orders, he made south to the Horn and entered the Pacific by the Strait which to this day bears his name, and which has been described so eloquently by Joshua Slocum, who took the same route in the sloop *Spray* in the stormy February of 1896. "The Scene", wrote Slocum, "was . . . real and gloomy; the wind, north-east, and blowing a gale, sent a feather-white spume along the coast; such a sea as would swamp an ill-appointed ship."

THE PACIFIC ISLANDS

Dotted about the Pacific are the hundreds of islands peopled originally by the Micronesians, Melanesians and Polynesians.

The Melanesians are said to have come from New Guinea and spread through the Solomon Islands and other groups to Fiji. The Micronesians, on the other hand, came from Indonesia to the Caroline, Marianas, Gilbert and such groups which lie to the north of the Equator as opposed to the south. The Polynesians peopled the islands east of the 180th degree of latitude in the main, and this fact lends some support to an interesting theory. The Polynesians were the last to migrate, but where they migrated from is not certain. In his book

"The Kon-Tiki Expedition" Thor Heyerdahl describes how he and his companions sailed a balsa-wood raft from Callao in South America to Raroia in the Tuamotu archipelago, in order to prove his theory that the Polynesians had come from South America. It is generally accepted that the Micronesians and the Melanesians came from south-east Asia. While many people hold that the Polynesians came also from that quarter, it may at least be said that Heyerdahl's expedition and written theories have thrown some doubt on this.

In our passage across the Pacific let us take a look at some of the typical islands where the circumnavigators have touched. The first group that we reach after leaving Panama is, as we have already seen, the Galápagos Islands. The Galápagos were first discovered by Bishop Berlanga of Panama in 1535. The name means "Tortoise" Islands, given them because of the giant tortoises which are to be found there. Perfect examples of volcanic islands, the Galàpagos are the home not only of the great tortoises but of the two types of lizard called Iguana, a land breed and a sea breed, as well as many other unusual creatures. Charles Darwin, the naturalist, was enchanted by the Galápagos and is said to have stated there that his famous theory of evolution had its roots in his studies on the islands. It is to this day the existence of all this variety of fauna that gives these islands their principal appeal to a circumnavigating yachtsman, apart from the convenience of a "stop" of any kind *en route* for the Marquesas Islands; for the anchorages are not good, being almost all open to the great ocean. The fact that a good many world wanderers do call in is attested by the famous barrel in Post Office Bay, on the north side of Charles Island, which is covered with the names of yachts. The barrel was originally used by whalers outward-bound. Letters placed in it would be collected by home-bound vessels. It is supposed to work to this day, and mail placed there is said to be collected by any yacht or fishing vessel calling in and bound for the mainland. However, Eric Hiscock placed a missive (and even took the trouble to put it in a plastic bag, with some money to cover postage), but (as one can read in his second great voyage, referred to later in this book) it never arrived. His explanation is that it was eaten, bag, money and all, by ants.

The usual route for a yacht with all those magic names like Moorea, Tahiti, etc., in mind is to sail for the Marquesas Islands. This is a group of eleven islands and they are French-owned, although they were discovered first by the Spanish in 1595. The islands are grouped in two archipelagoes, and they have fascinating names. In the northern groups are Nukuhiva, Hatutu, Eiao, Motuiti, Ua Huka and Ua pou; and in the southern group are Hiva Oa, Fatu Hiva, Fatua Huku, Tahuata and Motane. In spite of these haunting names, however, there is a sadness about the Marquesas, for they are a monument of man's inhumanity to man. These beautiful islands, once truly a paradise upon earth, have been the scene of bloody wars of conquest, and of disease that had reduced the total population of the group to 2,400 in 1941 (although this figure is reported to be increasing). It is unfortunate that William Robinson did not call at any of the islands of the group in *Svaap*, for his fearless comments upon the diseases and alcoholism introduced by white men would have been as stimulating as are his remarks about similar cases in other Polynesian islands. The original colonizers of the Marquesas, who came, it is said, via Samoa, must have thought they had indeed discovered Paradise. They found a fertile, beautiful land where they flourished and prospered and increased until there were more than 150,000 of them . . . until that is, the arrival of the Spaniards. But one can by no means blame the early Spanish adventurers for the fact that this race became almost exterminated; the real harm came from the introduction by Europeans, by no means all of them Spanish, of tuberculosis, smallpox, syphilis and leprosy. The artist Paul Gaugin, who died there in 1903, had reason to curse the French who brought in the latter part of the eighteenth century West Indian negroes to work on the plantations, and in doing so introduced opium into the islands. Of Nukuhiva, Eric Hiscock writes "we thought it a sad, silent and much too empty place". It is said that the population of the Marquesas Islands is now developing rapidly. Modern Medicine has doubtless something to do with this, and a more compassionate and intelligent understanding. Let us hope so. The white race has here much leeway to make up.

It must be emphasized, however, that these islands are by no means the only place where the arrival of the white man has for many reasons, some of them bad, some outside white man's control, had such a disastrous effect upon the indigenous population. It would seem a little unfair perhaps to single out the Marquesas Islands, but they are a bad case, there is no doubt of that, and—they come first on our course.

It is only fair to say, however that Mulhauser on his voyage in *Amaryllis* found much of interest in the Marquesas and was greatly impressed with their beauty. He mentions, too, how pleasant it was to be . . . "anchored for a change after twenty-six days at sea"; and the strategic position of the islands from the point of view of a yachtsman sailing these wide seas can be of considerable help, and one must not forget this.

The British trader, Bob McKetterick, who Mulhauser mentions, as does Hiscock (in fact, who doesn't!), gives a wonderfully warm welcome to yachtsmen who anchor at Nukuhiva. A man who has been at sea the best part of a month and lets go his anchor in such beautiful surroundings is not going to bother his head too much (to begin with, at all events) with the plight of the native inhabitants, particularly if that plight is on the mend. It is only fair to say this and it should be said, even if it only means that we can weigh anchor bound down for Takaroa, through the Tuamotu atolls to Tahiti, with a pleasant taste in our mouth. We must be alert, too, for sailing through low-lying atolls needs a watchful eye!

To sail to Tahiti from the Marquesas involves some delicate navigation, since there is a large group of atolls, some of them very low-lying and difficult to see, spread across the course. The problem has been solved in various ways by different yachtsmen, and it is no part of my intention here to discuss navigation and pilotage.

Most of the circumnavigators become lyrical in praise of Tahiti, but it is noticeable that the more recent ones speak of commercialization of the main island, especially Papeete, the famous waterfront town. With Honolulu, Hawai and Waikiki beach in mind, this is to the true "islomane" a depressing thought, but he can console himself with the knowledge that there are still many outlying islands in all these various groups where native life and freedom of expression and dance and song have not been overcome by the music of the cash register. Some idea of how things have changed in the main islands however, may be gleaned from the greeting given in Samoa to Joshua Slocum, at the turn of the century, as opposed to the welcoming words given, over fifty years later, to Eric Hiscock in "Quinn's" in Papeete, Tahiti:

To Slocum the Samoan girls said: "Talofa lee—"(Love to you, Chief).

To Hiscock a Tahitian girl sang a rude little song that began: "Hello, Capitaine, how are you?" and ended with: "God-damn son-of-a-bitch, what's the matter, you?"

Tahiti was discovered in 1767 by Captain Samuel Wallis, commanding officer of H.M.S. *Dolphin*. Although Captain Wallis annexed the island for the British, this fact seems to have escaped the notice of the French, who sent an expedition to appropriate it for themselves in the following year.

Few people have not heard about or read about or seen a film depicting the visit to Tahiti of the British ship H.M.S. *Bounty*, when she called there in 1788 to collect specimens of the breadfruit plants which were then taken to the West Indies; and of how the crew mutinied. Captain Bligh, who commanded the *Bounty*, is always depicted as a bully who drove his crew to the point where mutiny became inevitable. In fact, historians are of the opinion that Bligh was no severer a disciplinarian than any other captain in His Majesty's Navy at that time. He was a superb seaman and navigator, and the really wondrous thing about the whole episode is his journey, with those of the crew who did not mutiny, in an open boat. His feat in keeping the men under control, on very short rations of food and water and of navigating so well as to make her landfall after many days at sea, is quite remarkable, and he should be given more credit for it. The reason for the mutiny? Who can really say. Possibly the beautiful Vahines in their idyllic Tahitian background proved as strong a lure there as they do today, and this tipped the scale in favour of rebellion.

As those who are familiar with the story will know, Fletcher Christian, the officer who led the mutineers, realizing that a wrathful Admiralty would not be long in sending a search party to bring them to justice, sailed in the *Bounty* in search of another, less-known, island Paradise. This they discovered in Pitcairn Island, and some of their descendants are there to this day. Eleven of the mutineers were unable to tear themselves away from Tahiti, and were found in 1791 by H.M.S. *Pandora*, thus proving the wisdom of Christian's decision. Pitcairn Island being wrongly charted, however, *Pandora* was unable to bring the remaining mutineers to justice.

Tahiti is French to this day. When in the middle of the nineteenth century the native rulers sought the help of the British—the trouble arose over French Roman Catholic missionaries—the British refused to intervene. In 1877, after a long campaign, Tahiti was forced to become a full French possession. This has by no means been to their disadvantage, however. The French are excellent colonists and they permit local culture and customs to flourish and do not seek to influence them.

The fact that Tahiti, or at all events Papeete, has become a commercialized shadow of its former self is no fault of the French Government. Methods of travel have improved, and with them comes the tourist. Now runways permit the landing of the largest jet-liners, which arrive from the four corners of the world to disgorge their goggling, camera-clad passengers. It is nobody's fault—but is it progress?

For all this, Tahiti in some strange way remains a magic word. For the yachtsman it is at the very cross-roads of the Pacific, a meeting-place for small-boat world wanderers of every nationality, a nautical gathering as cosmopolitan as the town of Papeete itself. To the island-lover—the islomane—it is still the Mecca—the ultimate in the search for quiet blue waters seen through leaning palms, beautiful grass-skirted girls, the scent of flowers and always, mingling with the distant roar of surf, the plaintive haunting songs that once heard are always there for he who would listen, like the sigh of the breeze in a sea-shell held to the ear.

Eric and Susan Hiscock recorded much of this lovely music on tape, and sitting in their living-room, I enjoyed the pleasure of listening to it, on a winter's day not so long ago. As the sound of those oh! so sad little songs filled the room we were transported to a magic land, probably far more enchanting than the reality. But was there not also (and if I am guilty of an excess of imagination, I apologize) the pull of the South Pacific, a longing to be running before steady trades again always into warmer, bluer sea?

Having made the long passage from the Galápagos, the ocean wanderer now finds, as he progresses westwards, an embarrassment of islands claiming his attention. The Hiscocks, on their first voyage, sailed from Tahiti via Moorea, "the most beautiful island they know") and the Society Group to Samoa, Tonga and Fiji. The second time round they took in Raratonga, Tonga and Fiji. Bill Robinson pottered about among the islands, calling at Mopelia, Raratonga, Aitulaki, Palmerston Island, Samoa, Tonga, Nukualofa, Suva, Viti Levu, and many many more on his way to New Guinea. It was Robinson's intention to see as many of these wonderful islands as he could, and happy the man who has the time to do so.

For our purposes we need not concern ourselves with every Southern Pacific island, but let us take a look at three—the Samoa, Tonga and Fiji Islands —in that order, as we would, in fact, encounter them if we followed in the wake of Bill Robinson.

Samoa is thought by many to be the original nucleus of Polynesian colonization in the Pacific. From Tahiti and the Society Islands to Samoa is getting on for 2,000 miles, and a glance at the chart will show that we are more than half-way across the Pacific, and are approaching the 180th degree of longitude. The Samoan group consists of three large islands, seven small islands, and a number of smaller islands, which are not inhabited. They are volcanic in origin. Samoa is now part of the U.S.A., but it was a Dutchman, Jacob Roggeveen, who was the first white man to discover it, in 1722. The nineteenth century brought its inevitable crop of missionaries. Although the majority of these were British, and although Britain had certain commercial interests in the group, yet for some reason no effort was made to prevent the group being partitioned between Britain's two rivals in this particular area, namely Germany and the U.S.A.

At the time of the beginning of the First World War the German half, that is the islands of Savaii, Upolu, Apolima and Manono in the western half, was taken over by New Zealand, and after the Second World War this group continued to be administered by that country, under the auspices of the United Nations, until 1962, when on New Year's Day, Western Samoa made history by becoming the first Polynesian sovereign independent state.

The American half, that is to say, Tutuila, Aunuu, Rose Island, Swains Island and the three Manua Islands, was annexed in 1925. There is a Governor, who administers for the United States Department of the Interior, the centre of such administration being Pago Pago, on the island of Tutuila. Of Pago Pago, Eric Hiscock writes: "Mountain-girt Pago Pago is one of the best harbours in the South Pacific islands for large ships. It is landlocked and almost free from shoals, but for small boats it has the disadvantage of being very deep." An interesting observation also by Hiscock is that the native Samoan house, or fale, is a much more elaborate and skilful piece of building than its equivalent in the islands farther east. Hiscock was also impressed by the looks of the Samoan man but adds that the women were "more portly and less graceful than the Tahitian women . . ."

Bill Robinson has much to say in his forthright and entertaining way about American Samoa. "It was", he writes, "a tremendous change to drop suddenly from the indolence and leisure of the islands into a model of American efficiency with officials for ever consulting, reports being produced and read by the score, messengers dashing about as if their lives depended upon it, and typewriters and calculating machines rattling away frantically." He continues his tirade against "TIME" and "DETAIL". Robinson, perhaps of all the circumnavigators, is the most fervent advocate for the preservation of local culture and the damming of the flood of development for tourism and speculative financial gain. A reactionary, perhaps, fighting a losing battle, but at least he is a good fighter.

John Guzzwell, in little *Trekka*, called at Samoa. He also comments on the native houses, writing that they ". . . were set on a level stone platform, and the walls were plaited matting which could be raised or lowered according to the weather. They were ideal homes for the climate." Guzzwell also mentions the grave of Robert Louis Stevenson on the top of the mount overlooking Apia, and from Joshua Slocum onwards circumnavigators have usually paid homage in one way or another to the great author who lived here in his house, Vailima, for many years. Slocum was lucky enough to meet Mrs Stevenson, who gave him a book that had been a favourite possession of her husband's.

From Samoa we sail now to Tonga, which consists of over 100 islands covering nearly 200 miles. They are mostly low-lying and surrounded by formidable coral reefs, although certain high volcanic islands at the western end of the chain made good landmarks. The Tongans are Polynesian and are ruled over by Queen Salote Tupou. The group is also known as the Friendly Islands, a name given to them by Captain Cook. The islanders do not have the physical attractions of the Tahitians or Samoans, being somewhat stout in appearance.

East of the Tonga group of islands runs a rift in the ocean bed in which are some of the deepest places in any ocean in the world. It is known as the Tonga-Kermadec Trench and runs east of the Tonga and Kermadec Islands almost due north and finishes south of Samoa. It is 1,500 miles in length and depths of more than 35,000 feet have been recorded there.

In the Fijian Islands the third of our group of three, and a British Crown Colony, we have arrived at the most easterly home of the Melanesians, a different type altogether from the Polynesians. There is no complete transition, however, and, as would be expected, the islands contain an interesting mixture of the two cultures. Nevertheless, yachtsmen sailing across the international date-line into Melanesia *are* aware of a difference. The change in the appearance of the people is marked. The Polynesians are brown-skinned and have straight hair. The Melanesians have blacker faces, and their hair is fuzzy and mop-like. Their faces, too, are more negroid, with thicker lips and flatter noses. However, paradoxically enough, the population of Fiji today is predominantly Indian, stemming from the Indian immigration of 1879. There is also, as is commonly found in the South Pacific, a small Chinese population. The Fijians and the Hindus do not mix. There is no intermarriage; indeed there is little friendship between the two. One notices, too, that the vegetation and fauna have changed. On the larger islands one finds jungle, loud with the buzz of insects. There may be elephantiasis, tuberculosis, syphilis and leprosy in the Polynesian islands, but here there is malaria.

Fiji is a beautiful place with a striking variety of landscape. It has the golden sandy beaches, blue lagoons and surf-crowned reefs to which we have by now grown accustomed, but it also has great forests climbing the hillsides. In the dry zone the hills are arid as any desert, while in the forest areas the rainfall is torrential.

Life in the Fijian Islands presents contrasts to match the landscape. There is mining for gold, sugar refining, and large European plantations which produce copra and coconut oil. There are the Indian bazaars, with the noise and bustle one expects in such places, while inland is to be found the remains of the old way of life, the idyllic existence so beloved of Robinson.

Fiji was discovered by Tasman in 1643, but it did not come under British rule until 1874. Like most of the South Pacific islands, the inhabitants were cannibals. The islands are composed of volcanic rock and coral limestone. There are two large islands, Viti Levu (the largest) and Vanua Levu, and there are numerous small islands, about 300 of them, about 100 of which are uninhabited. On Viti Levu is the harbour of Suva.

From Fiji the circumnavigator is faced with a problem. It is usually one of time. Shall he visit New Zealand and Australia, or one or the other? The Hiscocks visited New Zealand on both circumnavigations and found it greatly rewarding. The first time round they visited Australia, too, but not the second.

Bill Robinson visited neither in his circumnavigation in *Svaap*, preferring to sail north of New Guinea via the Solomon Islands. Much has been written about the main harbours of those two great countries of Australia and New Zealand. For the purposes of our imaginary sail, let us continue through the groups of islands known as the New Hebrides and Solomon Islands to the island of New Guinea (one of the largest islands in the world), and so through the Torres Strait to Christmas Island and the crossing of the Indian Ocean.

THE NEW HEBRIDES AND NEW GUINEA

The New Hebrides, which were thoroughly explored by Bill Robinson in *Svaap*, are a group of volcanic and coral islands running virtually from Fiji to the Solomon Islands. These islands are Melanesian in population, with a small mingling of Polynesians and an even smaller number of Pygmies. This is another part of the South Pacific (like the Marquesas) where the white man has much to answer for. Although it must be conceded that the inhabitants of these islands were cannibals, yet there seems little evidence to justify the violence of the way in which their homes were ransacked and their crops destroyed. Whole villages were massacred. In the wake of the early sandalwood traders came those who traded in the natives themselves, capturing them and selling them to sugar-plantation owners. It can be argued that the early traders were naturally unwilling to take chances with an obviously hostile native population, and there is little doubt that each excess of violence produced a greater retaliation on both sides.

The native population of the New Hebrides, which was over 1,000,000 strong at the advent of the first traders, now numbers just over 50,000. This was, of course, grist to Robinson's mill, and the same picture was repeated in the Solomon Islands, and, as we shall see, in New Guinea. It was a Spaniard who originally discovered the islands in 1606. They are now an Anglo-French Condominium.

I have touched on this subject before, but I make no apologies for these remarks, since every circumnavigator who has sailed this way has written in similar terms. The yachtsman, travelling slowly and modestly, sees much of the game, and his opinion is worth attention. A single-hander or a man who sails with a small crew over great distances learns to rely on his opinions and not to make hasty judgements, and when he is as lucid as many of these people were and are, his arguments carry much conviction.

The Solomon Islands are also volcanic, and consist of a string of islands some 900 miles in length, running from the New Hebrides in a north-westerly direction. The inhabitants are for the most part Melanesian, with some Polynesians, a small number of Indians and Chinese and about 1,000 whites. Like other Pacific islanders they were cannibals and head-hunters, and in spite of the work of missionaries and others these 'unsavoury' practices exist in some parts to this day.

The first to discover Santa Isabel, one of the islands of the group of islands, Alvado de Mendaña, who sailed from Peru in 1567, and another island, Ontong Java, was discovered by Tasman, but almost a century later. The main chain of islands was not discovered until 1767 by Captain Carteret. The way was then open for traders and others to come to the islands. The selling of slaves for labour on the Fijian and North Australian sugar plantations was here, as in the New Hebrides, an unattractive feature of the early white occupation. In 1893 the South Islands became a British Protectorate. The Solomon Islands, particularly the Island of Guadalcanal, were the scene of heavy fighting in the Second World War. The Japanese occupied the group in 1942 and the counter-offensive by the Allied powers which followed (after many months of preparation) saw some of the bitterest fighting of the Pacific war.

The Solomon Islands are not the sort of place a visiting yachtsman would wish to linger in. The climate is hot and damp. Humidity is high, and the great tropical forests on the larger islands in the group testify to the high annual rainfall. It would seem to be a case of "if the head-hunters don't get you, the fever will".

New Guinea is about 1,500 miles in length. It boasts the highest island peak in the world in Mount Carstenz (16,400 feet). It is a hot, humid land, New Guinea, in the lowlands, but on the peaks there is always snow. It is a land of violent contrasts, and it bred a violent people whose ferocity was such that the early settlers, the missionaries, the slave traders and others by-passed it for slightly more tractable populations. As a result up to the 1914–18 War, New Guinea was an unknown country, and if it had missed some of the blessings of civilization it was fairly free from the diseases that followed in the white man's train in the Pacific islands. However, some missionaries did find their way to New Guinea, and it is about the New Guinea missionaries that Bill Robinson is at his most outspoken. Writing in 1930, he says: "The wealth and influence of the missions here amazed me." His remarks are not flattering. He mentions some names—the "Mission of the Sacred Heart of Jesus Christ, Limited", for example, and the "Catholic Mission of the Holy Ghost, Limited". Do these organizations, he asks, exist to cure souls—or to cure copra? One cannot help thinking that Robinson was unlucky in the missionaries he met, for, although it cannot be denied that corruption existed, the majority of the Christian missionaries were brave people, risking their lives and working under gruelling conditions, and supported only by a wonderful faith in their purpose. Such people compel nothing but admiration.

The western half of New Guinea is Dutch and until the First World War the eastern half was divided into two parts. Papua (Australian) and what was called the Territory of New Guinea which was German. On the outbreak of war Australia walked in. Between the two world wars this part of New Guinea was administered by Australia under a mandate. In 1949, Papua and the Territory of New Guinea were joined under a single administration from Port Moresby (in Papua).

To this day there are parts of New Guinea which are virtually unknown. It is said that in parts of the island cannibalism still exists, although the principal indigenous pastime of head-hunting has been pretty well eliminated.

However, in the Solomon Islands one should not be too certain about this, and a visiting yachtsman would be well advised to take a gun with him if he should venture far inshore, in case somebody thinks his head would look better shrunk to a quarter its size!

When Bill Robinson was in the New Hebrides he actually attended a "head-hunters' initiation ceremony", and came away with his head firmly on his shoulders, but then Robinson was an unusual man. He found, too, that tobacco was the perfect passport to safety. In his own words, "We found there people . . . to be simply insane for the flavour of nicotine". A habit presumably acquired from traders.

On one occasion, when *Svaap* was a good five miles from the shore, Robinson spotted a canoe being paddled by a single man as if his very life depended on it. On catching up with *Svaap* he clutched her rail, gasped out the one word "Tobacco", and fell exhausted in the canoe. He had brought three coconuts and a piece of carved wood to trade for the nicotine. Robinson threw some tobacco into the canoe. The native was alone on the sea, five miles from shore on a very dark night in a frail canoe. "All", writes Bill Robinson, "for a scrap of tobacco!"

THE CORAL SEA

Robinson sailed along the north coast of New Guinea by way of the Solomon Islands. He describes the passage aptly as ". . . a dangerous, reef-infested run". If, however, one decided to sail south of New Guinea, as most of the circumnavigators have done, one would sail through the rather indeterminate stretch of water known as the Coral Sea. It was Captain Joshua Slocum who wrote of the dangers from coral rocks in this part of the world, saying that he "trusted now to the mercies of The Maker of all reefs, keeping a good lookout at the same time for perils on every hand".

The Coral Sea is thus aptly named after the coral growths, which are really an extension of the Great Barrier Reef, lying along its western edge. Eric

Hiscock and his wife Susan, on their first circumnavigation, sailed up through the Great Barrier Reef from the Tasman Sea and Sydney on their way to the Torres Strait and so westwards to the Indian Ocean, and Hiscock's description of the reef is a vivid piece of writing. The Coral Sea saw one of the great battles of the Pacific war. It was indeed a turning-point in that war.

TORRES STRAIT

In order to pass from the Coral Sea into the Arafura Sea and so to the Indian Ocean, it is necessary to sail through the Torres Strait, a shallow, narrow stretch of water, dotted about with small islands, and named after its discoverer in 1606, the Spaniard, Luis Vaez de Torres. It is strewn with wrecks. In the southern part of it, just off Cape York, the most northerly tip of Queensland, is a small island that has been a "calling in" place for many a world voyager. It is a pearl-shell diving centre, just $1\frac{1}{2}$ miles by $\frac{3}{4}$ mile. Although small it has a population of 2,000. Hiscock describes it as ". . . a hilly, dried-up little place", and John Guzzwell as ". . . . dry and barren, with little greenery". Guzzwell arrived there appropriately on a Thursday, for it is called Thursday Island.

Actually Thursday Island is just one of a group of islands (including some very small islands called the Tuesday Islands), and its attraction as a port of call in the Torres Strait would seem hard to discover. It is true that there is a fair anchorage off Port Kennedy with the pearling luggers (long two-masted vessels with very low freeboard aft), but this can be very uncomfortable, especially if the south-east monsoon happens to be blowing. It just seems to have an attraction for people. Hiscock, in his second book, only heightens the mystery when he writes: ". . . Thursday Island, with its black inhabitants, sandy, wind-blown streets, tumbledown shacks . . . is a derelict-looking but entertaining spot." (Entertaining!)

THE INDIAN OCEAN

But the time has now come when we must begin the passage across the Indian Ocean, the third largest ocean in the world. The northern half of the Indian Ocean is ruled by the monsoons. From June to September the south-west monsoon blows on to the land men of Asia. As the land heats so the air over it rises and air from the cooler sea rushes in to fill the partial vacuum caused. So in reverse, between December and March, the land is cold by comparison with the sea (which retains heat for longer than land), and so air rises from the sea and colder air blowing from the land replaces it, causing the north-east monsoon.

The Indian Ocean, although often associated in people's minds with leisurely

S.G.B.—D

tropical cruising weather (and John Guzzwell called it "kindly"), is anything but a calm ocean. In the northern part (Bay of Bengal and Arabian Sea) one may meet with tropical storms of great violence, particularly at the "change" of monsoons, and in some parts of the ocean in midsummer the wind remains for days on end at gale force.

In the central and southern half of the ocean, the latitude of, say, the Cocos Islands, the south-east trades are the prevailing wind, while farther south still one may pick up the westerlies, sometimes known as the "roaring forties" from the latitude in which they mainly flow. This pattern of winds may be clearly seen in the chart on page 25.

The Indian Ocean has fewer areas of great depth than the Atlantic or the Pacific, and the deepest recorded depths are in the region of 24,500 feet. By comparison the Atlantic has depths of 30,250 feet, and the Pacific boasts the tremendous depth of just under 37,000 feet. The deepest parts of the Indian Ocean are found off South Australia.

THE ISLES OF HOSPITALITY

Most of the circumnavigators have followed in the wake of Joshua Slocum in the *Spray* and sailed west to the Cocos Islands and so to Mauritius and then south-west to the eastern seaboard of South Africa. The islands usually called at are Christmas, the Cocos group, Rodriguez and Mauritius; so let us consider each one in that order.

There are, in fact, two Christmas Islands, but one cannot possibly confuse them, for while one is located in the Indian Ocean about 250 miles south of Java Head, the other is in the central Pacific, almost due south of the Hawaiian Islands and virtually on the Equator. The Pacific Christmas Island is also much larger. Christmas Island (the Indian Ocean one) is part of the Crown Colony of Singapore. It measures about 11 miles by 5 miles. It was not annexed by the British until 1858, but it had, in fact, been discovered in the middle of the seventeenth century. It was, however, uninhabited, and nobody seems to have wanted to settle there until the end of the nineteenth century, when it was placed under the Straits Settlements for purposes of administration. It is in shape like the letter T, and the coastline consists of high cliffs, sometimes up to 70 feet in height. The island exports phosphate of lime; indeed it is the only export. However, the phosphate deposits are rich. The population consists of about eighty Europeans, about six times that number of Malays and some 1,500 Chinese. It is also inhabited by red land crabs and a variety of interesting birds; frigate birds, boobies, and bo'sun birds, to mention three. It is said that the bo'sun bird nests only here. All ocean voyagers who have called here report the contentment of the people and the warmth of the hospitality. The late A. G. H. MacPherson, the yachtsman whose logs have been edited into a delightful book by the late John Scott Hughes, called the islands of the Indian Ocean sailing route the "Isles of Hospitality".

Next on our course come the Cocos or Keeling Islands. To sail from Christmas Island to the Cocos Islands one must put about 525 sea miles astern—a mere nothing to one who has crossed the Pacific Ocean and learnt to think in terms of thousands! These islands consist of two atolls about 15 miles apart. The northern atoll is uninhabited and completely encloses its lagoon. The southern atoll shelters a lagoon about 8 miles wide and on it at intervals stand some twenty small islands. The islands are low-lying and although crowned with palm trees are not easy landmarks when at sea. Several yachtsmen sailing this way have missed them altogether, including Captain J. C. Voss in *Tilikum*, whose voyages we discuss in Chapter 5. The next island on course is Rodriguez, a good 2,000 miles farther on, so to miss the Cocos could be a serious business if stores and water were insufficient, and tiresome at the best.

The islands were discovered in 1609 by Captain William Keeling. In 1857 they became a British possession. Since 1951 they have been administered by Australia. The largest island measures about 5 miles by ¼ mile only, but it boasts an airstrip. Most people have heard of the Clunies-Ross family, who in 1886 were granted the islands in perpetuity by Queen Victoria, the original John Clunies Ross having settled there in 1827.

The present white "King" of the islands is Mr John Clunies-Ross, who is the great-great-grandson of the original settler.

The passage across the Indian Ocean from the Cocos Islands to Rodriguez can be a stormy one. It is interesting to read of the number of circumnavigators who have found this to be the case. Slocum, Voss, Pidgeon, Macpherson, the Hiscocks, all speak of strong, contrary winds. Slocum spoke of "rugged" weather—strong words for him, but John Guzzwell in the 18 foot 6 inch waterline *Trekka* found quite the reverse! "Looking back on this passage to Rodriguez," he writes, "I am amazed how easy it was. This was by far the fastest port-to-port passage *Trekka* ever made . . . day after glorious day . . ." And yet the Holmdahls on their crossing of the Indian Ocean estimated the wind force to average 7 in the Beaufort Scale the whole way across! All that seems to emerge from this is that the Indian Ocean is a fickle lady, and quite often a bad-tempered lady whose moods last for long periods!

The little island of Rodriguez, unlike the Cocos Islands, is a good landmark, for it is high. Coral reefs surround the island, which measures about 10 miles by 4. In places these reefs extend over 4 miles offshore. It is a British possession, being a dependency of Mauritius. It has a population of 10,000 and its exports are pigs, goats and cattle.

The last of our "Hospitable" islands on the route to South Africa is Mauritius. This is a much larger island than the others, measuring some 39 miles by 27. It is a British Crown Colony with a population of over 600,000. It was discovered by the Portuguese in the early part of the sixteenth century. It is said to have been inhabited solely by huge birds, Solitaires and Dodos, that were unable to fly. The story of the Dodo is surely one of the saddest tales of the extinction of an innocent victim of man ever told. Before the arrival of the Portuguese the Dodo, a huge blue-grey coloured bird, lived quietly at peace with its surroundings. Then came man the intruder, who not only slaughtered the Dodo for amusement and the pot, but also imported pigs into the island which completed the job of finishing off the Dodos, who could not defend themselves. In 1638 the Dutch arrived on the scene and colonized the island, and by 1692 the Dodo was extinct. There are a number of skeletons of Dodos in museums and reconstructed drawings of the bird show him as the possessor of a large beak, and it is said that he could bite with it. The trouble was that he never learnt to use it as a weapon of defence. One might not expect him to be able to escape the attacks of human beings, but at least he might (or so one would think) have learnt to defend himself against the pigs; but it was not to be.

I apologize to the reader for taking up time with this lament for the Dodo, and will come quickly back on course and report that the present inhabitants of the island consist of Europeans, Indians and people of various forms of mixed descent. The Europeans are mostly French, and this is explained by the fact that the Dutch, having named the island after Prince Maurice of Nassau, left the island in 1710, and the French took possession five years later. They changed the name to Île de France. It became the centre of French Government in this part of the world until a more suitable centre was found in Pondicherry in 1789. In 1810 the British landed and took possession in their turn. Strong links with the past remain, however, in that the French language has been preserved, as, surprisingly enough, has French law, while the island has reverted to its original name of Mauritius given to it by the Dutch. Currency is the rupee, and indeed the majority of the population is Indian and, according to Eric Hiscock, "swelling to an alarming degree".

THE CAPE OF GOOD HOPE

Circumnavigators round the Cape of Good Hope have called, apart from Cape Town itself, at places like Durban and Port Elizabeth; but it is no purpose of this section of this book to discuss large cities and harbours. There are things, how-ever, that may usefully be said about the Cape of Good Hope itself. This sheer, rugged cliff, rising at its highest point to 840 feet, juts into the South Atlantic, separating it from the Indian Ocean. This dividing point between the Eastern world and the Western is also called the Cape of Storms, which was the name given to it by the Portuguese Bartholomew Dias, who is the first man to be authentically recorded as its discoverer. The name is apt. The Cape is within the belt of westerly winds, the "roaring forties", and in the days of sail the Cape had an evil reputation. Ships bound for English and North American ports from the east, would often have to spend days tacking about and about in an effort to round the Cape, hoping always for a favourable slant. In this wild area gale force winds are the rule, not the exception. Actually the Cape itself is not the southern-most tip of the African continent; that distinction belongs to a relatively un-imposing low promontory called Cape Agulhas. Nevertheless it is generally accepted that it is the Cape of Good Hope that divides the Indian Ocean from the Atlantic, and not Cape Agulhas.

Although it was the westerly winds that baffled the old square-riggers, the most dreaded wind at the Cape is the "south-easter", which has a definite season of its own, in their summer (December–January, etc.) and our winter. The sure sign of an approaching south-easter is the layer of billowing white cloud on Table Mountain. Hiscock reported frequent gales with wind speeds from 45 to 60 knots in the squalls.

A glance at the current chart on page 27 will reveal the Agulhas current, which runs, as will be seen, in a south-westerly direction. In the region of Cape Agulhas this current runs strongly. There is a continental shelf (similar to the shelf we discussed in the Bay of Biscay) that projects in the neighbourhood of Durban about 15 miles from the shore, increasing as it runs south until off Cape Agulhas the 100-fathom line of the shelf lies 100 miles or so offshore. The rate of the Agulhas current, especially against a contrary wind, combines to produce on this 100-fathom line a steep and dangerous sea. When one realizes that such seas have the whole of the South Atlantic behind them it is not difficult to picture the conditions that one may be unlucky enough to meet with while rounding the Cape of Storms.

Bartholomew Dias erected a pillar on the Cape and pieces of it remain to this day. Vasco da Gama passed here on his circumnavigation in 1497. The colonial expansion of the Dutch in Cape Colony dates from the second half of the seventeenth century, when the Dutch East Indiamen now passing the Cape of Good Hope on their regular runs used the place as a half-way house for victualling and taking on stores. At the end of the eighteenth century the British arrived in force and captured the Cape.

A circumnavigator who sailed from either the eastern seaboard of the U.S.A. or from England would now have only the Atlantic Ocean before him. Some, however, like William Robinson and the Hiscocks on their second voyage, instead of rounding the Cape of Storms, chose to sail home via the Red Sea and the Mediterranean, so let us look first at that long narrow sea dividing Africa from Asia, the southernmost extension of the great Rift Valley.

THE RED SEA

The Red Sea is 1,400 miles long. Its width varies greatly between 15 to 20 miles to 200 miles. It is the great classic trade route of ancient times. In the fourteenth century B.C., and probably much earlier, a canal joined the Gulf of Suez and the Nile River, but in course of time it dried up. For centuries there was no direct communication with the Mediterranean Sea until the Suez Canal was opened in 1869. The prevailing wind in the northern part of the sea is north-westerly. In the southern part of the sea they are south-easterly, with the exception of the months of June to September, when they are northerly. It will be clear, therefore, that a vessel would find a headwind against her in the northern part of the sea all the year round, and in the summer months she would find a headwind for the whole length of the sea. In ancient times a vessel would hoist sail when making the passage south, and if she desired to go northwards sail would have to be lowered and oars used. The early Arab vessels had a large squaresail that was eminently suited for this purpose. A more enterprising fellow than the rest, however, hit upon a method of positioning his sail in relation to the wind that was to have far-reaching consequences. Without knowing, he founded a dynasty. What happened was this. It was discovered, quite probably originally by accident, that by tipping up the squaresail until the two spars, the yard and boom, made an angle of about 45 degrees to the mast, a new drive was given to the old sail. One corner of the sail was peaked right up and the top fore-corner of the sail came forward of the mast.

The new drive of the sail came from the fact that the yard could swing on the mast so that it presented a high, straight leading edge to the wind. By contrast with the baggy sagging fore-leech of the old squaresail the new sail had become very much more efficient as an aerofoil. The same principle that keeps an airplane, a glider or a bird in the air was being for the first time harnessed to a sailing ship. The thin, high-aspect-ratio mainsail of the modern racing yacht is the direct descendant of those early Nile boats, when a clever Egyptian conceived the idea of tipping up the yard of his squaresail.

THE SUEZ CANAL

Connecting the Red Sea and the eastern Mediterranean is the Suez Canal. Tremendous boon to shipping that this is, it had one sad effect. By shortening the long-route journey round the Cape of Storms, the Suez Canal killed the beautiful great sailing ships of the latter part of the nineteenth century, the clippers, like *Cutty Sark*, *Thermopylae*, *Tae Ping*, for they could not go through it, while the steamers could. A great piece of engineering, its history has been one of international intrigue and finance. It reads like a novel. Although various canals had been built (one noticeably by the Arabs in the seventh century A.D.), they usually consisted of a link between the Nile River and the Bitter Lakes, for in olden times the Red Sea extended as far as the Lakes. Small vessels of shallow draught could reach the Mediterranean by means of the Nile Delta. The actual cutting of a canal through the isthmus was a much bigger project. The formation, in 1854, of the Compagnie Universelle du Canal Maritime de Suez started the ball rolling. In spite of many setbacks and labour troubles, the work did get done eventually, and in 1869 the Canal was ready. On the 16th of November it was opened and the first vessel to cleave its still waters was the Royal Yacht of France, bearing the Empress Eugenie.

The British were somewhat out of the picture. Lord Palmerston openly mistrusted the idea, and short-sightedly could perceive no advantage to England in the scheme. Not so Disraeli, however! The immense importance of the Canal to a maritime nation like Britain was to him not only obvious—it was essential that his country should an have active say in it. In 1875 his opportunity came.

The Khedive of Egypt was bankrupt. It was learnt in London that the latter's holding of 177,000 shares in the Suez Company were for sale. Disraeli bought them for four million pounds, which he borrowed from the London Bank of Rothschilds. This gave Britain a stake in the Company of nearly 50 per cent. It was a triumph. One can imagine Disraeli puffed with pride of achievement as in his letter of information to Queen Victoria, he wrote "You have it, Madam!"

In 1888 the signing of the Suez Canal Convention agreed that "The Canal should always be free and open, in time of war as in time of peace, to every vessel of commerce or of war without distinction of flag". (Perhaps not surprisingly the Convention's lofty terms were disregarded during both world wars.)

Most people are familiar with the story of the seizing of the Canal by President Nasser of Egypt in 1956, in whose hands it still is, and upon whose Government now rests the responsibility of keeping the Canal in a dredged, sound and navigable condition. When the Hiscocks sailed through they were charged no dues, and although pilotage is compulsory no charge is made for it. The length of the Canal is 87 miles.

THE MEDITERRANEAN

The Mediterranean Sea, that must now be navigated before we can sail through the Straits of Gibraltar into the Atlantic, is all that remains today of a great ocean that at some point in the dawn of time is said to have girdled half the globe. To most people today the Mediterranean Sea means holidays, sparkling blue waters, villas, yachts, speedboats, water-skiing and everywhere human bodies browning in the sun. But this picture, whether it appeals to your taste or not, can also be an erroneous one. The Mediterranean in the winter can provide some of the most uncomfortable rough sailing in the world. In the summer months there is either too much wind or not enough.

Bill Robinson in *Svaap* found himself in the middle of one of the worst gales of his circumnavigation in the Mediterranean, and this within sight of Capri, with all its associations of the easy, sweet life! Extracts from Robinson's log read: "7 p.m. S.W. gale. Most dangerous sea have been in for a year . . . Took the biggest sea aboard at 5 p.m. *Svaap* has *ever* had—whole forward part of ship under green water." And this was in the middle of July!

As one sails from Port Said westwards to Gibraltar one passes through three distinct sections of the Mediterranean, each with its own characteristics. The first sector contains the Levant Basin in the south and the Aegean Sea in the north. Winds here are for the most part northerly. The central section contains the Ionian Sea and the Adriatic. The dominating wind here is the sirocco, a warm southerly wind, but there is also a northerly wind which is found in the Adriatic called the bora. The third sector, the largest, contains the Tyrrhenian Sea between Italy, Sicily and Sardinia; and the western basin, containing the Balearic Islands and in the northwest corner, the Gulf of Lions. Here, although one finds south-westerly winds at times, the principal wind is the mistral, northerly, from the Rhone Valley, which can rise to gale force with great rapidity. The wise seaman treats the Gulf of Lions, and the mistral, with respect; especially in winter.

The history of the Mediterranean has been chronicled many times, and most people are familiar with at all events the outline of it. No one would deny its fascination. In spite of the modern tourist industry, its almost tideless waters lap the shores of some of the most beautiful and interesting countries in the world. This inland sea, the cradle of our civilization, possesses, especially at its eastern end, a quality of timelessness all its own. And now only the Straits of Gibraltar lie between us and the Atlantic which we crossed many pages back.

There is a delightful description of life aboard a yacht based at Gibraltar in Joshua Slocum's great book, and what he has to say needs little addition from me. This strange limestone rock has dominated the western entrance to the

Mediterranean for the British for more than two centuries. One of the most famous landmarks in the world, it measures slightly more than $2\frac{1}{2}$ miles in length. It is a free port, everything except spirits and tobacco being free of duty.

And so, as we sail out into the Atlantic Ocean, our imaginary circumnavigation is, for our purpose, complete. There are certain omissions which are intentional. For example, not many circumnavigators sail round Cape Horn. One of these is Captain Slocum, and his description of sailing in those turbulent waters I have included in Chapter 4. The same applies to the Azores. I have also made no mention here of the English Channel, neither have I included the northeastern seaboard of the U.S.A.—Cape Cod, Massachusetts Bay, the Bay of Fundy, Cape Breton Island—all those places so dear to Captain Slocum. I am aware that there are numerous other islands which have not been mentioned, but I do not want to prolong this section any further. It has been a voyage of islands, headlands and two canals in the main, with some remarks thrown in about the seas through which we have been sailing. And now, with (I hope) some knowledge gained, let us meet the "first" man, Joshua Slocum.

4

JOSHUA SLOCUM

The First Man to Sail Around the World Alone

Of all those who have been driven by who knows what inspiration to sail small boats single-handed around this world of ours, pride of place belongs to Captain Joshua Slocum. Slocum was the first man to circumnavigate the world alone. This feat of endurance coupled with ability has been achieved a number of times, and one marvels each time at the skill and courage shown, but in one respect Captain Slocum stands alone, for he was the first man to do it.

"Sailing Alone Around the World" is the title of his book which was first published in the year 1900. It is a classic. Not only did the fact of being the "first" give him a position which none that followed could take from him, but he had the facility of setting down on paper the adventures that befell him and his own thoughts and reactions, in some of the best English that has ever been written by a sailorman. But the real appeal of Slocum's writing stems from the man himself. Master of his trade, he had true humility and also enormous interest and enjoyment of whatever came his way, in fair weather and in foul.

"Sailing Alone Around the World" has probably inspired more people to try their fortune on the sea than any other book that has been written. Moreover, people who can never hope to journey farther than, say, from the Solent to Poole Harbour, can still read it and dream. It is a book which forms part of any self-respecting library.

What kind of man was it who wrote such a book? One can build up something of a portrait from the main events of his life, a life so adventurous that it reads like maritime fiction—and "far-fetched" fiction at that!

Captain Joshua Slocum was born in 1844 in Nova Scotia. He came of seafaring stock, although his father was a farmer. He started work on his father's farm on Briar's Island when only 8 years old, and it is one of the most remarkable things about this man that with so little schooling he taught himself to write so well, so graphically and clearly. He was well aware of his lack of scholastic tuition and says in his book that he wrote with "a hand, alas, that has grasped the sextant more than the plane or pen".

Of course, master mariners under sail were used to keeping a ship's log; a form of writing which encourages simplicity of style and great economy of expression. But this is only half the story. There is surely something of genius in the manner in which this great sailorman communicates to us over the years his powers of observation, his modesty, his superb efficiency and, perhaps most important of all, his sense of humour. The book is full of sly humorous allusions.

His early life was not easy. Working as a young boy on his father's farm, love of the sea and ships waxed strongly in him and he spent all his free time messing about in boats. Such activities were not encouraged. The climax came when, at the tender age of 12, he was caught making a model of a ship during farm working hours. The model, lovingly fashioned, was smashed to pieces before his eyes, and he was soundly beaten. The farm lost a worker and the world gained a sailor; Slocum ran away to sea. He does not appear to have borne any grudge, however, because in the opening phrases of his book he says: "My father was the sort of man who, if wrecked on a desolate island, would find his way home, if he had a jack-knife and could find a tree. He was a good judge of a boat, but the old clay farm, which some calamity made his, was an anchor to him."

Having cast off from the farm, Joshua Slocum managed to get work as a ship's boy, and sometimes even as ship's cook, among the fishing craft around the Bay of Fundy. He never went back to the farm.

By the time he was 17 years old he had sailed before the mast in a full-rigged ship across the Atlantic. But this was nothing to what was to come, for he was shortly to ship aboard an English vessel bound for China.

By now he was fairly launched on his seafaring career. A bout of fever in Batavia did not stop him for long, for he is soon heard of as a member of the ship's company of the s.s. *Soushay*, in which vessel he made many long voyages in far Eastern waters. He was no stranger to Cape Horn either, twice rounding that formidable headland in British vessels. By the time he was 18 he had risen to second mate.

His first actual command of a vessel came in 1869, when he was 25. His ship was a schooner, sailing between Seattle and San Francisco. We are told she carried grain and coal, but probably she had been a grain carrier that had been down-graded to coal, when her holds were no longer good for carrying grain. His first command lasted for a year, after which he joined the bark *Washington* as master. This was a good step forward, for she carried general cargo to Australia, but was to continue on a special run from Sydney to Alaska on a salmon-fishing enterprise.

This is of particular significance, because the *Washington* carried on board boatbuilding materials, with which the craft to be used for the salmon fishing were to be built. Slocum had been given this command because earlier, while working for the fishing canneries on the Pacific coast of North America, he had designed and built his own boat. That both design and construction were good is proved by the fact that not only did he have a thoroughly testing season in the boat, but he sold her profitably afterwards.

It was the knowledge of his abilities in the field of design and construction, therefore, that had impressed the owners of the *Washington* sufficiently to put him in command of the Alaskan enterprise. His experience gained in the Alaskan venture were to stand him in good stead when it came to building a ship strong and seaworthy enough to take him round the world. He married while in Sydney and his wife accompanied him to Alaska. They did not have a smooth run, encountering severe gales which resulted in the *Washington* being driven ashore. She had to be abandoned, but Slocum refused to be beaten. He salvaged all the gear necessary for the expedition, set up some sort of accommodation for his crew and began work. He built a 35-foot whaler with the help of the local Indians and carried out a successful season's fishing, using the whaler and two smaller craft.

Slocum's next command was the *Constitution*, a barkentine plying between San Francisco, Australia and the Pacific islands. She had the same owners as the ill-fated *Washington*, so they clearly had a high opinion of Slocum and attached no blame to him for the loss of the latter. His next venture in shipbuilding came in the year 1873. While in command of a barque, *Benjamin Aymar*, he found himself landed at Manila, as the vessel had been sold there. While ashore he met a certain Mr Jackson, a designer of ships, who had with him the plans of a steamship. Slocum, in want of a job, undertook to build the vessel for Jackson.

He went about it in typical Slocum fashion. He cleared a patch of jungle and built a house. He needed a good home, for he had with him his wife and family. Having taken care of the domestic side of things, he set about building the ship from the materials at hand, cutting down trees and sawing them up into planking. The local natives helped Slocum and were friendly. Not so the Chinese shipwrights up the coast in Manila. They knew about Jackson's plans and resented this "foreigner" who had snatched a good job from under their noses! They planned to attack Slocum's home-made shipyard and would have been successful were it not for the loyalty of the local natives. This attack and a subsequent one, during the launching, were defeated, and Jackson's ship was duly launched.

As part payment Slocum took a ship. She was a schooner of 90 tons called the *Pato*. In the *Pato* he set out on a real story-book adventure, sailing her some 400 miles to the North Danger Reef, where the wreck of a British bark lay sunk in the reasonably shallow water on the reef. The *Pato* had been chartered by a group who had knowledge of the very valuable cargo of the bark.

But luck was not with Slocum and his colleagues. The wrecked vessel was located and salvage work begun. Indeed, the *Pato* made a number of trips from the reef to Manila, but before the job could be completed, the bark slid off the reef and sank to the sea bed many fathoms below.

Slocum continued his career, going from one vessel to another. There was nothing in the way of seafaring that he did not attempt at one time or another. Probably the finest ship he commanded (he was actually part-owner) was the *Northern Light*, a full-rigged vessel of great beauty. It was after his command aboard this vessel that he bought the little bark *Aquidneck* of which he wrote: ". . . a little bark which of all man's handiwork seemed to me the nearest to perfection of beauty, and which in speed when the wind blew, asked no favours of steamers". She was wrecked on the coast of Brazil, but Slocum turned to, and with such local material as there was to hand he built the *Liberdade*, a small 25-foot vessel, which he rigged in the Chinese sampan style, a rig which he says in his other book, "The Voyage of the *Liberdade*", is ". . . the most convenient boat rig in the whole world".

In this curious craft he returned to Boston, which journey aroused a great deal of interest in the American newspapers. However, such fame as this brought him could not get him the one thing he wanted, command of a ship. In the 1890s times were bad for masters of ships and work was very scarce. And so we come to where our story really begins.

It was after two years "on the beach" that Slocum was offered what remained of an elderly 35-foot sloop, the *Spray*, which was lying not even in a mud berth, but propped up, in an undignified manner in a field at Fairhaven, and covered with canvas.

The terms of the offer gave Slocum all the assistance necessary to fit out the *Spray* for sea, but when he arrived at Fairhaven and saw the vessel he realized, as he puts it, ". . . my friend had something of a joke on me". The old ship had, in fact, been lying propped up in the self-same field for well on seven years. She was, moreover, a very old vessel indeed and quite useless as she stood.

However, when Slocum saw her he decided that he who laughs last laughs longest, and began immediately to rebuild her. The vigour and determination with which he did so was characteristic: ". . . my axe felled a stout oak tree nearby for a keel . . ."

He built carefully and strongly. No one knew better than he the value of sound construction, and the whaling captains who came up from New Bedford to watch the progress pronounced his work "A1". The *Spray* cost Slocum $553.62 for materials, and she took one month over the year to build.

The first season Slocum spent fishing in his new boat, but all the while he was longing for deep water and distant lands, for, unlike some of the circumnavigators, he had decided that he would sail, not ". . . to this or that place and then see", but right round the world. When one considers that he was the first man ever to sail the globe single-handed it will be seen that this was quite a decision to have made!

In the following year, therefore, 1895, he sailed to Gloucester from Boston, where he did some additional fitting-out. His description of his arrival in Gloucester Harbour is a little masterpiece.

He had never come alone into a port and he found himself sailing in before the wind, which was blowing strongly. (He uses the expression "feather white" to describe the wave-tops.) Actually one schooner running alongside him was under bare poles, and another had had most of her sails blown away! The wharf was crowded with the fishermen of Gloucester, eagerly watching the new-comer. Before he hit the wharf for which the *Spray* was heading so rapidly, Slocum ran forward and downed the jib. This had the effect of making the ship round into the wind's eye and, of course, of slowing her up. He describes how she came to rest against a mooring post so that it ". . . would not have broken an egg".

Slocum says that he knew that some of the "ablest sailors in the world" were watching him and he did not wish to "appear green". Consequently he did not speak, because he was so out of breath.

Anyone who has ever tried to bring a heavy yacht of some 36 feet single-handed into harbour, with a very strong following wind and sea, will know that to execute the manoeuvre that Slocum did as well as he did required a deal of experience and know-how. The Captain's modesty and humility, always the mark of the great man, are apparent throughout his book, and add greatly to the pleasure of reading it.

Eventually Slocum was ready for his great adventure, and on the 2nd of July he sailed from Yarmouth, to cross the Atlantic Ocean, and this is a good moment for us to join him in his book. "I now stowed all my goods securely, for the boisterous Atlantic was before me, and I sent the top-mast down, knowing that the *Spray* would be the wholesomer with it on deck. Then I gave the lanyards a pull and hitched them afresh, and saw that the gammon was secure, also that the boat was lashed, for even in summer one may meet with bad weather in the crossing.

"In fact, many weeks of bad weather had prevailed. On July 1, however, after a rude gale, the wind came out nor'west and clear, propitious for a good run. On the following day, the head sea having gone down, I sailed from Yarmouth, and let go my last hold on America. The log of my first day on the Atlantic in the *Spray* reads briefly: '9.30 a.m. sailed from Yarmouth. 4.30 p.m. passed Cape Sable; distance, three cables from the land. The sloop making eight knots. Fresh breeze N.W.' Before the sun went down I was taking my supper of strawberries and tea in smooth water under the lee of the east-coast land, along which the *Spray* was now leisurely skirting.

"At noon on July 3 Ironbound Island was abeam. The *Spray* was again at her best. A large schooner came out of Liverpool, Nova Scotia, this morning, steering eastward. The *Spray* put her hull down astern in five hours. At 6.45 p.m. I was in close under Chebucto Head light, near Halifax harbour. I set my flag and squared away, taking my departure from George's Island before dark to sail east of Sable Island. There are many beacon lights along the coast. Sambro, the Rock of Lamentations, carries a noble light which, however, the liner *Atlantic*, on the night of her terrible disaster, did not see. I watched light after light sink astern as I sailed into the unbounded sea, till Sabro, the last of them all, was below the horizon. The *Spray* was then alone, and sailing on, she held her course. July 4, at 6 a.m. I put in double reefs, and at 8.30 a.m. turned out all reefs. At 9.40 p.m. I raised the sheen only of the light on the west end of Sable Island, which may also be called the Island of Tragedies. The fog, which till this moment had held off, now lowered over the sea like a pall. I was in a world of fog, shut off from the universe. I did not see any more of the light. By the lead, which I cast often, I found that a little after midnight I was passing the east point of the island, and should soon be clear of dangers of land and shoals. The wind was holding free, though it was from the foggy point, south-south-west. It is said that within a few years Sable Island has been reduced from forty miles in length to twenty, and that of three lighthouses built on it since 1880, two have been washed away and the third will soon be engulfed.

"On the evening of July 5, the *Spray*, after having steered all day over a lumpy sea, took it into her head to go without the helmsman's aid. I had been steering south-east by south, but the wind hauling forward a bit, she dropped into a smooth lane, heading south-east, and making about eight knots her very best work. I crowded on sail to cross the track of the liners without loss of time and to reach, as soon as possible, the friendly Gulf Stream. The fog lifting before night, I was afforded a look at the sun just as it was touching the sea. I watched it go down and out of sight. Then I turned my face eastward and there, apparently at the very end of the bowsprit, was the smiling full moon rising out of the sea. Neptune himself coming over the bows could not have startled me more. 'Good evening, sir,' I cried; 'I'm glad to see you.' Many a long talk since then I have had with the man in the moon; he had my confidence on the voyage.

"About midnight, the fog shut down again denser than ever before. One could almost 'stand on it.' It continued so for a number of days, the wind increasing to a gale. The waves rose high but I had a good ship. Still, in the dismal fog I felt myself drifting into loneliness, an insect on a straw in the midst of the elements. I lashed the helm, and my vessel held her course, and while she sailed I slept.

"During these days a feeling of awe crept over me. My memory worked with startling power. The ominous, the insignificant, the great, the small, the wonderful, the commonplace,—all appeared before my mental vision in magical succession. Pages of my history were recalled which had been so long forgotten that they seemed to belong to a previous existence. I heard all the voices of the past laughing, crying, telling what I had heard them tell in many corners of the earth.

"The loneliness of my state wore off when the gale was high and I found much work to do. When fine weather returned, then came the sense of solitude, which I could not shake off. I used my voice often, at first giving some order about the affairs of a ship, for I had been told that from disuse I should lose my speech. At the meridian altitude of the sun I called aloud, 'Eight bells,' after the custom on a ship at sea. Again from my cabin I cried to an imaginary man at the helm, 'How does she head there?' and again, 'Is she on her course?' But getting no reply, I was reminded the more palpably of my condition. My voice sounded hollow on the empty air, and I dropped the practice. However, it was not long before the thought came to me that when I was a lad I used to sing; why not try that now, where it would disturb no one? My musical talent had never bred envy in others, but out on the Atlantic, to realize what it meant, you should have heard me sing. You should have seen the porpoises leap when I pitched my voice for the waves and the sea and all that was in it. Old turtles, with large eyes, poked their head up out of the sea as I sang 'Johnny Boker,' and 'We'll Pay Darby Doyl for his Boots,' and the like. But the porpoises were, on the whole, vastly more appreciative than the turtles; they jumped a deal higher. One day when I was humming a favourite chant, I think it was 'Babylon's a-Fallin,' a porpoise jumped higher than the bowsprit. Had the *Spray* been going a little faster she would have scooped him in. The sea-birds sailed around rather shy.

"July 10, eight days at sea, the *Spray* was twelve hundred miles east of Cape Sable. One hundred and fifty miles a day for so small a vessel must be considered good sailing. It was the greatest run the *Spray* ever made before or since in so few days. On the evening of July 14, in better humour than ever before, all hands cried, 'Sail ho!' The sail was a barkentine, three points on the weather bow, hull down. Then came the night. My ship was sailing along now without attention to the helm. The wind was south; she was heading east. Her sails were trimmed like the sail of the Nautilus. They drew steadily all night. I went frequently on

SPRAY

After her rig was altered in South American
waters; by shortening bowsprit and boom, and adding
mizzen-sail to form the Yawl rig shown here.
Length overall: 36 feet 9 inches
Beam: 14 feet 2 inches; 9 tons net
(A flying jib could be set on a bamboo lashed to the bowsprit)

deck, but found all well. A merry breeze kept on from the south. Early in the morning of the 15th the *Spray* was close aboard the stranger, which proved to be *La Vaguisa* of Vigo, twenty-three days from Philadelphia, bound for Vigo. A lookout from his masthead had spied the *Spray* the evening before. The captain, when I came near enough, threw a line to me and sent a bottle of wine across slung by the neck, and very good wine it was. He also sent his card, which bore the name of Juan Gantes. I think he was a good man, as Spaniards go. But when I asked him to report me 'all well' (the *Spray* passing him in a lively manner), he hauled his shoulders much above his head; and when his mate, who knew of my expedition, told him that I was alone, he crossed himself and made for his cabin. I did not see him again. By sundown he was as far astern as he had been ahead the evening before.

"There was now less and less monotony. On July 16 the wind was north-west and clear, the sea smooth, and a large bark, hull down, came in sight on the lee bow, and at 2.30 p.m. I spoke to the stranger. She was the bark *Java* of Glasgow, from Peru for Queenstown for orders. Her old captain was bearish, but I met a bear once in Alaska that looked pleasanter. At least, the bear seemed pleased to meet me, but this grizzly old man! Well, I suppose my hail disturbed his siesta, and my little sloop passing his great ship had somewhat the effect on him that a red rag has upon a bull. I had the advantage over heavy ships, by long odds, in the light winds of this and the two previous days. The wind was light; his ship was heavy and foul, making poor head-way, while the *Spray*, with a great mainsail bellying even to light winds, was just skipping along as nimbly as one could wish. 'How long has it been calm about here?' roared the captain of the *Java*, as I came within hail of him. 'Dunno, cap'n,' I shouted back as loud as I could bawl. 'I haven't been here long.' At this the mate on the forecastle wore a broad grin. 'I left Cape Sable fourteen days ago,' I added. (I was now well across towards the Azores.) 'Mate,' he roared to his chief officer—'mate, come here and listen to the Yankee's yarn. Haul down the flag, mate, haul down the flag!' In the best of humour, after all, the *Java* surrendered to the *Spray*.

"The acute pain of solitude experienced at first never returned. I had penetrated a mystery, and, by the way, I had sailed through a fog. I had met Neptune in his wrath, but he found that I had not treated him with contempt, and so he suffered me to go on and explore.

"In the log for July 18 there is this entry: 'Fine weather, wind south-south-west. Porpoises gambolling all about. The S.S. *Olympia* passed at 11.30 a.m., long. W.34°50'.'

" 'It lacks now three minutes of the half-hour,' shouted the captain, as he gave me the longitude and the time. I admired the businesslike air of the *Olympia*;

but I have the feeling still that the captain was just a little too precise in his reckoning. That may be all well enough, however, where there is plenty of sea-room. But over-confidence, I believe, was the cause of the disaster to the liner *Atlantic*, and many more like her. The captain knew too well where he was. There were no porpoises at all skipping along with the *Olympia*! Porpoises always prefer sailing-ships. The captain was a young man, I observed, and had before him, I hope, a good record.

"Land ho! On the morning of July 19 a mystic dome like a mountain of silver stood alone in the sea ahead. Although the land was completely hidden by the white, glistening haze that shone in the sun like polished silver, I felt quite sure that it was Flores Island. At half-past four p.m. it was abeam. The haze in the meantime had disappeared. Flores is one hundred and seventy-four miles from Fayal, and although it is a high island, it remained many years undiscovered after the principal group of the islands had been colonized.

"Early on the morning of July 20 I saw Pico looming above the clouds on the starboard bow. Lower lands burst forth as the sun burned away the morning fog, and island after island came into view. As I approached nearer, cultivated fields appeared, 'and oh, how green the corn!' Only those who have seen the Azores from the deck of a vessel realize the beauty of the mid-ocean picture." At 4.30 p.m. the *Spray* let go her anchor at Fayal, having taken eighteen days from Cape Sable.

He did not stay long, four days to be exact (which was two days longer than he had intended), and hove anchor early on the 24th of July. The weather was squally. He had been given some plums to add to his provisions, and these eaten with some white cheese gave him such indigestion that he passed out during the night: ". . . By night-time I was doubled up with cramps. The wind, which was already a smart breeze, was increasing somewhat, with a heavy sky to the sou'west. Reefs had been turned out, and I must turn them in again somehow. Between cramps I got the mainsail down, hauled out the earings as best I could, and tied away point by point, in the double reef. There being sea-room, I should, in strict prudence, have made all snug and gone down at once to my cabin. I am a careful man at sea, but this night, in the coming storm, I swayed up my sails, which, reefed though they were, were still too much in such heavy weather; and I saw to it that the sheets were securely belayed. In a word, I should have laid to, but did not. I gave her the double-reefed mainsail and whole jib instead, and set her on her course. Then I went below, and threw myself upon the cabin floor in great pain. How long I lay there I could not tell, for I became delirious. When I came to, as I thought, from my swoon, I realized that the sloop was plunging into a heavy sea, and looking out of the companionway, to my amazement I saw

a tall man at the helm. His rigid hand, grasping the spokes of the wheel, held
them as in a vice. One may imagine my astonishment. His rig was that of a
foreign sailor, and the large red cap he wore was cockbilled over his left ear, and
all was set off with shaggy black whiskers. He would have been taken for a pirate
in any part of the world. While I gazed upon his threatening aspect I forgot the
storm, and wondered if he had come to cut my throat. This he seemed to divine.
'Señor,' said he, doffing his cap, 'I have come to do you no harm.' And a smile,
the faintest in the world, but still a smile, played on his face, which seemed not
unkind when he spoke. 'I have come to do you no harm. I have sailed free,' he
said, 'but was never worse than a *contrabandista*. I am one of Columbus's crew,'
he continued. 'I am the pilot of the *Pinta* come to aid you. Lie quiet, señor
captain,' he added, 'and I will guide your ship to-night. You have a *calentura*,
but you will be all right to-morrow.' I thought what a very devil he was to carry
sail. Again, as if he read my mind, he exclaimed: 'Yonder is the *Pinta* ahead; we
must overtake her. Give her sail; give her sail! *Vale, vale, muy vale !*' Biting off a
large quid of black twist, he said: 'You did wrong, captain, to mix cheese with
plums. White cheese is never safe unless you know whence it comes. *Quien sabe*,
it may have been from *leche de Capra* and become capricious—'

'Avast, there!' I cried. 'I have no mind for moralizing.'

"I made shift to spread a mattress and lie on that instead of the hard floor, my
eyes all the while fastened on my strange guest, who, remarking again that I
would have 'only pains and calentura,' chuckled as he chanted a wild song:

> *High are the waves, fierce, gleaming,*
> *High is the tempest roar !*
> *High the sea-bird screaming !*
> *High the Azore !*

"I suppose I was now on the mend, for I was peevish, and complained: 'I
detest your jingle. Your Azore should be at roost, and would have been were it a
respectable bird!' I begged he would tie a rope-yarn on the rest of the song, if
there was any more of it. I was still in agony. Great seas were boarding the *Spray*,
but in my fevered brain I thought they were boats falling on deck, that careless
draymen were throwing from wagons on the pier to which I imagined the *Spray*
was now moored, and without fenders to breast her off. 'You'll smash your
boats!' I called out again and again, as the seas crashed on the cabin over my
head. 'You'll smash your boats, but you can't hurt the *Spray*. She is strong!' I
cried.

"I found, when my pains and calentura had gone, that the deck, now as white
as a shark's tooth from seas washing over it, had been swept of everything
movable. To my astonishment, I saw now at broad day that the *Spray* was still

heading as I had left her, and was going like a race-horse. Columbus himself could not have held her more exactly on her course. The sloop had made ninety miles in the night through a rough sea. I felt grateful to the old pilot, but I marvelled some that he had not taken in the jib. The gale was moderating, and by noon the sun was shining. A meridian altitude and the distance on the patent log, which I always kept towing, told me that she had made a true course throughout the twenty-four hours. I was getting much better now, but was very weak, and did not turn out reefs that day or the night following, although the wind fell light; but I just put my wet clothes out in the sun when it was shining, and, lying down there myself, fell asleep. Then who should visit me again but my old friend of the night before, this time, of course, in a dream. 'You did well last night to take my advice,' said he, 'and if you would, I should like to be with you often on the voyage, for the love of adventure alone.' Finishing what he had to say, he again doffed his cap and disappeared as mysteriously as he came, returning, I suppose, to the phantom *Pinta*. I awoke much refreshed, and with the feeling that I had been in the presence of a friend and a seaman of vast experience. I gathered up my clothes, which by this time were dry, then, by inspiration, I threw overboard all the plums in the vessel."

The weather gradually moderated and by the 4th of August Slocum saw land ahead—Spain. At 3 p.m. the *Spray* cast her anchor in the harbour of Gibraltar, the first leg of his voyage over. He had always confidence in himself with his lifetime of experience at sea, and he now had unbounded confidence in his little vessel, that had looked after him and the pilot of the *Pinta* so well. There is a delightful description of the hospitality extended to the *Spray* while in Gibraltar. " '. . . Put it thar!' as the Americans say, was the salute I got from Admiral Bruce, when I called at the admiralty to thank him for his courtesy of the berth, and for the use of the steam-launch which towed me into dock. 'About the berth, it is all right if it suits, and we'll tow you out when you are ready to go. But, say, what repairs do you want? Ahoy the *Hebe*, can you spare your sailmaker? The *Spray* wants a new jib. Construction and repair, there! Will you see to the *Spray*? Say, old man, you must have knocked the devil out of her coming over alone in twenty-nine days! But we'll make it smooth for you here!' Not even her Majesty's ship the *Collingwood* was better looked after than the *Spray* at Gibraltar.

"Later in the day came the hail: '*Spray* ahoy! Mrs Bruce would like to come on board and shake hands with the *Spray*. Will it be convenient to-day?' 'Very!' I joyfully shouted. On the following day Sir F. Carrington, at the time governor of Gibraltar, with other high officers of the garrison, and all the commanders of the battleships, came on board and signed their names in the *Spray*'s log-book.

Again there was a hail, '*Spray* ahoy!' 'Hello!' 'Commander Reynold's compliments. You are invited on board H.M.S. *Collingwood*, "at home" at 4.30 p.m. Not later than 5.30 p.m.' I had already hinted at the limited amount of my wardrobe, and that I could never succeed as a dude. 'You are expected, sir, in a stovepipe hat and a claw-hammer coat!' 'Then I can't come.' 'Dash it! come in what you have on; that is what we mean.' 'Aye, aye, sir!' The *Collingwood*'s cheer was good, and had I worn a silk hat as high as the moon I could not have had a better time or been made more at home. An Englishman, even on his great battleship, unbends when the stranger passes his gangway, and when he says 'at home' he means it."

Slocum had sailed to Gibraltar with the intention of sailing eastwards through the Mediterranean Sea, through the Suez Canal and Red Sea and east about round the world. At Gibraltar he changed his plans. Naval officers, engaged in a continuous guerrilla sea warfare with the longshore pirates of the North African coast, urgently persuaded him of the dangers of taking the proposed route. Accordingly he sailed back into the Atlantic south-south-west for the Cape Verde Islands and South America.

I have always been interested in the original plans of Captain Slocum, for here was a sea captain of great experience, who knew, if anybody knew them, the great wind systems of the world, by which the old square-riggers shaped their courses. If you look at the chart of the world on page 25 you will see, without considering the Mediterranean for the moment, that the prevailing trade winds blow from a south-easterly direction in the Indian Ocean, and from a south-easterly direction also in the South Pacific Ocean. In other words, a course through the Red Sea from Aden south-east towards Torres Strait and Australia would be likely to encounter headwinds, and the same argument would apply to a ship sailing from Australia to South America until she got well south and into the belt of westerly winds that blow around the southernmost part of the globe.

When it came to rounding Cape Horn, however, she would be at a great advantage because of the westerly winds. A ship sailing west about, on the other hand, could make use of the north-east trades to get her to the West Indies, and this is the way about taken by pretty well all recent circumnavigators, but they, of course, could use the Panama Canal. Slocum *had* to go round by Cape Horn, where the westerlies blow so fiercely as to be a legend.

So one can conclude that Slocum intended originally to battle through the south-east trades in the Indian Ocean, reach Australia, then sail south-west to Cape Horn with the westerlies, from where, as can be seen from the map, he would have been able to sail up the South American coast, to the West Indies,

Alone on the vast Atlantic; the rising sun greets Joshua Slocum at the start of that "first ever" single-handed circum-navigation taking great advantage of the Renolds current which runs on the circular plan shown on the map, using the westerly set in the southern part of the North Atlantic to get him to the Gulf of Mexico.

Because of the warning of pirates, however, he had to face "the Blind Horn's Hate", and the ironical part of it all was that he did get attacked by pirates off the West African coast after all, to say nothing of even more tiresome attacks from Fuegians while rounding the Horn.

Here is his description of an attack by pirates off the African coast: ". . . Monday, August 25, the *Spray* sailed from Gibraltar, well repaid for whatever deviation she had made from a direct course to reach the place. A tug belonging to her Majesty towed the sloop into the steady breeze clear of the mount, where her sails caught a volant wind, which carried her once more to the Atlantic, where it rose rapidly to a furious gale. My plan was, in going down this coast, to haul offshore, well clear of the land, which hereabouts is the home of pirates; but I had hardly accomplished this when I perceived a felucca making out of the nearest port, and finally following in the wake of the *Spray*. Now, my course to Gibraltar had been taken with a view to proceed up the Mediterranean Sea, through the Suez Canal, down the Red Sea, and east about, instead of a western route, which I finally adopted. By officers of vast experience in navigating these seas, I was influenced to make the change. Longshore pirates on both coasts being numerous, I could not afford to make light of the advice. But here I was, after all, evidently in the midst of pirates and thieves! I changed my course; the felucca did the same, both vessels sailing very fast, but the distance growing less and less between us. The *Spray* was doing nobly; she was even more than at her best; but, in spite of all I could do, she would broach now and then. She was carrying too much sail for safety. I must reef or be dismasted and lose all, pirate or no pirate. I must reef, even if I had to grapple with him for my life.

"I was not long in reefing the mainsail and sweating it up—probably not more than fifteen minutes; but the felucca had in the meantime so shortened the distance between us that I now saw the tuft of hair on the heads of the crew—by which, it is said, Mohammed will pull the villains up into heaven—and they were coming on like the wind. From what I could clearly make out now, I felt them to be the sons of generations of pirates, and I saw by their movements that they were now preparing to strike a blow. The exultation on their faces, however, was changed in an instant to a look of fear and rage. Their craft, with too much sail on, broached to on the crest of a great wave. This one great sea changed the aspect of affairs suddenly as the flash of a gun. Three minutes later the same wave overtook the *Spray* and shook her in every timber. At the same moment the sheet-strop parted, and away went the main-boom, broken short at the rigging. Impulsively I sprang to the jib-halyards and down-haul, and instantly downed the jib. The head-sail being off, and the helm put hard down, the sloop came in the wind with a bound. While shivering there, but a moment though it was, I got the mainsail down and secured inboard, broken boom and all. How I got the boom in before the sail was torn I hardly know; but not a stitch of it was broken. The mainsail being secured, I hoisted away the jib, and, without looking round, stepped quickly to the cabin and snatched down my loaded rifle and cartridges at hand; for I made mental calculations that the pirate would by this time have recovered his course and be close aboard, and that when I saw him it would be better for me to be looking at him along the barrel of a gun. The piece was at my shoulder when I peered into the mist, but there was no pirate within a mile. The wave and squall that carried away my boom dismasted the felucca outright. I perceived his thieving crew, some dozen or more of them, struggling to recover their rigging from the sea. Allah blacken their faces!"

In shaping his course from Gibraltar to the Cape Verde Islands, Slocum was following the route of the big sailing vessels, who always tried to pass to the westward of these islands. If bound for the Cape of Good Hope, they would then set a course to cross the Equator somewhere about longitude 25° west, using the north-east trade winds, and so through the doldrums, meeting the south-east trades, which would mean sailing close-hauled until they caught the westerlies to take them round the Cape, after which, all would be a fair wind for Australia.

By the 16th of September Slocum had reached the doldrums ". . . a gloomy region" he calls it, and the *Spray* tossed fitfully here for ten long days, making only 300 miles. At the end of this very trying period he picked up the south-east trades, which, as he puts it, ". . . gave her sails now a stiff breeze, sending her handsomely over the sea towards the coast of Brazil". So it looks as if his mind may have been made up for him by the wind. When he picked up the south-east trade he was in latitude 4° N. and longitude 29° 30′ W., and a glance at a map or chart will show that he was a good deal nearer South America than Africa!

It was while off the South American coast, having left Buenos Aires, that the *Spray* encountered one of those enormous waves which appear occasionally and provide subject-matter for debate, rather like a very large salmon that "got away"—one has only the story-teller's word as evidence. Anyone, however, who has read as far as this in Slocum's book, will be inclined to trust the old man completely not to exaggerate. Slocum writes:

". . . My ship passed in safety Bahia Blanca, also the Gulf of St Matias and the mighty Gulf of St George. Hoping that she might go clear of the destructive tide-races, the dread of big craft or little along this coast, I gave all the capes a berth of about fifty miles, for these dangers extend many miles from the land. But where the sloop avoided one danger she encountered another. For, one day, well off the Patagonian coast, while the sloop was reaching under short sail, a tremendous wave, the culmination, it seemed, of many waves, rolled down upon her in a storm, roaring as it came. I had only a moment to get all sail down and myself up on the peak halyards, out of danger, when I saw the mighty crest towering masthead-high above me. The mountain of water submerged my vessel. She shook in every timber and reeled under the weight of the sea, but rose quickly out of it, and rode grandly over the rollers that followed. It may have been a minute that from my hold in the rigging I could see no part of the *Spray*'s hull. Perhaps it was even less time than that, but it seemed a long while, for under great excitement one lives fast, and in a few seconds one may think a great deal of one's past life. Not only did the past, with electric speed, flash before me, but I had time while in my hazardous position for resolutions for the future that would take a long time to fulfil. The first one was, I remember, that if the *Spray* came through this danger I would dedicate my best energies to building a larger ship on her lines, which I hope yet to do. Other promises, less easily kept, I should have made under protest. However, the incident, which filled me with fear, was only one more test of the *Spray*'s worthiness. It reassured me against rude Cape Horn."

Slocum had indeed a wearisome time round the Cape. He entered Magellan Strait, rounding Cape Virgins, and had to beat to windward against an easterly wind. Having threaded his way through Broad Reach, round Cape Froward, he emerged into the Pacific, leaving Cape Pillar to port. But he was not to be let off so lightly! Out in the Pacific he ran into a violent storm. In the tide race off Cape Pillar he admits to being sea-sick. The farther offshore he got the higher rose the seas to mountainous proportions. He stuck it for four days. Picture what that means, alone, in a small vessel like the *Spray*!

". . . It was the 3rd of March when the *Spray* sailed from Port Tamar direct for Cape Pillar, with the wind from the north-east, which I fervently hoped might hold till she cleared the land; but there was no such good luck in store. It soon began to rain and thicken in the north-west, boding no good. The *Spray* neared Cape Pillar rapidly, and, nothing loath, plunged into the Pacific Ocean at once, taking her first bath of it in the gathering storm. There was no turning back even had I wished to do so, for the land was now shut out by the darkness of night. The wind freshened, and I took in a third reef. The sea was confused and treacherous. In such a time as this the old fisherman prayed, 'Remember, Lord, my ship is so small and thy sea is so wide!' I saw now only the gleaming crests of waves. They showed white teeth while the sloop balanced over them. 'Everything for an offing,' I cried, and to this end I carried on all the sail she would bear. She ran all night with a free sheet, but on the morning of March 4 the wind shifted to south-west, then back suddenly to north-west, and blew with terrific force. The *Spray*, stripped of her sails, then bore off under bare poles. No ship in the world could have stood up against so violent a gale. Knowing that this storm might continue for many days, and that it would be impossible to work back to the westward along the coast outside of Tierra del Fuego, there seemed nothing to do but to keep on and go east about, after all. Anyhow, for my present safety the only course lay in keeping her before the wind. And so she drove south-east, as though about to round the Horn, while the waves rose and fell and bellowed their never-ending story of the sea; but the Hand that held these held also the *Spray*. She was running now with a reefed forestaysail, the sheets flat amidship. I paid out two long ropes to steady her course and to break combing seas astern, and I lashed the helm amidship. In this trim she ran before it, shipping never a sea. Even while the storm raged at its worst, my ship was wholesome and noble. My mind as to her seaworthiness was put to ease for aye.

"When all had been done that I could do for the safety of the vessel, I got to the fore-scuttle, between seas, and prepared a pot of coffee over a wood fire, and made a good Irish stew. Then, as before and afterward on the *Spray*, I insisted on warm meals. In the tide-race off Cape Pillar, however, where the sea was marvellously high, uneven, and crooked, my appetite was slim, and for a time I postponed cooking. (Confidentially, I was sea-sick!)

"The first day of the storm gave the *Spray* her actual test in the worst sea that Cape Horn or its wild regions could afford, and in no part of the world could a rougher sea be found than at this particular point, namely, off Cape Pillar, the grim sentinel of the Horn.

"Farther offshore, while the sea was majestic, there was less apprehension of danger. There the *Spray* rode, now like a bird on the crest of a wave, and now like a waif deep down in the hollow between seas; and so she drove on. Whole days passed, counted as other days, but with always a thrill—yes, of delight."

It was while passing for the second time through the Strait of Magellan that Slocum, fearing an attack by Fuegians while he slept, took the advice of an old friend, Captain Pedro Samblich, who had advised him to scatter tin tacks liberally on the deck before turning in. This simple precaution appears to have worked like a miracle. The marauding Fuegians ". . . howled like a pack of hounds", and jumping back into their canoes paddled hastily for the shore, not before Slocum had speeded their departure with a shot or two over their heads. He always kept a gun and ammunition handy.

From Cape Pillar Slocum's next landfall was the island of Juan Fernandez, a beautiful island which he describes movingly in his book. He enjoyed a wholly delightful stay there before sailing west to pick up the trade winds, to take him to the Marquesas and all the romantic islands of the South Pacific. Of this period Slocum wrote: "To cross the Pacific Ocean, even under the most favourable circumstances, brings you for many days close to nature, and you realise the vastness of the sea." Of this passage from Juan Fernandez to Samoa, Slocum writes:

". . . To be alone forty-three days would seem a long time, but in reality, even here, winged moments flew lightly by, and instead of my hauling in for Nukahiva, which I could have made as well as not, I kept on for Samoa, where I wished to make my next landing. This occupied twenty-nine days more, making seventy-two days in all. I was not distressed in any way during that time. There was no end of companionship; the very coral reefs kept me company, or gave me no time to feel lonely, which is the same thing, and there were many of them now in my course to Samoa.

"First among the incidents of the voyage from Juan Fernandez to Samoa (which were not many) was a narrow escape from collision with a great whale that was absent-mindedly ploughing the ocean at night while I was below. The noise from his startled snort and the commotion he made in the sea, as he turned to clear my vessel, brought me on deck in time to catch a wetting from the water he threw up with his flukes. The monster was apparently frightened. He headed quickly for the east; I kept on going west. Soon another whale passed, evidently a companion, following in its wake. I saw no more on this part of the voyage, nor did I wish to.

"Hungry sharks came about the vessel often when she neared islands or coral reefs. I own to a satisfaction in shooting them as one would a tiger. Sharks, after all, are the tigers of the sea. Nothing is more dreadful to the mind of a sailor, I think, than a possible encounter with a hungry shark.

"A number of birds were always about; occasionally one poised on the mast to look the *Spray* over, wondering, perhaps, at her odd wings, for she now wore her Fuego mainsail, which, like Joseph's coat, was made of many pieces. Ships are less common on the Southern seas than formerly. I saw not one in the many days crossing the Pacific.

"My diet on these long passages usually consisted of potatoes and salt cod and biscuits, which I made two or three times a week. I had always plenty of coffee, tea, sugar, and flour. I carried usually a good supply of potatoes, but before reaching Samoa I had a mishap which left me destitute of this highly prized sailors' luxury. Through meeting at Juan Fernandez the Yankee Portuguese named Manuel Carroza, who nearly traded me out of my boots, I ran out of potatoes in mid-ocean, and was wretched thereafter. I prided myself on being something of a trader; but this Portuguese from the Azores by way of New Bedford, who gave me new potatoes for the older ones I had got from the *Colombia*, a bushel or more of the best, left me no ground for boasting. He wanted mine, he said, 'for changee the seed.' When I got to sea I found that his tubers were rank and inedible, and full of fine yellow streaks of repulsive appearance. I tied the sack up and returned to the few left of my old stock, thinking that maybe when I got right hungry the island potatoes would improve in flavour. Three weeks later I opened the bag again, and out flew millions of winged insects! Manuel's potatoes had all turned to moths. I tied them up quickly and threw all into the sea.

"Manuel had a large crop of potatoes on hand, and as a hint to whalemen, who are always eager to buy vegetables, he wished me to report whales off the island of Juan Fernandez, which I have already done, and big ones at that, but they were a long way off.

"Taking things by and large, as sailors say, I got on fairly well in the matter of provisions even on the long voyage across the Pacific. I found always some small stores to help the fare of luxuries; what I lacked of fresh meat was made up in fresh fish, at least while in the trade-winds, where flying-fish crossing on the wing at night would hit the sails and fall on deck, sometimes two or three of them, sometimes a dozen. Every morning except when the moon was large I got a bountiful supply by merely picking them up from the lee scuppers. All tinned meats went begging.

"On the 16th of July, after considerable care and some skill and hard work, the *Spray* cast anchor at Apia, in the kingdom of Samoa, about noon. My vessel being moored, I spread an awning, and instead of going at once on shore I sat under it till late in the evening, listening with delight to the musical voices of the Samoan men and women.

"A canoe coming down the harbour, with three young women in it, rested her paddles abreast the sloop. One of the fair crew, hailing with the naïve salutation, 'Talofe lee' ('Love to you, chief'), asked:

" 'Schoon come Melike?'

" 'Love to you,' I answered, and said, 'Yes.'

" 'You man come 'lone?'

"Again I answered, 'Yes.'

" 'I don't believe that. You had other mans, and you eat 'em.'

"At this sally the others laughed. 'What for you come long way?' they asked.

" 'To hear you ladies sing,' I replied.

" 'Oh, talofa lee!' they all cried, and sang on."

Amongst the people Slocum met in Apia was Mrs Robert Louis Stevenson, who invited him to Vailimi, her home, and the house in which Robert Louis Stevenson had written so many tales. Slocum was a great admirer of the author, and to his delight Mrs Stevenson gave him four volumes of "Sailing Directions for the Mediterranean". Although not likely to be of use on Slocum's voyage, the Mediterranean sailing directions had a special significance, as having been some of Stevenson's favourite books to pore over, when in "wandering mood". Mrs Stevenson wrote a short note on the fly-leaf of the first book and signed it.

From Samoa, Slocum, unlike many of the later circumnavigators, sailed straight for the coast of Australia. After dropping the Fiji group astern, and while passing south of New Caledonia, he met with a really strong gale in what appeared to be a season of gales. He had had stormy weather to contend with ever since leaving Samoa. During this bad gale, the *Spray* was sighted by a French mail ship, who reported her on arrival in Sydney as being ". . . in the thick of the storm". She was perfectly all right, however, and was as dry as a bone, while the passengers in the mail ship ". . . were up to their knees in water in the saloon". It is, of course, a fact that a heavy steamship will often fare worse in a gale than a small sailing vessel, which bobs about on the top of the waves, while the large steamship forces her way through the big seas and is subjected to the force of hundreds of tons of water.

Even so, Slocum's characteristic modesty no doubt greatly understates the difficulties he met with before arriving at Newcastle, from where, after a short rest, he sailed south to Sydney, arriving there after a passage of one day.

In Sydney the *Spray* and Slocum were news. He was asked no harbour charges in Sydney, or for that matter in any port on his voyage (except Pernambuco) until he got to Melbourne. However, by charging 6*d*. a head for each sightseer who boarded the *Spray*, he soon made up the modest harbour charge of 6*s*. 6*d*. Reading between the lines, however one gets the impression that the old sea captain considered his being charged anything as very bad form!

"Summer was approaching and the harbour of Sydney was blooming with yachts. Some of them came down to the weather-beaten *Spray* and sailed round her at Shelcote, where she took a berth for a few days. At Sydney I was at once among friends. The *Spray* remained at the various watering-places in the great port for several weeks, and was visited by many agreeable people, frequently by officers of H.M.S. *Orlando* and their friends. Captain Fisher, the commander, with a party of young ladies from the city and gentlemen belonging to his ship, came one day to pay me a visit in the midst of a deluge of rain. I never saw it rain harder even in Australia. But they were out for fun, and rain could not dampen their feelings, however hard it poured. But, as ill luck would have it, a young gentleman of another party on board, in the full uniform of a very great yacht club, with brass buttons enough to sink him, stepping quickly to get out of the wet, tumbled holus-bolus, head and heels, into a barrel of water I had been coopering, and being a short man, was soon out of sight, and nearly drowned before he was rescued. It was the nearest to a casualty on the *Spray* in her whole course, so far as I know. The young man having come on board with compliments made the mishap most embarrassing. It had been decided by his club that the *Spray* could not be officially recognized, for the reason that she brought no letters from yacht-clubs in America, and so I say it seemed all the more embarrassing and strange that I should have caught at least one of the members, in a barrel, and, too, when I was not fishing for yachtsmen.

"The typical Sydney boat is a handy sloop of great beam and enormous sail-carrying power; but a capsize is not uncommon, for they carry sail like vikings. In Sydney I saw all manner of craft, from the smart steam-launch and sailing-cutter to the smaller sloop and canoe pleasuring on the bay. Everybody owned a boat. If a boy in Australia has not the means to buy him a boat he builds one, and it is usually one not to be ashamed of. The *Spray* shed her Joseph's coat, the Fuego mainsail, in Sydney, and wearing a new suit, the handsome present of Commodore Foy, she was flagship of the Johnstone's Bay Flying Squadron when the circumnavigators of Sydney harbour sailed in their annual regatta. They 'recognized' the *Spray* as belonging to 'a club of her own,' and with more Australian sentiment than fastidiousness gave her credit for her record.

"Time flew fast those days in Australia, and it was December 6, 1896, when the *Spray* sailed from Sydney. My intention was now to sail around Cape Leeuwin direct for Mauritius on my way home, and so I coasted along toward Bass Strait in that direction."

Slocum spent some time in Australia, as was to be expected. He liked the people and they liked him. It was after he sailed from Melbourne south and west into Bass Strait that separates the mainland from the Island of Tasmania that he started giving lectures on his voyage. His first talk given in a hall lent by a Scots lady brought him £3. After that he gave several similar lectures, always with great success, at places farther north, like Cooktown, which he reached on the 31st of May.

An example of Slocum's superstition is contained in those paragraphs that describe how he touched the edge of the "M" Reef, while passing through the Great Barrier Reef Channel. The *Spray* struck, but swung off immediately. Slocum could see ugly-looking rocks beneath his keel, and as he did so he recalled that M (for "M" Reef) was the thirteenth letter of the alphabet. To have got off so lightly from striking part of a submerged reef while sailing at full speed with sheets eased certainly lends force to the old seaman's conviction that thirteen was his lucky number!

The *Spray* was now rigged as a yawl; that is to say with two masts, a mainmast and a (much smaller) mizzenmast. Slocum had altered the rig while in South American waters, by shortening the bowsprit and main boom, and stepping the small mizzen in the stern. He had experienced so much variety in the weather conditions that he decided that the yawl rig with its smaller mainsail and its mizzensail would be of more all-round use, and so it turned out.

While in Australian waters Slocum had an amusing encounter with three "dandy" yachtsmen.

". . . I had just finished reading some of the most interesting of the old voyages in woe-begone ships, and was already near Port Macquarie, on my own cruise, when I made out, May 13, a modern dandy craft in distress, anchored on the coast. Standing in for her, I found that she was the cutter-yacht *Akbar*,[1] which had sailed from Watson's Bay about three days ahead of the *Spray*, and that she had run at once into trouble. No wonder she did so. It was a case of babes in the wood or butterflies at sea. Her owner, on his maiden voyage, was all duck trousers; the captain, distinguished for the enormous yachtsman's cap he wore, was a Murrumbidgee[2] whaler before he took command of the *Akbar*; and the navigating officer, poor fellow, was almost as deaf as a post, and nearly as stiff and immovable as a post in the ground. These three jolly tars comprised the crew. None of them knew more about the sea or about a vessel than a newly born babe knows about another world. They were bound for New Guinea, so they said; perhaps it was as well that three tenderfeet so tender as those never reached that destination.

"The owner, whom I had met before he sailed, wanted to race the poor old *Spray* to Thursday Island *en route*. I declined the challenge, naturally, on the ground of the unfairness of three young yachtsmen in a clipper against an old sailor all alone in a craft of coarse build; besides that, I would not on any account race in the Coral Sea.

" '*Spray* ahoy!' they all hailed now. 'What's the weather goin' t'be? Is it a-goin' to blow? And don't you think we'd better go back t' r-r-refit?'

"I thought, 'If ever you get back, don't refit,' but I said: 'Give me the end of a rope, and I'll tow you into yon port farther along; and on your lives,' I urged, 'do not go back round Cape Hawk, for it's winter to the south of it.'

---

[1] *Akbar* was not her registered name, which need not be told.
[2] The Murrumbidgee is a small river winding among the mountains of Australia, and would be the last place in which to look for a whale.

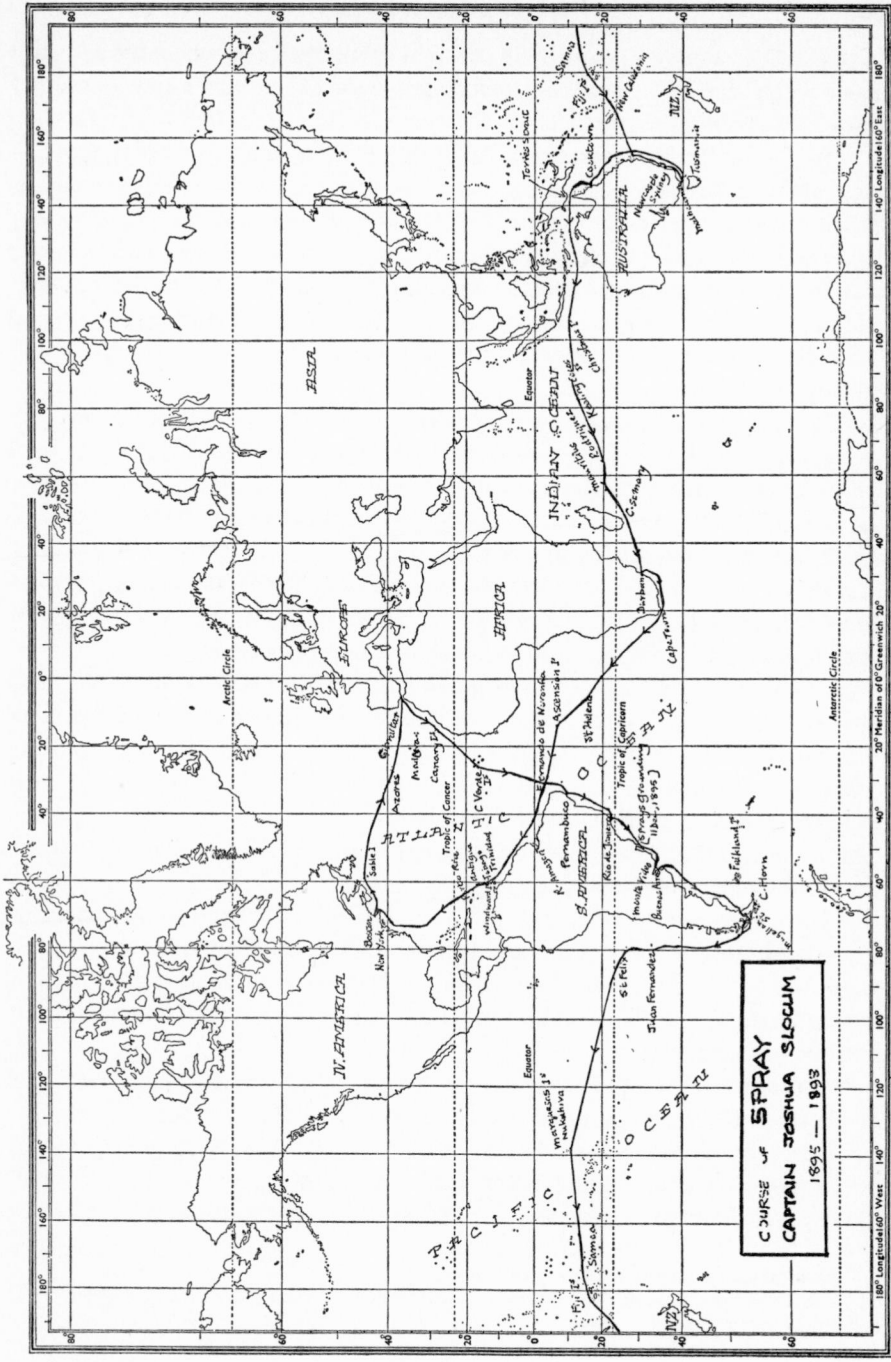

COURSE of SPRAY
CAPTAIN JOSHUA SLOCUM
1895 — 1898

S.G.B.—F

"They purposed making for Newcastle under jury-sails; for their mainsail had been blown to ribbons, even the jigger had been blown away, and her rigging flew at loose ends. The *Akbar*, in a word, was a wreck.

" 'Up anchor,' I shouted, 'up anchor, and let me tow you into Port Macquarie, twelve miles north of this.'

" 'No,' cried the owner; 'we'll go back to Newcastle. We missed Newcastle on the way coming; we didn't see the light, and it was not thick, either.' This he shouted very loud, ostensibly for my hearing, but closer even than necessary, I thought, to the ear of the navigating officer. Again I tried to persuade them to be towed into the port of refuge so near at hand. It would have cost them only the trouble of weighing their anchor and passing me a rope; of this I assured them, but they declined even this, in sheer ignorance of a rational course.

" 'What is your depth of water?' I asked.

" 'Don't know; we lost our lead. All the chain is out. We sounded with the anchor.'

" 'Send your dinghy over, and I'll give you a lead.'

" 'We've lost our dinghy, too,' they cried.

" 'God is good, else you would have lost yourselves,' and 'Farewell' was all that I could say.

"The trifling service proffered by the *Spray* would have saved their vessel.

" 'Report us,' they cried, as I stood on—'report us with sails blown away, and that we don't care a dash and are not afraid.'

" 'Then there is no hope for you,' and again 'Farewell.'

"I promised I would report them, and did so at the first opportunity, and out of humane reasons I do so again. On the following day I spoke the steamship *Sherman*, bound down the coast, and reported the yacht in distress and that it would be an act of humanity to tow her somewhere away from her exposed position to an open coast. That she did not get a tow from the steamer was from no lack of funds to pay the bill; for the owner, lately heir to a few hundred pounds, had the money with him. The proposed voyage to New Guinea was to look that island over with a view to its purchase. It was about eighteen days before I heard of the *Akbar* again, which was on the 31st of May, when I reached Cooktown, on the Endeavour River, where I found this news:

"May 31, the yacht *Akbar*, from Sydney for New Guinea, three hands on board, lost at Crescent Head; the crew saved.

"So it took them several days to lose the yacht, after all."

Meanwhile Slocum continued on his voyage, passing Home Island and Sunday Island, sailing through the Torres Strait that divides Australia and New Guinea. He weighed anchor for a short stay in the harbour of Thursday Island, sailing from there on the 24th of June for the long passage in the Indian Ocean.

He was able to count on the trade wind helping him on his way to Madagascar at least. One must remember that the 24th of June in this part of the world represented early winter, and not midsummer! Slocum's plan was not to arrive off the Cape of Good Hope before summer, as he had had experience of the very bad weather that can be met with there during the winter months.

Accordingly he planned to sail quietly westwards, calling in at islands *en route* such as the Keeling Cocos Islands and Rodriguez. He spent further time by putting the *Spray* ashore (deliberately) while in the Keeling Islands in order to coat her bottom with a mixture of coal tar and 'other stuff'. Slocum found the Keeling Islands greatly to his taste:

"On the 22nd of July arrived H.M.S. *Iphegenia* with Mr Justice Andrew J. Leech and court officers on board, on a circuit of inspection among the Straits Settlements, of which Keeling Cocos was a dependency, to hear complaints and try cases by law, if any there were to try. They found the *Spray* hauled ashore and tied to a cocoa-nut tree. But at the Keeling Islands there had not been a grievance to complain of since the day that Hare migrated, for the Rosses have always treated the islanders as their own family.

"If there is a paradise on this earth it is Keeling. There was not a case for a lawyer, but something had to be done, for here were two ships in port, a great man-of-war and the *Spray*. Instead of a lawsuit a dance was got up, and all the officers who could leave their ship came ashore. Everybody on the island came, old and young, and the governor's great hall was filled with people. All that could get on their feet danced, while the babies lay in heaps in the corners of the room, content to look on. My little friend Ophelia danced with the judge. For music two fiddles screeched over and over again the good old tune, 'We won't go home till morning.' And we did not.

"The women of the Keelings do not do all the drudgery, as in many places visited on the voyage. It would cheer the heart of a Fuegian woman to see the Keeling lord of creation up a cocoa-nut tree. Besides cleverly climbing the trees, the men of Keeling build exquisitely modelled canoes. By far the best workmanship in boat-building I saw on the voyage was here. Many finished mechanics dwelt under the palms at Keeling, and the hum of the band-saw and the ring of the anvil were heard from morning till night. The first Scotch settlers left there the strength of Northern blood and the inheritance of steady habits. No benevolent society has ever done so much for any islanders as the noble Captain Ross, and his sons, who have followed his example of industry and thrift.

"Admiral Fitzroy of the *Beagle*, who visited here, where many things are reversed, spoke of 'these singular though small islands, where crabs eat cocoa-nuts, fish eat coral, dogs catch fish, men ride on turtles, and shells are dangerous man-traps,' adding that the greater part of the sea-fowl roost on branches, and many rats make their nests in the tops of palm-trees.

"My vessel being refitted, I decided to load her with the famous mammoth tridacna shell of Keeling, found in the bayou near by. And right here, within sight of the village, I came near losing 'the crew of the *Spray*'—not from putting my foot in a man-trap shell, however, but from carelessly neglecting to look after the details of a trip across the harbour in a boat. I had sailed over oceans; I have since completed a course over them all, and sailed round the whole world without so nearly meeting a fatality as on that trip across a lagoon, where I trusted all to some one else, and he, weak mortal that he was, perhaps trusted all to me. However that may be, I found myself with a thoughtless African negro in a rickety bateau that was fitted with a rotten sail, and this blew away in mid-channel in a squall, that sent us drifting helplessly to sea, where we would have been incontinently lost. With the whole ocean before us to leeward, I was dismayed to see, while we drifted, that there was not a paddle or an oar in the boat! There was an anchor, to be sure, but not enough rope to tie a cat, and we were already in deep water. By great good fortune, however, there was a pole. Plying this as a paddle with the utmost energy, and by the merest accidental flaw in the wind to favour us, the trap of the boat was worked into shoal water, where we could touch bottom and push her ashore. With Africa, the nearest coast to leeward, three thousand miles away, with not so much as a drop of water in the boat, and a lean and hungry negro—well, cast the lot as one might, the crew of the *Spray* in a little while would have been hard to find. It is needless to say that I took no more such chances. The tridacna were afterward procured in a safe boat, thirty of them taking the place of three tons of cement ballast, which I threw overboard to make room and give buoyancy.

"On August 22, the *kpeting*, or whatever else it was that held the sloop in the islands, let go its hold, and she swung out to sea under all sail, heading again for home. Mounting one or two heavy rollers on the fringe of the atoll, she cleared the flashing reefs. Long before dark Keeling Cocos, with its thousand souls, as sinless in their lives as perhaps it is possible for frail mortals to be, was left out of sight, astern. Out of sight, I say, except in my strongest affection."

But perhaps his longest "stay" while on this part of his voyage was at Mauritius Island. It was the "fine weather" season there, although off the Cape of Good Hope storms still raged. Slocum gave lectures in the so-called "Opera House" and generally enjoyed himself among good friends. While in Mauritius he was given free use of the Military Dock, and the *Spray* was thoroughly refitted for the remaining part of her voyage. He sailed eventually on the 26th of October, with the boom broad-off before a gentle breeze, while the hospitable island faded slowly astern.

However, although he had hoped to escape bad weather by waiting this long he was not to get off so lightly! By the 30th of October he had reached the limits of the south-east trade winds and during the first week of November he had to compete with a really hard south-westerly gale, preceded by a thunderstorm of unusual violence. Slocum himself admits that this gale was as severe as any he had met with on the voyage with the exception of Cape Horn.

It was not until the 17th of November that the *Spray*, somewhat battered by a succession of gales, arrived at Port Natal, Durban.

It was while in Durban that Slocum met emissaries from President Krüger, the "flat earthist", and had a most entertaining argument with them almost ending in violence.

During his long stay in South Africa, Slocum naturally met President Krüger, who took occasion to remind him that he was sailing "in the world", and not "round" it!

"The trip to Kimberley, Johannesburg, and Pretoria was a pleasant one. At the last-named place I met Mr Krüger, the Transvaal president. His Excellency received me cordially enough; but my friend Judge Beyers, the gentleman who presented me, by mentioning that I was on a voyage around the world, unwittingly gave great offence to the venerable statesman, which we both regretted deeply. Mr Krüger corrected the judge rather sharply, reminding him that the world is flat. 'You don't mean *round* the world,' said the president; 'it is impossible! You mean *in* the world. Impossible!' he said, 'impossible!' and not another word did he utter either to the judge or to me. The judge looked at me and I looked at the judge, who should have known his ground, so to speak, and Mr Krüger glowered at us both. My friend the judge seemed embarrassed, but I was delighted; the incident pleased me more than anything else that could have happened. It was a nugget of information quarried out of Oom Paul, some of whose sayings are famous. Of the English he said, 'They took first my coat and then my trousers.' He also said, 'Dynamite is the corner-stone of the South African Republic.' Only unthinking people call President Krüger dull."

Slocum remained in South Africa until the 26th of March 1898, whence he sailed on the last leg of her voyage. Her course was now north-westerly almost all the way home, and the end was beginning to be in sight, although she still had a long way to go. Her first step in the South Atlantic Ocean was the Ascension Islands, which she reached on the 27th of April, having been a month at sea.

Slocum writes:

"On March 26, 1898, the *Spray* sailed from South Africa, the land of distances and pure air where she had spent a pleasant and profitable time. The steam-tug *Tigre* towed her to sea from her wonted berth at the Alfred Docks, giving her a good offing. The light morning breeze, which scantily filled her sails when the tug let go the tow-line, soon died away altogether, and left her riding over a heavy swell, in full view of Table Mountain and the high peaks of the Cape of Good Hope. For a while the grand scenery served to relieve the monotony. One of the old circumnavigators (Sir Francis Drake I think), when he first saw this magnificent pile, sang, 'Tis the fairest thing and the grandest cape I've seen in the whole circumference of the earth.'

"The view was certainly fine, but one has no wish to linger long to look in a calm at anything, and I was glad to note, finally, the short heaving sea, precursor of the wind which followed on the second day. Seals playing about the *Spray* all day, before the breeze came, looked with large eyes when, at evening, she sat no longer like a lazy bird with folded wings. They parted company now, and the *Spray* soon sailed the highest peaks of the mountains out of sight, and the world changed from a mere panoramic view to the light of a homeward-bound voyage. Porpoises and dolphins, and such other fishes as did not mind making a hundred and fifty miles a day, were her companions now for several days. The wind was from the south-east; this suited the *Spray* well, and she ran along steadily at her best speed, while I dipped into the new books given me at the cape, reading day and night. March 30 was for me a fast-day in honour of them. I read on, oblivious of hunger or wind or sea, thinking that all was going well, when suddenly a comber rolled over the stern and slopped saucily into the cabin, wetting the very book I was reading. Evidently it was time to put in a reef, that she might not wallow on her course.

"March 31 the fresh south-east wind had come to stay. The *Spray* was running under a single-reefed mainsail, a whole jib, and a flying-jib besides, set on the Vailima bamboo, while I was reading Stevenson's delightful 'Inland Voyage.' The sloop was again doing her work smoothly, hardly rolling at all, but just leaping along among the white horses, a thousand gambolling porpoises keeping her company on all sides. She was again among her old friends the flying-fish interesting denizens of the sea. Shooting out of the waves like arrows, and with outstretched wings, they sailed on the wind in graceful curves; then falling till again they touched the crest of the waves to wet their delicate wings and renew the flight. They made merry the livelong day. One of the joyful sights on the ocean of a bright day is the continual flight of these interesting fish.

"One could not be lonely in a sea like this. Moreover, the reading of delightful adventures enhanced the scene. I was now in the *Spray* and on the Oise in the *Arethusa* at one and the same time. And so the *Spray* reeled off the miles, showing a good run every day till April 11, which came almost before I knew it. Very early that morning I was awakened by that rare bird, the booby, with its harsh quack, which I recognized at once as a call to go on deck; it was as much as to say, 'Skipper, there's land in sight.' I tumbled out quickly, and sure enough away ahead in the dim twilight, about twenty miles off was St Helena.

"My first impulse was to call out 'Oh what a speck in the sea!' It is in reality nine miles in length and two thousand eight hundred and twenty-three feet in height. I reached for a bottle of port wine out of the locker, and took a long pull from it to the health of my invisible helmsman—the pilot of the *Pinta*."

In St Helena, the "Isle of Napoleon's exile", Slocum once more gave lectures to an appreciative audience, first the people of Jamestown, and another time to the Governor the officers of the garrison and their friends, at Government House. He stayed in St Helena until the 20th of April, when he sailed after a great luncheon with the Governor, taking with him a "Royal Mail" for Ascension Island, his next port of call.

He met with the same friendliness at Ascension, being entertained by the Commander of the island. It was here that, wishing, as he puts it, ". . . to clench beyond doubt that it was not at all necessary in the expedition of a sloop around the world to have more than one man for the crew, all told, and that the *Spray* sailed with only one person on board", he arranged for the executive officer, one Lieutenant Eagles, to fumigate the sloop, making it impossible for a person to live concealed below, and proving ". . . that only one person was on board when she arrived". This was accordingly done and Slocum was given a certificate to this effect. The value of such a certificate may perhaps be open to question. The fact that Slocum was patently incapable of deceit is of much more significance.

So the *Spray* sailed from Ascension on an east-north-easterly course, and on reaching longitude 30° west she shortly afterwards crossed her outward-bound track that she had made on the 2nd of October 1895. She had thus circumnavigated the globe.

Although from the point of view of the circumnavigation, therefore, the rest of the voyage might be something in the nature of an aftermath, it was by no means uneventful. Joshua Slocum, was, if not exactly accident-prone—adventure-prone. He was unaware that war had been declared with Spain, and this leads to an amusingly described encounter with the battleship *Oregon*.

On the 17th of May he passed Devil's Island, and the following night he was able to write in his log "Tonight in latitude 7° 13' N, for the first time in nearly three years I see the north star". He was now almost home. In the lovely island of Grenada he gave a lecture before clearing for the U.S.A. on the 4th of June 1898. There he received back for the last time on the voyage his licence to sail single-handed (round the world), which document was eventually to be housed in the Treasury Department in Washington.

Slocum headed for Cape Hatteras. The *Spray* floundered for a while in the horse latitudes and the weedy morass of the Sargasso Sea and then on the 18th of June a southerly gale brought escape to the north and he soon picked up the Gulf Stream.

So often within sight of victory there comes one or more setbacks as if to subject us to one last test. So it was that, having passed latitude 30° north, the *Spray* ran into a storm which broke the jibstay at the masthead. The mast being unstayed from ahead, whipped about, but it had to be climbed and a makeshift stay rigged. The far-sighted Captain had spare blocks and rope to hand, and also the energy to carry out what must have been no easy job. He admitted afterwards that if his mast had not been very stout it would have broken when the stay broke. (The mast was a spruce from New Hampshire.) All was soon put to rights and with a reef in it the jib was rehoisted and the ship put back on her course.

But the elements were still out to get their pound of flesh. On the 25th of June, off Fire Island, and very nearly home, she encountered a tornado, which had an hour earlier devasted part of New York city. The ever-watchful skipper spotted advancing trouble in time to down sail and meet the wind's force under bare poles. Slocum's account of this storm leaves no doubt as to its violence, but like all the other disasters, now so many wonderful memories of man's triumph over the elements, he and his stout little ship came boldly through it, and on a beautiful afternoon on the following day she rounded Montauk Point.

At 1 a.m. on the 27th of June 1898 Slocum cast anchor after a cruise of more than 46,000 miles which had taken just over three years and two months. The *Spray* was as sound a ship as when she had left and had never leaked a drop. By way of rounding off his voyage completely, Slocum sailed the *Spray* round to Massachusetts, and moored her at Fairhaven to the same cedar pile that he "had driven in the bank to hold her when she was launched". He could, as he said, "bring her no nearer home".

Slocum was 51 years of age when he started on his circumnavigation. His voyage took him more than 46,000 miles. He had gained in health and experience and truly seen the "works of the Lord and His wonders of the deep".

After returning, Slocum continued to sail the *Spray* until the year 1909, when he was 65 years of age. In that fateful year, having fitted out for a long passage, he sailed from Bristol R.I. bound down for the Orinoco. His journey took him across several steamship routes, and steamships were multiplying fast. The ocean was no longer the (relatively) safe place it was. It is not known whether Slocum was run down by a steamer. All that is certain is that he and his stout little vessel were never seen again.

As a lesson to would-be cruising sailors, whether afloat or in a comfortable arm-chair with pipe lit and the fire glowing, his book is unbeatable—the legacy he has left is without price, both as an example of numerous instances of practical seamanship, often in the face of great difficulty, and as an example of a simple, lucid, wonderfully readable account of that first voyage alone around this world. The latest publication of the book is by Rupert Hart-Davis, which first appeared in 1948. The original book was published in 1900. Judged by whatever yardstick you choose, "Sailing Alone Around the World" is one of the world's great books.

What of the *Spray* herself, the stout little vessel that "never leaked a drop"? She was originally a type of vessel called a "North Sea fisherman" and had been built (according to Slocum) somewhere about the turn of the eighteenth century. This was largely guesswork on his part, as there was no record of her building. She was rigged as a sloop; that is to say she had one mast stepped fairly well forward in her hull. She belonged latterly to Captain Eben Pierce of New Bedford, and it was he who gave her to Joshua Slocum. There was not much of philanthropy in this gift, as she could be said with truth to have reached the end of her days.

In consequence Slocum had entirely to rebuild her, which he did with great thoroughness and knowledge. He quoted that it is a law in Lloyds that ". . . the *Jane* repaired all out of the old until she is entirely new is still the *Jane*". He also said that the vessel changed her being so slowly that it was impossible to say at what point she ceased to be the old *Jane* and became the new.

Slocum used carefully selected wood in her construction. Her keel was of "pasture white" oak, as were her timbers and her breast hooks. (The breast hook is a crook or knee-shaped piece of wood whose purpose is to hold the gunwales to the stem of a vessel.)

The *Spray*'s planking was of $1\frac{1}{2}$ inch Georgia Pine. Her bulwarks were of pine and also her deck planking. She measured 36 feet 9 inches overall and had a beam of 14 feet 2 inches. She measured 4 feet 2 inches deep in the hold and the cabin coamings rose 3 feet from deck-level, so as to give headroom in the cabin. Slocum slept in the main cabin, which was aft. In the fore cabin he cooked, while provisions were stored in the midship hold situated between the two cabins. Her net tonnage was nine.

The hull was typical of her type, having rather flat sections aft and not much draught. She had a good strong sheer which was drawn out to end in a fine bowsprit. When she sailed from Boston the *Spray* was rigged as a sloop, but in South American waters Slocum shortened both the bowsprit and main boom and stepped a small mizzenmast aft, thus converting her into a yawl. He was able to set a flying jib on a bamboo stick fastened to the bowsprit. The wheel was well aft and Slocum used "tiller lines" to lash it, belaying the ends, one over the other, on the top spokes. Directly in front of the wheel was a compass enclosed and viewed through a small "window".

The main cabin was entered by a companion-way on the port-hand side, while the forecabin had its own companion-way placed amidships. For a tender Slocum shortened a "Cape Ann" dory which he stowed and lashed, bottom upmost, amidships between the two cabins. Just aft of the dory and ahead of the main cabin was the ship's pump, flanked by two water casks.

The mainsail was of the four-sided "gaff" rig and the mizzen was a small lug sail. The *Spray* was apparently adept at "sailing herself", a useful attribute in a lone ocean wanderer! Slocum wrote that ". . . it never took long to find the amount of helm, or angle of rudder, required to hold her on her course".

She had little weather helm in light airs, but like any well-balanced vessel, needed some weather helm as the wind increased. On her run from Thursday Island to the Keeling Cocos Islands, a distance of 2,700 miles, which took her twenty-three days, Slocum was at the helm for only one hour! This must still surely be a record. How proud he was of her! It shows in every line he wrote about her. The last words of his account of the *Spray* were "The days passed happily with me where my ship sailed".

Joshua Slocum was, indeed, a happy man.

THE "VENTURESOME" CAPTAIN VOSS

A book alliteratively entitled "The Venturesome Voyages of Captain Voss" was first published in Yokohama in 1913. It contained the accounts of three voyages made by one of the most remarkable seafarers who ever lived; a Canadian, Captain John Claus Voss. The first voyage was the outcome of a conversation in the Queen's Hotel, Victoria, British Columbia, in the summer of the year 1897, when a certain Mr Haffner introduced himself to Voss as the bearer of a letter from an old friend. The letter explained that Haffner knew the position where a great treasure lay buried on Cocos Island.

Haffner, moreover, had a permit from the Government of Costa Rica to secure such treasure as he was able to find. His proposition to Voss was that the latter should find him a suitable vessel for the journey, fit her out, sail her to the Cocos Island, help to get the treasure aboard, and then sail with it back to Victoria. Voss's share of the reward was to be one-third of the treasure, the other two-thirds going to Haffner and the Costa Rican Government respectively.

The treasure had been valued at £7,000,000 sterling, so that Voss's share would come to about £2,333,000! Small wonder that he says in his book "Turning those gigantic figures over in my mind, my brain almost became dizzy".

Alas for Voss and his dizziness; Haffner belatedly realizing that he needed a vessel of some size to carry out his projected treasure hunt efficiently, abandoned Voss to enlist the aid of Admiral Pallister of the North West British Squadron, who agreed to make the trip to the Cocos Island in his flagship. On the journey aboard the flagship Haffner learnt to his dismay that even if they found the treasure it would eventually have to be handed back to its rightful owner—the Peruvian Government. Accordingly he deliberately misled the search party, who returned empty-handed.

Haffner who was exceedingly lucky to get away with his lame story, was put ashore by the good-natured English at Acapulco, Mexico, from where he wrote to Voss, putting up to him the original proposal again. Voss, showing even more good nature, agreed, and bought and fitted out a sloop of some 10 tons, 30 feet on the waterline, called the *Xora*. On the trip *Xora* sailed some 7,000 miles, and although they did not find the treasure, they had, it is recorded, a "thoroughly enjoyable sail"! Moreover, Voss learned something of great value to those who venture far offshore in small boats, as he puts it: "I also learned something which I had not known in all my previous experience at sea, that a small vessel is just as safe in a heavy gale as a large one."

Like Joshua Slocum, Voss writes in a simple straightforward seaman's style. If he has not the sly humour of Slocum, he nevertheless writes extraordinarily readably, and once one starts his book it is difficult to put it down. The events of this first voyage may be judged from some of the chapter headings: "In a Sloop on the High Seas", "Encounter with the First Gale", "History of the Great Treasure—Where is it Hidden?" "Prospecting and its Difficulties" etc. Ordinary enough headings; but the chapters they head hold the attention and quicken the pulse.

Alas for Voss's dreams of becoming a multi-millionaire, the difficulties proved too great, but in one respect he *had* found treasure—the knowledge of how to ride out a gale at sea. This self-confidence in handling a small vessel in all conditions led to his fantastic voyage of 40,000 miles in a converted Indian war canoe—the *Tilikum*.

The *Tilikum*'s voyage started in this way. In the year 1901 Voss, who was in Victoria, was approached by a fellow Canadian called Luxton, a journalist. The world had been thrilled by the remarkable circumnavigation in 1895 by Captain Joshua Slocum in the 36-foot vessel *Spray*. Luxton asked Voss if he thought he could make a similar voyage, but in a smaller vessel, adding that there was £5,000 in it to be shared between them, since Luxton proposed to accompany Voss and write a book about the voyage.

The following extract from Voss's book gives an excellent idea of his style of writing, even if it does leave one sympathizing somewhat with his "greenhorn" crew!

"My mate looked at me and then at the waves, and I know he was wishing himself ashore. I then tied a lifeline round his waist, and told him to go forward and stand by to drop the sea anchor over the bow when I gave the word. This time he obeyed my orders, as I assured him that I would pull him in again if he should get washed overboard. He managed to get forward on his hands and knees, and when forward held on to the foremast to wait for orders. By this time there was quite a large sea running, and some of the waves were breaking heavily. I waited for a fairly smooth sea to come along, and when she got on top I put the helm down, and as she came round inside of a few seconds, and just before swinging head to sea, I pulled the small sail down which I had set for that occasion.

"When the boat got head to sea a breaker came up in front of her which for a few moments looked very much like a brick wall. I shouted at the top of my voice 'Throw the sea anchor over,' but instead of doing this he dropped it on

John Voss riding out a gale to his sea-anchor in *Tilikum*

deck and climbed up the foremast, and owing to the smallness of the boat his weight on top of the mast almost caused her to turn over. I quickly took a pull on the lifeline and told him to come down, and as the sea had passed the boat by that time he came down just about as quickly as he went up. After throwing the sea anchor over, the *Tilikum* drifted along with the wind and sea and soon tightened the anchor rope; then the boat lay about five points from the wind, and, considering the sea which was running at the time, was fairly comfortable and apparently out of danger. I thought that she would be more comfortable and safer if I could manage to get her to lay closer to the wind; I therefore set my leg-of-mutton spanker and hauled the sheet in flat, which made a riding sail instead of a driving sail out of it. No sooner was the sail set than she swung her head to the wind and seas to about two and a half points. The *Tilikum* certainly rode fine that way.

"I then said to my mate, 'The *Tilikum* is all right now and we are as safe here as in the Victoria Hotel in Victoria, B.C. Now, tell me, why did you climb the foremast instead of attending to the sea anchor when I asked you?'

" 'Well,' Luxton replied, 'when I saw that sea coming up in front of us I made sure it was coming clean on top of us!'

"During the afternoon, while running before the strong wind and large seas, the boat had taken some spray over, and both my mate and myself got pretty wet; in fact, we were soaked to the skin; but now that she was hove-to, the decks, with the exception of the forward end, were quite dry. We then changed our clothes, had our supper, and then both of us sat down in the cockpit to have a smoke and talk about the poor people on shore, who at that very moment may have trees and houses blown about their heads.

"The wind and sea was increasing fast towards evening, but the bow of the *Tilikum* rose finely to every sea.

" 'By Jove, John,' said Luxton, at the same time tapping me on the shoulder, 'I thought sure it was all off with us when we hove-to and I saw that big sea in front of us, but to see this little canoe going over the top of those big monsters without rolling or tumbling about is most wonderful. Well, if ever we do get back to land, when I publish our experiences in this gale, not one person in a hundred will believe my story.'

"I may say that my mate, a young man, had never seen salt water until we went out in the *Tilikum*. Nevertheless he proved himself a first-class shipmate in every way, good sailor, good cook, and quick of action, but he acknowledges himself that the quickest move he ever made was in going up the mast."

In choosing an Indian canoe in which to make the trip Voss had decided to go one better than just a "smaller vessel than the *Spray*". Even when she was decked over this odd-looking vessel drew less than 2 feet of water! Voss's argument was that a buoyant hull will rise over the waves in bad weather, provided that that hull be kept moving sufficiently slowly through water. If, he argued, a ship runs too fast, the hull creates a suction which will defeat its natural buoyancy and bring breaking seas aboard. To slow down the ship Voss had developed a technique using a sea anchor or drogue, which, streamed on a stout line from the stern, slowed her speed down so that following seas passed harmlessly beneath the hull without breaking aboard and swamping her. Furthermore, if streamed from the bows, the sea anchor could be used to keep the vessel's head into the wind.

Pride of place, in being the first man ever to circumnavigate the globe in a small vessel, belongs to Joshua Slocum. No other man can take that away from him. Moreover, Slocum's voyage was single-handed, whereas Voss's was not. Further, Voss did not go west round the Horn and have to face that awe-inspiring experience.

Nevertheless Voss's achievement was a very remarkable one, especially when one considers the unlikely vessel in which he sailed. But for his masterly use of the sea-anchor technique, *Tilikum* would have found a watery grave.

Voss's passage took him from Victoria southwards and westwards through the Pacific islands to Australia. Thence via New Zealand and the New Hebrides, along the northern seaboard of Australia to the Keeling Cocos Islands in the Indian Ocean. From there he sailed westwards via Cape Town across the South Atlantic to Pernambuco, so completing his circumnavigation. He thence sailed into the North Atlantic, called at the Azores, and so arrived in the cold, choppy waters of the English Channel, finishing the voyage in London. In England Voss lectured before large audiences, was elected a Fellow of the Royal Geographical Society, and *Tilikum* herself was exhibited at Earl's Court Western Garden during the Navy and Marine Exhibition in 1905. From the start the voyage from Victoria had taken three years, three months and twelve days.

Packed with excitement as the first two accounts of the voyages are, the third and shortest account, called "The *Sea Queen*", contains a graphic description of being in a small yacht in the centre of a typhoon off Japan. The experiences of Voss and his crew in this adventure are scarcely credible, but fortunately chance has given us an eyewitness of the condition of *Sea Queen* when she arrived back at Yokohama.

It so happened that James Weston Martyr, yachtsman/author, whose classic "The South Seaman" brought him world-wide fame, was present when the little *Sea Queen* entered harbour. Now, Weston Martyr was a seaman of experience and one not given to exaggeration, and I cannot do better than quote from his introduction to the 1926 edition of Voss's book, published by John Lane the Bodley Head Ltd. (A later edition, by Rupert Hart-Davis Ltd., appeared in 1949.) Weston Martyr writes:

"She [the *Sea Queen*] was so battered and bruised that she looked as if she had been rolled down the shaft of a very deep coal-mine, and the appearance of her crew confirmed this impression. I hardly recognised Vincent, and as for Stone, he was so covered with cuts and sores that he might have been an over-ripe Stilton. . . . I observed the following facts myself: (a) the *Sea Queen*'s mainmast was broken in two places and her mizzen in three places; (b) the rudder was torn in half; (c) on one of the deck beams in the cabin there was a perfect impression of a leg of the ship's embossed and cast-iron stove. . . . Putting all else aside, the imprint of that stove on the deck beam is evidence enough for me." Evidence that the *Sea Queen* had turned turtle! For briefly what had happened was this.

Voss and his companions had sailed from Uraga Harbour in the 19-foot waterline yawl on the 29th of July 1912, bound on a cruise round the world. Her captain was Voss and her crew consisted of two young Yokohama yachtsmen F. Stone and S. A. Vincent.

They were unlucky enough to run into a typhoon so severe that it lifted the roof off Yokohama Station, which was only on the fringe of it, and 200 miles from its centre. The *Sea Queen* went right through that centre! Both her masts were broken and one really vicious sea rolled her right over. Stone and Vincent were imprisoned in the cabin, but Voss, who had been washed from the cockpit, managed to sit astride her keel until she righted herself. The *Sea Queen* was built on the lines of *Sea Bird*, the famous vessel designed by Thomas Fleming Day, Editor of "Rudder" magazine. She was thus a sister of Harry Pidgeon's *Islander* (see Chapter 7).

Here is the incident of the *Sea Queen*'s turning turtle in Voss's own words:

"Shortly after nine, when I noticed the boat fell sideways into the sea, the mizzen sheet parted. 'All hands on deck!' I yelled. In a second my two mates were alongside me. All three of us were crawling about the deck on all fours on the after-end of the vessel, and with the seas washing over us we managed to take in the mizzen and save the sail. We then found that our sea anchor was lost. Stone managed to get forward and pull the anchor rope on board, and Vincent and I got busy and made a temporary sea anchor by tying together the cabin ladder and one of our anchors. All this had to be done while lying flat upon deck. After fastening the anchor line to the temporary sea anchor we dropped it overboard, and as it was impossible to set the mizzen again we were obliged to let the vessel lay to this temporary arrangement alone. Owing to the fact that this

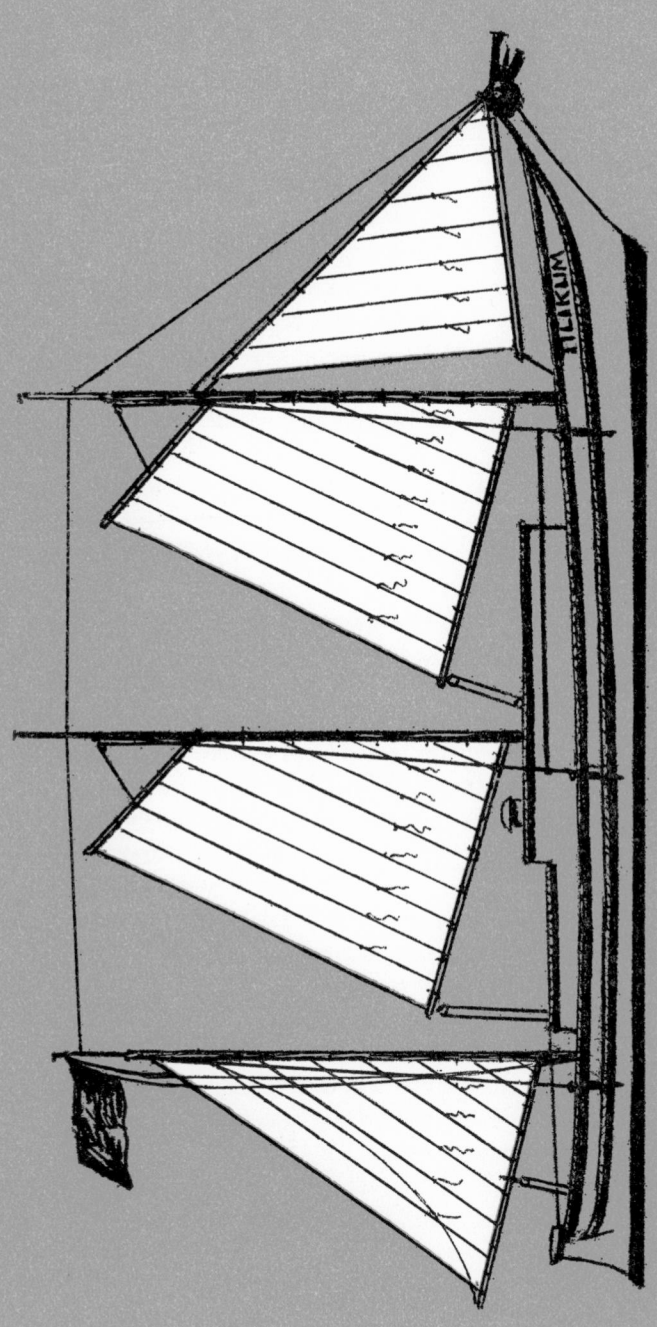

TILIKUM

Length overall: 38 feet Length on bottom: 30 feet
Beam: 5 feet 6 inches Beam at water-line: 4 feet 6 inches
Beam on bottom: 3 feet 6 inches Draught: forward: 1 foot 10 inches; aft: 2 feet

sea anchor was not much of a drag, and being without the aid of the storm sail, it did not do much good. Shortly before eleven o'clock we lost the temporary sea anchor also, and the boat then lay sideways to the sea. The rudder up to this time had been lashed amidships, but as the boat was lying sideways to the sea, I took the rudder lashings off to allow it to swing about and give her a better chance to drift sideways with the seas.

"My two mates were down in the cabin again and I was lying in the cockpit holding on with one hand and with the other keeping the oil bags in the water when a huge sea struck the boat and put her on her beam ends, in which position she remained for just a second or two. I wondered what would happen next; whether she would recover or turn turtle. I was not left long in doubt, for I then felt a little jerk which told me that the boat was turning bottom up, and to save myself from getting under her I let go my hold. The next moment I was in the water, and felt certain that it was all up with us; in fact I took two big mouthfuls of water, thinking to go down quickly and be done with it. When a man gets into a fix of that kind, however, many thoughts will run through his mind, and after I had said good-bye to the world and taken in the water ballast I thought of my two young shipmates who were inside the boat and unable to get out, and wished just to see them once more to say good-bye. By that time I had been under water long enough to be dead, but wasn't. I popped up again behind the stern of the boat and saw the *Sea Queen* in front of me, with her keel pointing to the sky. I made one kick and grabbed hold of her stern, and then made up my mind to get on her bottom and do something towards righting her again.

"I have heard it said that 'While there's life there's hope' and 'Where there's a will there's a way'. At that time I was still alive and had a little will left, but I thought it was going hard with the hopes and ways. Anyway, I made use of the little determination that remained and climbed over the stern of the boat. Just as I got on the bottom I saw an enormous breaking sea coming towards us, so I dug my nails into the keel to avoid getting washed off again. In a second the sea struck the boat along the keel, but I managed to hang on. The same sea caused the boat to heel over, and the weight of the iron on the keel slowly but surely brought her right side up again, and as she turned over I scrambled over the gunwale, and by the time the little vessel was floating on her bottom again I was in the cockpit. The next thing I saw the scuttle open, and heard Vincent shouting at the top of his voice, 'Are you there, Captain?' And then my two shipmates leaped out of the cabin.

"No doubt some of my readers have seen two porpoises jumping out of the water at sea, one after the other. Well, it looked just like that to me. In spite of being on a small craft which was broadside on to the worst storm and largest sea

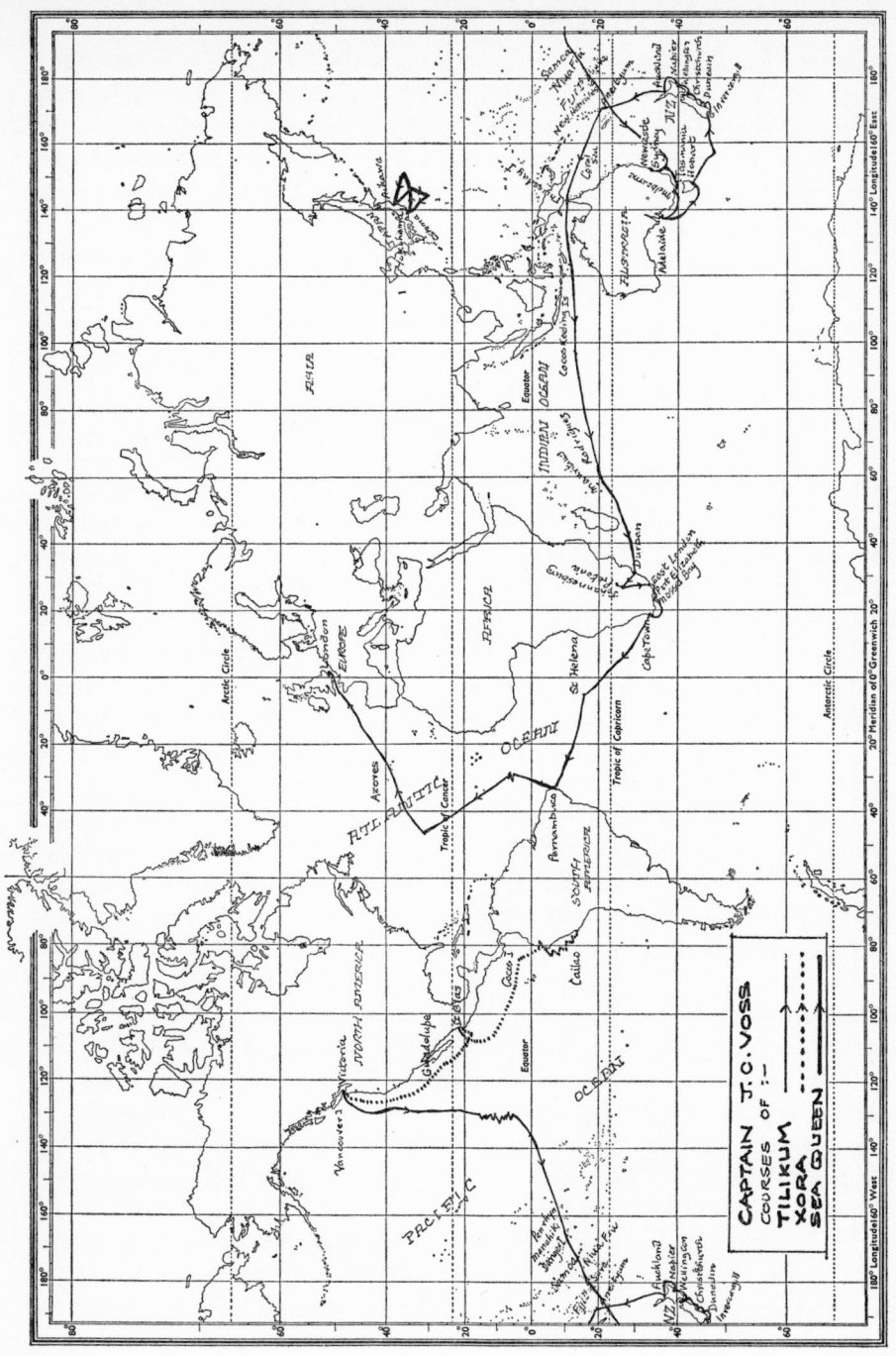

CAPTAIN J. C. VOSS
COURSES OF :—
TILIKUM ————→
XORA ············→
SEA QUEEN ————

that I ever experienced in all my years at sea, and all three of us lying down in the cockpit and hanging on for dear life, our meeting after the incident was quite joyous, and if the boat got smashed up in the typhoon, it would have given us a chance to say good-bye to each other."

The next two extracts from Voss's book show the indomitable spirit of the man. Of course, this is all written after the event, in the quiet and calm of a study, but who can doubt that at the time Voss exhibited the same sang-froid and the calm assessment of the situation which is the hall-mark of every man of action worthy to lead and inspire others.

"We had been working hard for three hours, and in spite of the boat being thrown on her beam ends time after time she never turned turtle again, and the water was then pretty well out of her. Vincent opened the scuttle again and said, 'Captain, I think we are in the centre of the typhoon.' 'No, not in the centre yet,' I answered, 'but I think we will be shortly, and the sooner we get there the better.' I knew by that time that in spite of the tremendous size of the breaking seas they could not harm our little vessel, but that it was the terrible strength of the wind that forced her bottom upwards, and put her on her beam ends time after time. I knew also that in the centre of the typhoon there would be no wind, and we should be all right.

"I have heard ship captains say that once a vessel gets into the centre of the typhoon she will never get out again. After my experience, I can quite agree where a large vessel is concerned, as with such tremendous seas and without a breath of wind she would roll herself to pieces. But the *Sea Queen* did not mind it in the least; she just simply bobbed up and down as the seas came along. I never had a better chance to prove my statement, both while the typhoon was blowing and after we got into the centre of it, that in a heavy gale, be they large or small, as long as their headway is stopped and they are allowed to take a natural drift with the sea and wind, a sea has no power on vessels, and if it does roll on board a large vessel there is no force behind it."

John Voss stands out from this book as a remarkable man. He is also something of an enigma. Very little is known of his life beyond what is told in his book. It is generally believed that he was born in Nova Scotia, but the Canadian Luxton, who sailed with Voss in *Tilikum*, wrote in the Vancouver "Sunday Province" in March of 1932 that Voss was born in Sweden! He died in his late sixties in Tracy, a town near San Francisco, on the 2nd of February 1922. He is said to have been earning his living by driving a pitney, which, since it is defined in the Oxford Dictionary as "a motorbus carrying passengers at low rates", cannot have been a very lucrative occupation. It is more than likely that he died a poor man, an inconspicuous death—but he has joined the immortals, not only because of his achievements as a seaman, but because of his ability to chronicle those achievements in such a very readable form. He has also left us with some of the most practical advice on how to handle a small craft in heavy weather that has ever been written. His wide experience well qualified him to do this. He sailed in many vessels, ranging in size from the small canoe *Tilikum* to great ships capable of carrying some 3,000 tons of cargo.

His book closes with an appendix in which he sets out the lessons he learnt from using his sea anchor in varying conditions of bad weather. These are somewhat technical, and also of absorbing interest to the "offshore" yachtsman, but would be out of place in this book.

We turn now to another pioneer of small-boat cruising either alone or with a small crew. Not a world-girdler, or even an "ocean-crosser", but nevertheless a man whose activities and writings greatly influenced those who came later, as the following chapter will show.

6

R. T. McMULLEN

Victorian Martinet and Pioneer of Small-boat Cruising

In 1869 there appeared in the bookshops a work entitled "Down Channel".[1] It was written not by a mercantile captain with a gift for the pen, but by a hard-headed stockbroker, and a typically Victorian one at that. Richard Turrell McMullen was a strict Protestant, a staunch conservative, who disliked such innovations as "screw steamers" and "mechanically propelled vehicles". He was also a yachtsman and a practical seaman of the first order, and in two aspects he was outstanding.

Firstly he was the pioneer of cruising either alone or with a very small crew, so that the owner/skipper had to be navigator, helmsman and deckhand, and not be dependent upon a paid hand. Secondly he was not only a fine seaman, he was a magnificent teacher. This stems from two things. He could write, express himself well; but perhaps his greatest asset was that he was not too proud to describe in detail the messes he got into when he was relatively inexperienced. In his book he tells almost with relish how his first boat *Leo* sank on the day she was launched; how he came near to sinking her again on her first sail.

He was determined to become a really competent seaman, however; as he puts it himself, his plan was "to persevere in sailing by day or night in all weathers, and never to let want of confidence stand in the way".

McMullen's book can be read today, read and reread with the same delight that it gave to its first readers; it does not date. Unlike the works of Slocum, Voss, Robinson, Pidgeon, and others, it in no way relies for its appeal and interest on some feat of endurance and magnitude. Its place in the history of yachting literature derives from the fact that he set himself a far higher standard of seamanship and general efficiency at sea than had ever been set by an amateur skipper of a small yacht before. He usually sailed with one or more paid hands, but he considered that he should give no orders to another that he could not perform himself, and perform it to perfection. In the middle of the nineteenth century this was a very novel line to take. Moreover, he taught that too much dependence on the shore and harbours could be dangerous for a small vessel caught out in bad weather. This again, in the days when small boats cruised by day mostly, dodging from port to port, came as a new idea. One of the greatest

[1] It can now be obtained in the "Mariner's Library" Edition, published by Rupert Hart-Davis Ltd.

of cruising yachtsmen, the late Mr Claud Worth, whose two books "Yacht Cruising" and "Yacht Navigation and Voyaging" are sailing classics, tells the story of how when he was fitting out his first boat he met McMullen, who was similarly engaged.

When he heard that Worth intended to sail down Channel McMullen gave the young sailor the benefit of his advice, and Worth remembers him saying: "If it looks like blowing hard on shore, get in somewhere in good time, or else give the land a very wide berth."

In his own writing Worth recalls how when at sea in a gale single-handed he found comfort in reading of McMullen's *Sirius*, which vessel is the subject of two of the chapters of the latter's book. In this account of nursing a small vessel through heavy weather Worth found inspiration for the courage and philosophy to carry on successfully. Worth later wrote that he "first learned from McMullen's writings and personal example that the deep sea is reasonably safe in bad weather, even for the smallest craft, a secret which otherwise one might only have found out after half a lifetime of timid dependence upon harbours".

McMullen writes with charm and wit. In *Sirius* he finds time, as the weather improves, to note the behaviour of sea birds; for example—"If disturbed while resting on the water, these birds, (Razorbills and Guillemots), never attempt to rise, but paddle a few strokes in great trepidation, and then dive perpendicularly, disappearing with a 'flop' like a stone.

"Gulls, on the contrary, always rise when disturbed. Not being divers, they seize their prey in a very elegant manner by stooping for it on the wing. If an unhandy morsel, they carry it to a distance from their robber comrades who have very indistinct notions of the rights of property."

Born in 1830, Richard McMullen became a member of the Stock Exchange in 1853, one year before his fellow (if somewhat wealthier) member, Lionel Rothschild, floated the £16,000,000 that enabled Great Britain to prosecute the Crimean War.

He lived mainly at Greenhithe. He was married, and his wife accompanied him on many of his cruises. It is typical that not once does he mention her in his logs. This was not so much an expression of the Victorian attitude towards women, but was in keeping with his policy of leaving out of his writings anything that had not to do with the "serious business of sailing the boat". As he puts it himself in his preface, the book "is not intended . . . to form an addition to the numerous accounts of domestic life on board a small yacht . . . but little more than a bare record of sailing". Nevertheless one cannot escape noticing that while no space is given to the activities of Mrs McMullen the author did include quite lengthy descriptions of the habits of sea birds! If in

ORION

(Before conversion to a yawl)
Length overall: 42 feet. Length water-line: 38 feet
Beam: 10 feet 5 inches. Draught: 7 feet
Built by G. Inman of Lymington, in 1865

this he shows a certain inconsistency, he was far from inconsistent in his continual crusade against "yachting" as opposed to "sailing".

The following three paragraphs make this attitude clear:

"Amongst some of my non-sailing acquaintances, the crudest notions of an amateur sailor's life prevail. Because the vessel is called a yacht, they think there is a royal road to every place, where the sea is neither rough, salt, nor deep—a sort of Elysium, where you anchor when you please, eat and drink when and what you please, and live for the time being in perpetual enjoyment of the sun, moon, and stars. A glance at the following pages will convince them that they have formed too high an estimate of the pleasures of yacht sailing, and perhaps save them the vexation of fitting out a yacht under a misapprehension.

"For years I have been accustomed to hear remarks implying that a yachtsman's time must be heavy on hand, and hard to kill. It may be so in yachting proper, which consists chiefly in promenading on quays, esplanades, and piers, in suitable attire, of course, and in passing to and fro in a steam launch or gig, with colours flying; a delight indulged in only by the extremely affluent, or by those who ought to be so.

"Yacht sailing, however, is a very different affair from 'yachting', and when carried on with spirit, as it is sometimes in large yachts as well as small, is anything but an idle recreation. It is always healthful and exciting, though not always a source of unalloyed pleasure. But even when the work is heavy and continuous, as it must be occasionally, more than ample compensation is found in the contrast of a pretty and quiet anchorage, which no one who has not been buffeted about can appreciate and thoroughly enjoy. If I may compare sailing with equestrian sports, I should say that yacht sailing stands in about the same relation to 'yachting' as the hunting field does to Rotten Row. The comparison is inadequate, but those who know the delight of being well and comfortably housed after a long and hard day's hunting in bad weather will understand the compensation to be found by the yachtsman in a quiet anchorage."

Let us take a look at the little vessels in which McMullen made his strenuous (and perfectionist) cruises.

First in his book comes *Leo*. She was a very small vessel. Built in 1850 by J. Thompson of Rotherhithe, of pine, she measured only 20 feet overall, and 18 feet between perpendiculars. In her McMullen made eight cruises from 1850 to 1857. He sailed in those seven years a total of 8,222 miles.

It is said that seafaring people are superstitious, and there were enough ill omens at the very start of McMullen's career as a yachtsman to daunt the stoutest heart. This is how he tells the story:

". . . Nothing could seem more ill-omened than the first incident related in the log for 1850, at the very commencement of my novitiate.

"The day the *Leo*, 3 tons [described on a previous page], left the builder's yard, she was so carelessly moored by the man who had charge of her, that she grounded during the night on the edge of a camp-shed at Charlton, between the Marine Society's ship and the shore. Being a deep boat, only half-decked, and heavily ballasted, the tide flowed into and filled her. Words will not describe the intense feeling of disappointment and mortification I experienced when I went down the next morning to try my new boat, and saw only a few feet of the mast above water.

"With assistance kindly rendered from the Society's ship, she was got up at the following low water, and taken to Greenwich to be cleared of the mud and filth with which she was well plastered inside.

"Since that time I have launched two new vessels, and took the precaution to have them christened in due form; my neglect of that ceremony in the case of the *Leo* being, no doubt, the pretext for Father Thames taking it into his own hands.

"The first sail was as far as Gravesend and back, with a waterman in charge, and this was the only apprenticeship I served. A confiding kinsman, whose judgment was almost equal to my own, accompanied me, and, his opinion coinciding with mine, that there was nothing to do which we could not easily do ourselves, I resolved to dispense with pilotage services from that day as a waste of money.

"My first attempt, with only the boy on board and a chart for guide, though a very mild and unambitious little cruise from Charlton to Erith and back, was not concluded without a narrow escape. Passing between the collier brigs off Charlton at 10 p.m. to anchor for the night, I made allowance for the two I wished to pass ahead of, and then discovered a third vessel at anchor by itself, upon which we were helplessly driven by the tide. Our mast-head fouling his bowsprit, the *Leo* was beginning to fill, when the crew of the brig got the mast clear and she righted.

"The second cruise was regularly planned and more pretentious. It was voted a jolly thing to drop down to Gravesend on the afternoon of the one day, and start early next morning for a sail round the Nore, my confiding kinsman to do duty as mate upon this grand occasion.

"Great was our rejoicing when the anchor was let go at Gravesend, after having providentially passed safely inside the ships to the anchorage below the Custom House. After tea, which was made in a bachelor's kettle on deck, all hands turned in—the boy, the bachelor's kettle, and sundries occupied the forecastle, in which there was just room for all when properly packed. We, the quarter-deckers, of course occupied the cabin. Though the boat was only 3 tons, each had a properly constructed berth 6 feet by 2 feet, with bed and leeboard complete. Nothing could be more comfortable, if you could only remember that the deck beams were within 6 inches of your head. What with glorious anticipations for the morrow, bright ideas that would not keep, but must be communicated immediately, and what with laughing and giggling, being too hot and too cold, and the novelty of the situation generally, there was not a wink of sleep got all night.

"At last the day broke on which we were to make our mark in the sailing world. O dear! I shall never forget that day, though a veil is thrown over it in the log-book, where it is mentioned in these suspicious terms: 'Sailed out the first season in the Thames, etc. etc. Once venturing to the Nore; but in this adventure got into such trouble that there was no chance of repeating the attempt until the recollection of it had quite blown over, which was not earlier than the following year.' Nevertheless, as an act of penance for unpardonable rashness, I will confess a few scrapes.

"After washing and dressing in the sharp air of an early June morning, with a nice breeze from the westward, we got the anchor up at 5 a.m. This was no sooner done, and the jib set, than we fell athwart a yacht, about ten tons, which brought out two wrathful and unlucky wights in their night shirts, who, with chattering teeth and much bare flesh exposed to the fresh wind, worked well and successfully to get us clear. Having given us a parting benediction, they dived precipitately below, and no doubt drank health and success to us in a well-earned glass of brandy. I must further confess that, being in a state of bewilderment on account of the getting athwart hawse not being in the day's programme, we did nothing whatever towards clearing the vessels, nor even thought of thanking the gentlemen for their exertions until they had probably fallen into a sound sleep again.

"It is usual, I think, after a confession to find, if possible, some excuse for the fault you have confessed. Now my excuse for getting athwart hawse was this; after much cogitation I made up my mind to cast the boat's head to the northward, but happening to spy a swell on board a yacht close by, with a gold band on his cap and a great many gilt buttons on his coat, I was greenhorn enough to think he knew something, so modestly asked his advice, and followed it to our grief and confusion.

"Since then I have grown older, and have learnt one or two little secrets which I will disclose for the information of brother greenhorns. When you hear a man talking so loudly that you are in doubt how many yachts he owns, be sure his nearest approach to ownership is knowing a friend, who is or was an owner. Therefore be careful not to ask the name of his yacht. And when you see a yachting gilt-bespangled dandy, trust rather to your 'Seaman's Manual and Vocabulary of Sea-terms,' and do not disgust the gentleman with awkward questions before company unless you wish to make an enemy.

"Running down the 'Hope' under all sail on a beautiful sunny morning was such a delightful novelty, and so exhilarating, that confidence was restored sooner than might have been the case if we had not been able to charge our first misfortune upon the lubber with the gold band and gilt buttons. After a good breakfast we were in high spirits, and every fresh gust of wind was answered with an inward chuckle of satisfaction.

"All went merrily as a marriage bell until we were about a mile below the Nore, when our enjoyment was at its height, and it was thought time to turn back. Finding, on coming to the wind, that it was necessary to take a reef down, we ceased all at once to see beauty anywhere, had misgivings, and secretly began to 'wish we were at home.' "

McMullen's next boat, *Sirius*, which we have already mentioned, was a larger craft altogether than *Leo*. She measured 32 feet overall and 29 feet between perpendiculars. She came from the same builder's yard, but was built of teak. She was not unlike *Leo* in profile, and was, in fact, built on the same lines as the latter. She had, however, a rounded stern, because McMullen had found that riding at anchor in a boat with a long counter was an uncomfortable business. In *Sirius* McMullen sailed from 1858 to 1865, logging a total of 11,693 miles, and it was in *Sirius* that in 1863 he achieved one of his ambitions, which was to sail round Great Britain.

Sirius was succeeded in 1865 by *Orion*. Once again McMullen went for a larger vessel, *Orion* being 42 feet overall and 38 feet between perpendiculars. She was also of teak, but was built in Lymington by G. Inman. She was rigged as a cutter originally, but in 1873 McMullen altered her rig to that of a yawl, and lengthened her some 6 feet by the stern. In *Orion* McMullen sailed 5,182 miles during the years 1865 to 1868. Although the distances were not so great as some of his earlier cruises, he saw some very heavy weather in *Orion* and one of the delightful engravings in the book depicts her "lying to" under headsail at midnight, September 28th, 1868. It is one of those awesome representations of mountainous, toppling seas, with the vessel herself at an alarming angle of heel, and with two apparently quite unmoved sailormen in the cockpit sitting down to leeward!

Here is McMullen's description of sailing through the Needles Channel on that same cruise, arriving at last at Cowes "wet through, tired, and hungry":

"For hours I had been most uncomfortably nervous about the passage of the Needles Channel, which is a gradually shoaling bar of considerable extent connecting the Shingles Shoal and the Bridge Reef, and I thought about sailing round the Island to avoid the difficulty. This wretched feeling of anxiety died away considerably as the morning advanced, and I saw how safely we were borne on by some of the most alarming breakers. Several times in the deep water, huge seas broke in our wake, and came rushing on in a mountain of foam. To those unacquainted with the power of the vessel destruction would have seemed inevitable, but owing to her powerful quarters and short elliptical stern, she rose steadily and regularly, and the seas passed harmlessly under her, excepting the little head before mentioned, which was heaped up high and thin by collision with our own wave, and was driven on deck by the wind.

"Shortly after 8 a.m. the sky was tolerably clear, and the wind less violent; but the clouds, thick with rain, were banking up heavily again in the S.W. For a while there seemed reason to hope we should outstrip them and make the Bar before they dispensed their favours, but they came on at such a rattling pace that we were overtaken in less than an hour, and the gale raged more furiously than ever, driving clouds of spoon-drift before it, and forcing us through the water at 9 knots, with only the little reefed trysail drawing.

"The steering was so hard, that my left hand and arm were benumbed. I could use them as a log, feeling pressure at the shoulder, but could not feel the tiller. My mate was a first-class seaman, but his sight was not sharp enough to dodge the sea by night, nor to anticipate its course at any time; and the man who understands the vessel best, especially a small vessel, must be at the helm when a mistake or a little carelessness may cause all to be overwhelmed in a moment.

"It was of such vital importance to cross in the best water, that, as the dreaded time drew near, I would have given a good deal for a reassuring glimpse of the chart; but as it did not occur to me at the time to send a man into the forecastle to force the door of communication between the fore and after cabins, by which it might have been obtained, I had to trust to memory. I recollected passing close to the buoy two years before, and fortunately remembered the appearance of the Needles and Alum Bay sufficiently well to run through the Channel on that mark, viz., the N.W. side of the rocks and the long white cliff just coming into view out of a right line.

"9 a.m. passed close to the Nun-buoy of the S.W. Shingles without seeing it. Though the man and the lad were keeping an anxious look-out, it was not sighted until we were past, and on the top of the next great sea beyond. It was not wanted, however, to show that we were in the Channel—the appearance of the sea proved that, it being the only spot free from dangerous breakers. While remarking this, we were picked up like a feather and carried over the inner edge of the Bar into deeper water by three or four enormous waves that towered up in walls of water just short of breaking. After this the sea lost its dangerous character.

"The general scene, viewed from just inside the Bar, was awfully grand and imposing. On the Shingles the surf was tremendous; great seas closing in upon the knolls (shoal spots) came into collision with each other, and leaped high into the air in immense columns of spray. From the Needles to a quarter of a mile S.W., and thence across to Sun Corner, a space including all Scratchell Bay, was a confused mass of breakers, a cauldron of raging surf, from which arose a cloud of spray to the height of about 150 feet, shrouding the weather side and the upper part of the Needles Point and Rocks in a thick haze. Thence, assuming the form of a well-defined stratum of cloud, the spray travelled at a great rate up Alum Bay until it came to the coloured cliff, a mile distant, over which it curved gracefully on to the land above. Upon the Bar itself, over which the ebb tide was just beginning to run, were about four prodigious rollers, through which there could have been little chance of passing in safety, had we unfortunately taken the course that is usual for any but the largest ships and run the log, which marked 28 knots, or 13 for 1 hr. 35 min. Allowing the same rate of sailing from 8 to 9 as for the previous two hours, leaves 5½ knots for the last 35 min.—equal to 9½ per hour—which was not surprising considering the hurricane it blew after 9 o'clock. 10 a.m. passed inside the Points, tide running hard out. Off Yarmouth there was a small fleet of vessels at anchor, including four steamers. One of them, the *Duke of Cornwall*, Dublin paddle-steamer, was canted partly athwart the tide, and had a considerable list from the power of the wind. Passengers and crew were comfortably sheltering in the lee scuppers. The sea in the Solent was extremely rough and violent, but seemed like smooth water after our recent experience. We saw only one vessel under way between Hurst and Cowes—a pilot cutter beating down under reefed trysail. 12.30 p.m. arrived at Cowes, wet through, tired, and hungry, having had 13 hours at the helm, besides very heavy work when lying-to.

"I am too great a novice to accept safety as a matter of course. The reaction upon my feelings after crossing the Bar was greater than I care to express, or desire to experience again if there be equal cause for it, however agreeable a successful result may be.

"One feeling of unmixed satisfaction I had in the knowledge that my vessel was equal to such an occasion."

McMullen must have dearly loved *Orion*. In her he made in the years following, that is to say from 1869 to 1877, a series of cruises to Bantry, to the Forth, to the west coast of Scotland, and finally in 1877 we come to his well-known single-handed sail, when having dismissed his crew of two for incompetence, he sailed this heavily sparred vessel of some 19½ tons home from Cherbourg by himself.

This was a prodigious feat. He lost "between two and three pounds" in weight during the preparation for sea and the single-handed passage to England. He was, in the words of the sailing writer Frank Cowper, "the first to show how one man could handle a large boat". But not only was this fact alone memorable, but when one thinks of a vessel of 42 feet overall, fitted with the heavy gear of those days, and without any modern labour-saving devices, some idea of the effort and skill involved becomes clear.

His account of his worsening relations with the crew, leading to their dismissal, is far too entertaining to be omitted. I quote it here in full:

"On Sunday morning after breakfast I found them evidently suffering from a suppressed sense of injury. It was not until the next day I learnt, at least according to their statement, that none of the men belonging to other yachts were turned out to wash down on Sunday morning. If true, it cannot be regarded as a praiseworthy remission of duty, out of regard for the sanctity of the day, unless extended to the cook and stewards, who have harder and more disagreeable work at anchor than all the rest of the crew put together. At all events, it was a new and happy discovery in favour of another hour in bed, and was seized upon accordingly. Not that they cared a bit for the sanctity of the day, for, by their own statement and my own observation, I found that their custom, at home, was to spend the day in listless idleness—and on board also, unless I could induce them to act differently. Those who are most loud in their objections to Sunday 'duty' are, generally, those who least regard it as a day of religious observance.

"When this matter of washing down was mentioned, I replied—that I cared nothing at all for what they did or did not do on other yachts—that it had always been a rule of *mine* to have a clean vessel on Sunday, before flying colours, and that it always would be.

"As regards sailing on Sunday. If under way—making a passage—it is a matter of course. If in port, I prefer not to leave. But if we are at anchor in an open roadstead, the rules of common sense must be observed on *that* day as on any other. Pitching bows under, on Sunday, in a state of anxiety about the anchor holding, I can answer for it by experience, is anything but a day of rest. If the men were conscientiously engaged in devotional exercises I should be sorry to disturb them. But if the choice lay between danger, discomfort, and idleness on the one hand—and safety combined with fair and legitimately imposed duties on the other—I should unhesitatingly choose the latter.

"*Monday, July 30*, opened with a fine treat. They quarrelled violently over the work on deck—each accusing the other of shirking. I thought to myself, 'Go it, my lads, you are on the right tack at last.' The day being fine, I ordered a coat of black paint—to make her more 'fit for the glass case in the park.' On shore it was frightfully hot; the people were asleep in the shops and beside the stalls in the markets; streets were deserted; the gutters 'quite French,' and business almost at a standstill. Before the painting began, I went ashore to make arrangements in furtherance of my plans—amongst other things, ascertained the expense to London, and that the steamer would sail next night at 10 o'clock.

"In the evening, after dinner, I went forward on deck to enlighten the men as to the 'bag and baggage' policy. It sounds harsh, it is perhaps historical, but really, it is only an intimation, that you may pack up your traps and go if you like.

"I began by informing them that the idea of the cruise to Dartmouth had been abandoned soon after our arrival at Cherbourg, in consequence of their disgraceful conduct—and continued, 'I remember, the first day out, you said that you hated the sea. Your notices prove that you desire to join your families as soon as possible. Now, there is a chance of your doing so by a steamer sailing from here to-morrow, and you had better avail yourselves of it.' Of course they were surprised, and a fuss ensued about being dismissed at a foreign port. I said, 'Very well, you may please yourselves. You owe me a week's service from to-day. The proposed cruise is abandoned through your misconduct. If you refuse my terms, whatever the weather is—if we have four reefs down—I intend to go to sea to-morrow, and have a cruise for my own pleasure to the Land's End. You can serve your time and be landed at an English port, or go by steamer to Southampton. I will leave you to make your choice.'

"Not many minutes elapsed before they came to tell me that they would agree to leave by the steamer.

"Having heard that I had been out of bed before, just the number of days coincident with the length of their notice, they shrewdly suspected that what had happened before might happen again, and let them in for a harder week's work than would agree with their constitution. Then a money difficulty arose, which, after some unpleasantness was settled to my satisfaction. Later on, one came aft to the companion to inform me that they were both completely satisfied and agreed to have a special cleaning up next day, put the forecastle in nice order, and do everything I desired.

"*July 31.*—I felt unwell, and attributed it partly to the heat of the weather, and the smell of the back streets of the town on the previous day. Everybody knows that in all French towns the poor inhabitants of the upper floors pour their waste water down pipes into the street gutters. Before it is 'wasted' all the good properties of water are exhausted so that our analysts would have to reverse the order of their investigation, and ascertain the percentage of 'pure water' the sample contained. I tried sulphuric acid, laudanum, and granular magnesia—all in turn. The former is my favourite medicine, and, I believe perfectly safe; but, without advice, I thought it best to have a turn at champagne, which, after all, proved the best physic for a very busy day.

"I had new wicks, saturated in spirits of turpentine, put into the lanterns, and a fresh supply of oil into the feeders; had topmast housed; extra tackles prepared—one 30 feet long, with spare trysail sheet blocks for taking the main-sheet in along the deck—others for various purposes, such as hauling the fore-sheet to windward and getting the jibsheet aft; strops of different-sized ropes to suit every requirement; short white ropes with an eye in one end, to break the canvas in, etc. The making of all these things may have occasioned some sur-prise, and probably led to the conclusion that sailors of less stamina than Englishmen would take their berths. It was not likely they would have the faintest suspicion of the truth, for it is characteristic of men of this stamp, to think that if they are taken away there will not be a man left. However, I was very careful not to drop a hint on the subject, for several reasons, two of them being: 1. The possibility of failure in getting the vessel under way at all, and the knowledge that a false report might get abroad and be a source of anxiety to my friends. 2. The fear of that would have added to the worry of a delay on the passage, and perhaps have induced me to act against judgment, in the desire to hasten on. The letters, securing five or six days' liberty, left me untrammelled. I was determined to go ahead, but free to 'ease her', 'stop her', or 'go astern.' It was a position that almost ensured success and speedy execution. Talking beforehand is—to those who are ashamed to fail—like burning the traditional boats that should accompany one on every difficult expedition; it leads to preci-pitancy, and is likely to be the cause of failure.

"I had no complaint against them the next day. Everything was honestly done, as per arrangement. After an earlier dinner than usual, for me, they put their bags into the boat, and we started for the shore. Upon their thanking me again for the fair treatment they had received, I said, 'I am glad to hear you acknowledge it; there is no vindictive feeling on my part, but our acquaintance must end here, as I cannot consent to know you if we meet again.' The rest of the distance was rowed in silence."

In 1887, the Jubilee year, McMullen sailed *Orion* in another circumnaviga-tion of Great Britain, with two paid hands and an amateur mate. It was this feat which, according to himself, gave him the most satisfaction. He sold *Orion* in 1889.

The majority of McMullen's cruises were carried out in the English Channel, although in *Orion* he ventured farther afield, as we have seen. His annual cruise would average 1,500 miles. When he sailed round Great Britain the first time he logged 2,640 miles, but these longer cruises were the exception rather than the rule. True to his original vow, he kept the sea in all weathers, always paying great attention to the many details involved in handling and navigating a small vessel. He left nothing to chance. He was blessed with good health. A small man, he was capable, as the *Orion* episode alone showed, of long, unrelieved hours of work. After his death the "Field" in an obituary notice said "Mr McMullen was unlike any other yachtsman we ever met. . . ." There is little doubt that various recalcitrant paid hands would agree!

In the year 1873 McMullen had sailed a 28 foot 6 inch lugger called *Procyon* single-handed from Greenhithe to the Isle of Wight. *Procyon* was built for McMullen in 1867. She was not exactly a comfortable vessel, her sleeping accommodation consisting of a hammock slung from the foremast in a small "cuddy".

An account of a trial cruise in 1878 made in *Procyon* is sandwiched in the book between the single-handed passage in *Orion* in 1877 and a cruise in the latter vessel in 1882, this time with an all-amateur crew.

Although this vessel occupies but a small section of McMullen's book, yet this section contains what is one of the best pieces of descriptive writing in the book. I quote from it:

"If I seem to have given too much prominence to the item of meals, it is because I regard their healthy enjoyment as the mainspring of work which otherwise could not have been carried on beyond a very limited time. Thus, in gauging the physical or mental condition of a crew, meals are an unfailing index to the state of the social barometer, discovering the existence of 'waves of depression,' whether caused by anxiety, debility, or discontent.

"Enlivened by a gleam of sunshine occasionally, the day was not entirely bad, though the wind was so extremely violent as to cause the lugger to ride to lee-ward with a great strain on the anchor, when in ordinary weather the tide would have forced her to ride to windward. In addition to a turbulent short sea off the land, on the port bow I had the big 'Channel sea' rolling partly athwart wind into Pegwell Bay, the two together creating a compound motion that threw the recollection of the Whitstable anchorage into the shade. Routine work and about two hours' carpentering below furnished plenty of occupation until four o'clock, when the wind once more veered to the westward with a rising barometer, according to its now almost established daily custom. As fresh supplies were again running short, and marketing cannot be done on Sandwich flats for love or money, in the hope—if not firm faith—that the clouds had drained themselves dry and the wind blown itself out at last, I determined upon another advance towards Dover, and at 5 p.m. set the mainsail double reefed for a reach down against tide to Deal. I had 35 fathoms of rope out, and not the least chance of getting any of it in by hand as in the morning; so I cast to windward with the sails hard sheeted, and when about on the other tack sailed straight for the anchor, my only difficulty this time being that of over-hauling the rope enough. The instant it tautened in my hand I 'took a turn' and lifted the anchor out of the ground. This was my first experience of rope *versus* chain, which, instead of exhausting me to speechlessness, enabled me to laugh approvingly the while at its charming simplicity and complete success. I used to think rope was used by smacks only in the absence of chain, but now, for temporarily anchoring small craft at sea, am convinced of its superiority, and shall adopt it in future.

"Under a brilliant sky, I had a delightful little sail, 'gunwale down,' that in the absence of sea-sickness must have approved itself to the most fastidious taste; and that even an 'unhappy sufferer' would have regarded as a welcome change who had passed the previous twelve hours on board. The position I chose was in four fathoms low water, abreast of Upper Deal, and about three-quarters of a mile from the pier. The sea was toning down when I brought up with the same riding gear as before, and, having started my preparations for dinner—which, fortunately in point of time, promised to be on the table at a less fashionable hour than usual—proceeded to make snug for the night. A boat had been alongside with a proposal to take me ashore for the trifling sum of six shillings, which considering the wind was off shore—and excepting a moderate swell on the beach was only like landing at Gravesend—I said would make the few things I required rather expensive. Upon their requesting me to name the sum I was willing to give, my reply was 'Nothing.' 'Then it's no use to wait?' 'Not the slightest.' 'Good night.'

"What a superb night it was! One might almost have been excused for supposing it would never rain again—yet the stars were overbright! Excepting for the long easy pitch and roll, I seemed to have come home after the rude buffeting of the day, and to be the centre of an illumination got up for my especial gratification. On the starboard hand were the lights of the town—on the port hand, the lights of between two and three hundred sail at anchor—and astern, the concentrated, but rather faint illumination of Ramsgate, looking not unlike Vauxhall Gardens in the time of their prosperity. I enjoyed the scene thoroughly, deeply, and little cared to think how quickly it could change.

"*Aug. 27.*—I had only just turned out after an unusually refreshing sleep—such as follows a gale and dispersion of clouds, but, with me, never precedes it if the clouds are gathering towards night—when one of my visitors of the previous evening came alongside, and immediately agreed to land me and put me on board again for two shillings. Of course! considering he would have rowed a whole family about for an hour for that money, or even have contended with another boat in a race of a mile home to pick up an old box for firewood not worth sixpence. Besides, I could have landed myself for nothing had I chosen to have done so.

"Having posted letters and purchased a few necessaries, I returned on board to breakfast, right glad to have attended to business first, since it had rained already, and was looking exceedingly dirty in the south-west, with an unmistakably dull barometer.

"The wind soon made itself heard in strong gusts from the direction of Lower Deal, and, while attending to my duties below, I felt the lugger rising higher and plunging deeper every minute as the sea came rolling up in constantly increasing volume from the South Foreland. Had not a miserable rain accompanied the sea, I should have found entertainment in watching its effect upon my neighbours; but rain and spray combined were too drenching for me to leave the cabin except on business.

"After breakfast I was hailed from a large lugger standing off under storm-sails to know 'If I would give them a trifle to take me into Ramsgate?' to which I replied, 'I would rather give you a trifle to keep me out.' The last words that reached me were, 'We'll come alongside,' which, though not attempted to be put into execution, I accepted as a warning not to bandy words that, on one side, it might possibly be convenient to misconstrue. My custom is to fly a club burgee, whatever the weather; but to fly an ensign in a gale is extravagant and unusual, unless there is a special motive. I had such a motive now, and ran mine up to its proper place—the mizenmast head; the purpose being to intimate plainly that assistance was not needed, and would be declined. As to my knowledge nothing passed within hailing distance during the next twenty-four hours, I presume its signification was understood; though it is doubtful if, after twelve o'clock, any but a very powerful crew or a steamer could have come, if they would.

"The wind increased in force, and gradually southed until it set straight through the Downs with a tremendous sea, which would not have occasioned me much inconvenience—though occasionally the lugger seemed to leap almost out of water with its violence—if the wind had not caught her in that position, first on one bow and then on the other, and caused her to range considerably. The effect of ranging with so large a scope was to expose her broadside more or less to the sea, and cause her to lurch heavily until she regained her position astream of the anchor. To correct this, I set the mizen and hoisted a small jib as

Orion, reefed, runs before a breaking following sea. [After an old print]

a trysail—sheet upwards and aback against the mast to prevent it being blown to pieces—cast to the westward, and when the sheer had forged her sufficiently ahead, let go a second anchor and hauled down the jib. Paying out 20 fathoms of rope, she fell into her former position and remained tolerably steady for a time with an equal strain upon both anchors. The ropes were 'parcelled' to protect them from chafing in the 'gammon-iron,' which answered admirably as a 'hawse-pipe'; and to prevent the strain being thrown directly upon the short nip of the belaying cleats, a turn was first taken round the mast.

"After a substantial luncheon and a pipe, I looked up at 3.30 p.m. to see if there were any prospect of the usual afternoon clearance, and discovered that she had dragged the two anchors in line. As the heavier one, with 40 fathoms of rope, now fairly backed the smaller one, with 20 fathoms, I had no reason to be dissatisfied; for the question was no longer one of personal comfort below, but of holding ground against the wind, which by this time was terrific.

"The fleet had increased in number by vessels running in under very short canvas from the Channel; but, to my knowledge, none passed to the southward. Nor is it likely any ordinary vessel did so, since I heard afterwards of a steamer due at Boulogne from the Thames at nine o'clock that night which failed to reach there until twelve hours later; and of a cutter-rigged smack which failed to weather the North Foreland.

"Observing that the barometer continued to decline, and that there was no indication of a break in the clouds, it became necessary to make the preparations for the coming night, during which, if the wind backed to the south-east without moderating, the anchors would probably have to be slipped, and the sea encountered under way. Moreover, it was certain she could not carry the mainsail, even close-reefed, and that the work of preparation would be far too long and heavy to be undertaken excepting in daylight—especially as the deck was slippery and unprotected with bulwarks.

"First, the mainsail had to be unbent from the mast; then, to enable it to be covered and stowed in the berth I contemplated, between the waist coaming and the gunwale, it had to be opened out on the deck, and, notwithstanding its wet and harsh condition, be furled almost as snugly as if it were dry. This, on account of the high sea running, the most trying task of the day, required time and perseverance; but it was accomplished at last to my satisfaction, and the sail lashed securely to the gunwale on the starboard side, where its weight counterbalanced the dinghy and spars on the opposite side. This heavy gear would have been stowed on the lower platform, had not my comfort below and complete freedom from any sort of obstruction been far more important than the trifling disadvantage of a moderate deck load.

"To avoid spending more time on deck forward than was absolutely necessary, the stormsail, being dry and in every way easier to handle than the mainsail, was opened out below and reefed there; then lifted forward and bent to the mast. When the tackles were overhauled and seen to be clear for hoisting almost beyond the possibility of a hitch, and the sheet bent on, I furled the sail and partially covered it—so that there would be nothing to do but uncover, cast off stops, and hoist away. The precaution of covering may seem superfluous, since rain and spray wetted it considerably before the cover could be put on; but if the canvas and tackles had been permitted to harden by saturation the difficulty of hoisting would have been increased, and the latter, probably, have kinked and jammed at a critical moment. The ensign, in a 'reasonably' tattered condition, had been hauled down at sunset, and shortly afterwards the riding light got up—which, in spite of the violence of the elements, I contrived to keep burning with steady brilliance throughout the night by partially closing the ventilator with thin canvas.

"Beyond an occasional glance towards the landmarks, to see that the anchors were holding firm, for several hours my attention was so exclusively directed to my own affairs, that if the whole fleet had vanished I should have been unconscious of the fact. It would be absurd to pretend that such work, in itself, was agreeable; yet the pleasure of knowing it was done, and that everything was in a reasonable state of efficiency and preparation to meet a more adverse change, if it should come, was immense. As with the most highly favoured mortals on shore comfort is only comparative, it cannot be difficult to understand how thoroughly jolly it was below when the stove was lighted, wringing wet garments exchanged for dry, and a savoury rump-steak and potatoes under way for dinner. Besides the powerful beam thrown across the cabin from the stove—I had an oil lamp with reflector at the after end of the cabin, and a candle lamp forward—for the more gloomy it is on deck the more desirable is cheerfulness below. Outside the cabin, the larger riding light belonging to the *Orion*, and specially chosen for duty upon this occasion, shed a strong light over the vessel; its rays, as I sat by the open cuddy doors, seeming to be absorbed immediately beyond the gunwale and the mizenmast in a wall of impenetrable darkness.

"Though I have passed many a suspicious-looking night at anchor upon various parts of the coast of Great Britain and Ireland, the situation struck me as novel when at 10.30, in a condition of wistful expectancy, I was tending the sputtering and odoriferous steak, compelled, for the credit of my occupation, to follow attentively and even anticipate the violent plunges and lurches of the vessel—listening, the while, to the roar of the wind and the dashing of rain and spray against the after bulkhead; and, at times, watching almost with curiosity the sudden depression of the stern followed by as sudden a rise above my head, according to the position she occupied on the passing wave. In such circumstances it sounds strange that there should be anything short of actual discomfort in sitting down to dinner at a late hour of the night by the open doors of the cuddy; but, excepting the motion, there was none whatever, as the thermometer was fairly high, and the wind too strong from ahead to allow any rain to fall within several feet of the entrance to the cabin. I was very curious to see the barometer—which, from an early hour of the day up to the last time of seeing it, had moved steadily downward—but restrained my curiosity for the present; considering that if the fall was checked nothing would be gained by ascertaining it, whereas if a serious further decline had taken place, knowledge of it might interfere with the dinner, which, with a pint of Bass, plumcake for pudding, and a pipe for dessert, was in every respect a most successful performance."

The final yacht in the book is *Perseus*. *Perseus* was a 6-ton lugger built by Holloway in 1890. She was built of elm on oak frames and measured 27 feet 2 inches overall. The drawing shows her sail plan.

The following are the entries Mr McMullen made in his journal after setting out on his last cruise in the *Perseus*, 1891, in the high spirits usual with him when setting out on a single-handed cruise:

"*June 8.*—Went out of dock, and alongside pier (causeway), to scrub the copper and take in water. Hauled off during night to moorings.

"*June 10.*—4 p.m., sailed from Greenhithe; wind high, N.E.; cool, but sunny. Off Northfleet the breeze freshened, and below Gravesend became strong; weather cloudy and hazy. With no jib, and towing the dinghey, she eventually beat every barge in a long turn to windward. 6.30 p.m., anchored in Mucking Bight.

"*June 11.*—Sunshine. Turned out 4.15; had some trouble with the anchor. 5.30 a.m., set mainsail. 7.40, passed the Nore; weather very gloomy and cold; wind N., puffy. Noon, Reculvers, S.W.; gladdened by a gleam of sunshine; touched both the Spaniards, but did not stay. 1 to 3, wind very light with swell. 3 p.m., tacked off Westgate; wind fresh, E.; large jib set; after rounding the North Foreland, wind fell lighter, with troublesome swell. 7, anchored with rope on Sandwich Flats; rolled dreadfully all night.

"*June 12.*—Wind N.E., fresh and fine. 6 a.m., under way with mainsail only; very much work. Eventually got early tea. Set jib and mizen; washed, and prepared breakfast before reaching Dover. 9 to 10, hove-to in Dover Bay, had breakfast, etc., and sailed again. 10.30, set large jib. 11, off Folkestone, going grandly, but the wind soon fell light. 2.30 p.m., passed Dungeness against tide; wind E.S.E., light. 7 p.m., St Leonards; wind S.S.W., light; boat making good way, owing to smoother water and the large jib. 8.30 p.m., anchored off Bexhill; night fine. (Bexhill is between St. Leonards and Eastbourne.)"

That is the last entry in his log. He is recorded as having posted a letter at Eastbourne, having presumably anchored and landed on the 13th of June. This was the last action of his that is known, for on the evening of the 15th he was found dead, by some French fishermen. He had been dead for twenty-four hours when he was discovered, but his little ship was sailing herself along as if there was a living hand upon the tiller. He was sitting in the cockpit, his face looking towards the sky, while *Perseus*, sailing as true as if he was still guiding her, continued on her course, the course "down Channel".

7

HARRY PIDGEON

His Sea Was Bluer

"The Cruise of the *Islander*" is the subtitle of a book which was published in 1933 called "Around the World Single-handed". The writer was an American called Harry Pidgeon. Since the first great lone circumnavigation of Joshua Slocum the feat of sailing a small yacht around the world had been successfully accomplished a number of times—and indeed in the previous year, 1932, a fellow American, William Robinson (who we meet in Chapter 15), had published his own version of the feat. Nevertheless there was something unusual about Harry Pidgeon's cruise. He made it in a vessel built entirely by himself. Add to this the fact that he could write entertainingly, was observant, and this result adds up to an unusual book.

Harry Pidgeon's love of his ship sprang not only from the fact that he built her, and that she was strong enough to carry him through the bad weather that no circumnavigator can really avoid, but because she made his dream come true. One can sense the enthusiasm and wonder he felt at each new encounter—his first flying-fish, his first breathtaking sight of a coral island ". . . a feathery line . . . on the horizon . . . just a wreath of verdure cast upon the sea".

The ship in which he made his voyage was built to plans by one Captain Thomas Fleming Day, a very experienced seaman, designer of small boats and editor of the magazine "Rudder". Day had drawn plans for three similar but slightly different types of vessel. They were called *Sea Bird*, *Naiad* and *Seagoer*. In the original *Sea Bird* he made a remarkable cruise from New York to Rome. The *Sea Queen* in which Voss turned turtle was built to the same plans (see Chapter 5). Harry Pidgeon, although choosing *Seagoer*, borrowed some ideas from the other two plans as well as adding some of his own. He started work in 1917 by laying down the keel.

He did not come from a seafaring background, being born on a farm in Iowa, and until he was 8 years of age had never even seen the sea. He spent some time on a ranch in California and while there built himself a canvas canoe. After a while he went to Alaska and while there he built with the help of another young farmer a wooden canoe in which they planned to navigate the Alaska River. He describes how they launched the boat off the ice into a bit of open water and how he found himself with a pair of oars in his hands for the first time in his life.

Their travels took them through the Five-finger Rapids on the Yukon River, which they navigated until the summer was over. This early taste of the pleasures of boating had been enough to sow the fatal seed of sea fever and Pidgeon was soon to join the ranks of small-boat owners, building his own small craft for use in his hunting trips along the rivers of Alaska. Undoubtedly the experience in building river boats and the toughening process of life in the wilds stood Pidgeon in good stead when he came to build his own sea-going ship and to sail her round the world. It was while cruising in a "flat boat" of his own construction on the Mississippi River that the wanderlust really caught him. He resolved as he puts it ". . . to see more distant lands in a vessel of my own".

He had by this time acquired some reputation as a naturalist photographer and spent some years among the trees of the Sierras earning a living in this way. And all the time his dream of sailing to distant lands was in the back of his mind, so that when one day he chanced upon the plans of Captain Day, and realized that here was a craft that an amateur could build, a craft moreover that could look after herself in the open sea, he knew that his opportunity had come. Accordingly he descended from the mountains to the shore of Los Angeles harbour, found a vacant lot, and began, with characteristic determination, to build his boat.

The plans were of a V bottom or chine construction, which is easier for the amateur to lay down and build. The wood used was mostly Douglas fir or Oregon pine, and the timbers were not only very heavy but reinforced at the bilge with steel plates that Pidgeon cut from tank plate.

Islander measured 34 feet overall and had a beam of 10 feet 9 inches. Her cabin was 12 feet long, giving enough, if somewhat spartan living room. She was rigged, as can be seen from the drawing, as a gaff yawl and her sweet and beautiful lines are eloquent of Captain Day's designing genius.

She had no engine and carried a 10-foot skiff as a dinghy, built also by her owner. The total cost of building was near enough $1,000 and she had taken almost exactly a year and a half to build. As she sat on the water after her launching one can readily imagine Harry Pidgeon's chest bursting with pride of achievement and delight in her beauty.

After some preliminary cruising with friends and some hard study of the mysteries of navigation, Harry Pidgeon and the *Islander* were ready for serious business.

His first voyage took him to Hawaii. He describes how after taking his little ship through her first gale the dark clouds gradually disappeared and '. . . when the sunlight broke through . . . the water was bluer than any I had ever seen", and how later on the thirteenth day out ". . . a beautiful white tropic bird, the

ISLANDER

Length overall: 34 feet
Beam: 10 feet 9 inches
Draught: 5 feet. Sail area: 630 square feet
This vessel, like the *Sea Queen* (see
Chapter 5) was of a type developed by
Captain Thomas Fleming Day and the
designing staff of *Rudder Magazine*.
They were designed for amateur
building, and Pidgeon built her himself.

first I had ever seen, paid the *Islander* a visit, and I began to realise that I was in the tropics at last". What a wonderful sense of adventure it must have given him. How far behind him the caustic remarks of those who had prophesied disaster as he worked on building the ship that was now carrying him so well to wherever his fancy took him.

He was accompanied on the return passage to California by a fellow country-man he met in Honolulu. They ran into uncertain weather varying from light winds to a gale, and Pidgeon's seamanship and navigational skill were daily increasing.

The Hawaiian cruise gave him the confidence that experience brings and he set about preparing for a voyage to the South Seas, and those fabulous islands in the Southern Pacific Ocean, and at noon on November the 18th, 1921, he sailed from Los Angeles for the Marquesas Islands.

Pidgeon says in his book that his intention was to voyage to the Marquesas, Society Islands and Samoa and then return to California. He does not seem to have set out with the definite intention of circumnavigating the globe, but he admits that he would probably ". . . extend the voyage if circumstances were favourable". Indeed, even after he had cruised as far westwards as Samoa with plans to continue as far as the Fiji group, we still find him writing that "I was enjoying my cruise so well that I decided to continue the voyage".

The decision to sail right round the world appears to have been taken at Thursday Island, the bleak gravelly island set in the reef-strewn Torres Strait. "Thursday Island", wrote Pidgeon, "is a sort of cross roads of the sea, where I could go south . . . to Australia, or pass through the East Indies to the Phil-lipines."

He did, however, do neither, but decided finally to sail home by way of the Cape of Good Hope and the Panama Canal. From Thursday Island the *Islander* followed fairly closely in the ghost of the wake of Captain Slocum's *Spray*, which had passed through Torres Strait in June 1897. At Trinidad, however, the *Spray* had sailed northwards to Boston, whereas the *Islander* continued west-wards to the Panama Canal.

It is impossible to sail alone round the world without having a good many adventures, whether you want them or not.

One of the hazards of single-handed sailing is fatigue, falling asleep during a time when great vigilance is necessary. All the great circumnavigators have managed to sleep perfectly adequately, lashing the helm, and like Captain Slocum trusting in the pilot of the *Pinta* to sail the vessel for them while they slept. But there are bound to be times when continuous bad weather brings such fatigue that it becomes almost impossible to keep awake. This is commented upon particularly by Eric Hiscock, who found fatigue a real problem for himself and his wife in *Wanderer III*.

While sailing for the island of St Helena, Pidgeon was drifting for two days along the coast, and being close inshore could not get proper sleep on account of dangers to navigation. On the third night, as he was a little farther from the shore, he turned in, exhausted, only to be woken by his ship raking the ground amidst breakers. He writes that when he saw he was stranded he said to himself: "My voyage ends right here."

But he was lucky. His ship had grounded on a sheltered sandy beach protected by rocks on either side and, apart from a battered rudder and some damage to the after part of the keel, no great harm had been done to the *Islander*. She had not filled with water, and by digging the sand away and raising the hull with jacks until planks could be worked underneath her she was eventually relaunched. It was indeed a miraculous escape, for if he had grounded on any other place on that stretch of coast the *Islander* would undoubtedly have been wrecked.

Another occasion when Pidgeon was rudely awakened was when the *Islander* was cruising just after midnight under jib and mainsail well out at sea off the South American coast. Anyone would be forgiven for taking the chance of a little sleep. Pidgeon was in his bunk below decks when suddenly there was a great crash as something struck the ship. He leaped on deck to find to his astonishment the hull of a large steamship alongside him, sailing the same course and speed as the *Islander*. He could see a line of faces peering down at him and somebody threw him a line. He was understandably bewildered, but then realized that he was being rescued. He was expected to climb the rope to safety and leave his ship.

A fairly irrascible dialogue ensued during which Pidgeon was asked if he wanted "assistance" and replied that he did not! At this point a more than usually large wave raised the *Islander* so that she was level with the steamer's rail, then the backwash of the same wave threw her clear and she came up into the wind clear of the steamer. She was not left without a scar, however, for as she rounded into the wind the steamer, rolling back towards her, broke off the mizzen boom at the gooseneck. Pidgeon confesses that although the whole episode did not last more than five minutes . . . "it was the most thrilling five minutes of my voyage".

The steamer turned out to be an oil tanker bound for Buenos Aires. She returned within hailing distance, asking repeatedly if Pidgeon wanted to be taken off, before continuing on her course to Buenos Aires.

Pidgeon spent a sleepless night, but with the morning was able to splice the

Islander in Moorea

broken mizzen rigging and hoist the mizzensail reefed. He was able to heave-to so that he would be free to work. The bowsprit had been broken with the first blow from the steamer, and Pidgeon had to cut off the broken end and refit it. He describes how while he lay out on it trying to splice a new wire bobstay a yellow-and-brown-spotted shark swam underneath, keeping him in close observation! Eventually the job was finished and *Islander*, with reefed mainsail and a small jib, was put on her course for Trinidad Island, Panama and home.

Curiously enough, it was the passage from Panama Bay to California that turned out to be the longest and most difficult, taking eighty-five days! He sailed via Clipperton Island, passing two degrees to the west of it, beating against contrary winds and squalls.

However, he took the capricious weather with his usual philosophic good temper, and was able to find entertainment in watching the antics of the fish all round him:

". . . One of the most startling sights that I saw was when a whole school of flying-fishes, numbering thousands, took to the air, a gleaming, silvery band spread out across the course of the *Islander*. Whether they were startled by my onrushing craft or were flying for the joy of it I could not tell, but they all left the water at the same time, and at the end of the flight came down together.

"I could have fared quite well on the flying-fishes to be found lying about where they fell on deck after striking sails or rigging at night. As I lay in my berth I could hear them plump against the side of the cabin. In their frantic efforts to escape the rushes of the albacore and dolphins, they often collided with the *Islander* in broad daylight, and I have been struck by them as I sat at the tiller. When one struck some part of the rigging and fell back into the water, there would be a violent commotion, as half a dozen albacore came together in a head-on collision in their rush to be first at the stunned flying-fish.

"One day I found a flying-fish that had lodged under the dinghy and lain there till it was not so fresh as it might have been. I tossed it over the side, where a large fish of the tunny variety snapped it up and disappeared in the depth. A moment later the decayed flying-fish came to the surface, having, no doubt, turned the stomach of the fish that takes its food alive and raw. A shark that was cruising beside the *Islander*, looking for just such dainties, now had a chance, and slid leisurely up, rolled on his side, and took in the second-hand dinner. The difference in the manner in which the shark and the tunny took their meals was very noticeable. There was the trap-like snap of one compared to the leisurely movements of the other. I never saw a shark make a move towards an albacore, though it be swimming close by, and I believe he is too slow to take one unless it is disabled or dead. There is some mystery about the pilot fish, so often seen

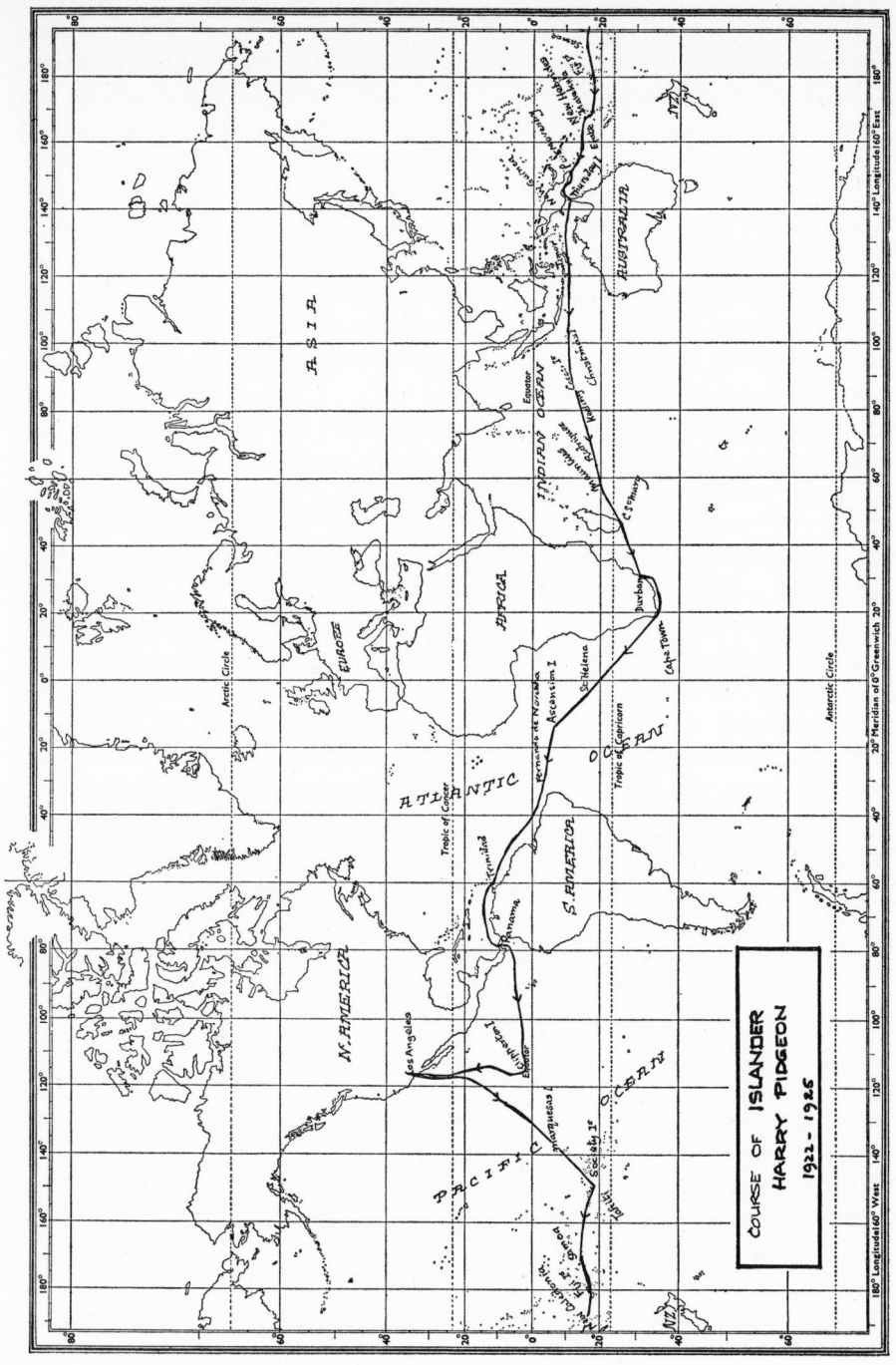

COURSE OF ISLANDER
HARRY PIDGEON
1921 - 1925

swimming just in front and above the shark's nose. It appears to me that it takes up this position as a safety measure. It is too quick for the shark, and at the same time, the predatory fishes hesitate when it comes to rushing in front of the mouth of so formidable-looking a fish as the shark."

Eventually weather conditions improved and at noon on October 31st, 1925, the *Islander* was moored in Los Angeles harbour. Her voyage had taken three years, eleven months and thirteen days.

At the end of his book Harry Pidgeon states that his voyage was "not undertaken for the joy of sailing alone. It was my way of seeing some interesting parts of the world", and he concludes: "Those days were the freest and happiest of my life." Who can doubt him?

8

E. F. KNIGHT

Yachtsman, Adventurer, Journalist

On the 3rd of July, 1925, there died one of the most adventurous rolling stones of a yachtsman that ever sat in a small dinghy off the Cuban coast in wartime or sailed from London to the Baltic in an old ship's lifeboat bought for £20; his name was E. F. Knight.

He led a remarkable life. Born in Cumberland in 1852, he spent his early years in Touraine, in France, whither his father, a soldier, had retired. As a result he was bilingual. It is claimed that he could be mistaken for a Frenchman, but this was not so on the occasion when, at the age of 18, he volunteered to fight in the Franco-Prussian war. He and his father were at Honfleur at the time and Knight walked to Lisieux in order to volunteer. He was rejected because he was a foreigner, whereupon he walked back, a total distance of 40 miles, without saying a word to his father.

Throughout his life he was in one scrape after another. Before he went up to Cambridge he had marched 250 miles into the Sahara with French troops; had wandered around in the desert on his own, before finally being arrested as a spy. It was at Cambridge that his tremendous enthusiasm and energy became channelled into sailing and boats. In France on holiday, he bought a small sailing dinghy and taught himself to sail in the Seine estuary. In this boat he painfully learnt something of the art of seamanship. At the age of 21, still at Cambridge, his father died, and Knight, coming into a little money, was able to buy his first yacht.

She was a yawl of 5 tons, and she was called *Ripple*. In her he learnt to cruise. He taught himself pilotage and some navigation, and he learnt to handle a small yacht single-handed; for he loved to go off alone and explore the beautiful coast-line of the west coast of France. After leaving Cambridge, he read law success-fully enough to be called to the Bar, but he did not practise. Indeed, he seems to have frittered away his (undeniable) talents on a variety of schemes, one of which almost involved him in fighting a duel!

His first long voyage in a boat began in 1880. He was 28 years old. With another friend he bought a yawl called *Falcon* of the same tonnage as Knight had years. Having collected two other friends (also barristers) and a boy to do the donkey-work, they sailed for South America in August. They arrived without mishap, and were away for almost two years, cruising, exploring South American rivers and riding over the Pampas. Knight's first real book was the result. He called it "The Cruise of the *Falcon*", and it had a great success, and he was able thenceforward to earn his living by writing. Writing of his adventures that is; for although he tried his hand a number of times at fiction, he could not write novels.

Armed with his new-found confidence as a writer, Knight was able to continue his wanderings, visiting the West Indies in 1885. It was in the following year, however, that he bought an old converted lifeboat. He could not afford much, because the majority of the small amount of money that his father had left him had been stolen by a solicitor while he was in South America. However, the writing income could at least afford an old ship's lifeboat, and she was, with her strong construction and shallow draught, very suitable for his purpose. This vessel he also named *Falcon*.

With a young yacht hand called Wright, who, as Knight puts it, "has luckily had nothing to do with Cowes and yachts", he sailed this creaking, leaking but game little vessel from Hammersmith to the Baltic, and up through the Danish fiords to Copenhagen. This adventure, far more humble than the voyage to South America, is the one which gained E. F. Knight immortality. It is just an account of a leisurely, coasting cruise—but what an account! It sparkles with enthusiasm and good humour. It is every yachtsman's dream cruise, if only because, as you read it, it sounds such tremendous fun. No one who loves boats and is remotely susceptible to that wonderful feeling of "escape from routine" that a sailing holiday brings can fail to "live it all again" in the pages of Knight's book, because Knight's writing is clear and readable and his enthusiasm so infectious. The book was published in 1951 in the Mariner's Library of Rupert Hart-Davis Ltd., the original version first appearing 1888. It is called "The Falcon on the Baltic".

Knight's cruise to the Baltic was by no means a venture of great hardihood. In these days we have become so used to people "popping across to New York or the West Indies" that a cruise like that of the *Falcon* seems quite tame by comparison. It is not for any accounts of disaster overcome or of mountainous seas that we go to this book; nevertheless, apart from the great enjoyment to be had from the reading of it, there are certain lessons that anyone may learn, if so minded.

One of the chief of these lies in the route which Knight took. A glance at the chart will show that apart from the North Sea crossing and passage from Wilhelmshaven to Tonning on the Eider River, the rest of the time Knight was sailing in canals and inland waterways or able to use the shelter (if he wanted to) of the Frisian Islands. In unsettled weather a small boat can therefore still reach

Baltic Harbour

the Baltic without having to face a long passage in the North Sea, which, as all who have sailed its waters knows, can be a very unhospitable host. With the mass of northern water funnelling down towards Dover Strait, with a northerly gale blowing and an ebb tide running, the North Sea can show an ugly face and should be treated with respect. This may sound a policy of unnecessary caution, one expects "some" bad weather at sea; but there is no point in taking unnecessary risks. I personally have sailed in the North Sea in varying conditions and in various types of vessel both in winter and summer, and have experienced winter gales in it of two to three days' duration, so I claim to be acquainted with the ugly side of its face. If the weather blows up on an ocean race in the North Sea one must, as always, take it as it comes, but a small cruising yacht can study her courses in relation to the expected weather, and if it looks unsettled may well decide to take a similar route to that of the little *Falcon*, so as to get to the Baltic fiords, where in spite of dirty weather in the former "German Ocean" one can find oneself, in the words of Erskine Childers ". . . sailing under warm sunny skies through one of the most beautiful regions of Northern Europe".

Of course, things did not run all that smoothly for Knight. Somehow, in sailing, they never do. But he did not help matters by buying a boat with an incurable leak! This was discovered in the Thames estuary at the start of the passage, and Knight found himself ". . . not feeling by any means so sanguine about the seaworthiness of our boat as we had done on starting".

At Rochester they put *Falcon* ashore to try to discover the source of the leak. At low water examination revealed that the leak lay along the garboard strakes, which required caulking. *Falcon*, which started her career as a wooden ship's lifeboat, was of the double-skin form of construction, in which the planking runs diagonally, one skin across the other. In such construction the garboard strakes, which are the range of planks along the vessel's keel, are the only planks which are caulked. This has always been a difficult seam to caulk, and in the old days of wooden sailing vessels was known as the Devil. From which we get the saying—"The Devil to pay, and no pitch hot". Another saying which, like so many originating from the sea, has become a part of our language stems from the fact that the projecting ridge of pitch along the "Devil" might be the last thing a man overboard could clutch as he sank down the ship's side. This, however, would be of small comfort, and so when a person is caught between two unpleasant situations we speak of him as being "between the Devil and the deep blue sea".

The garboard strakes being duly caulked, Knight and crew sailed with more confidence; confidence, however, that was soon to be dashed to even lower depths of gloom than hitherto. On anchoring for the night off Port Victoria,

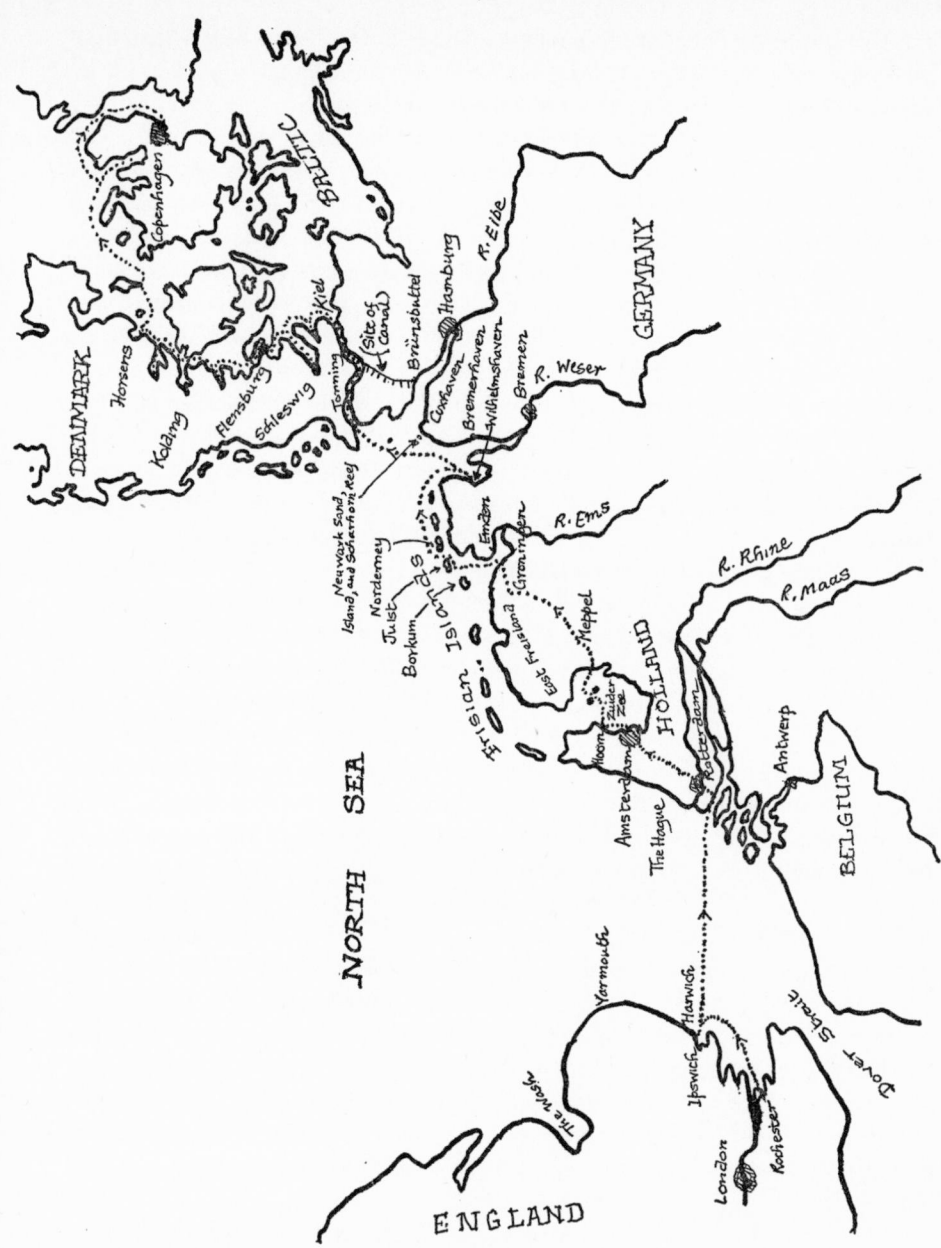

The course of the *Falcon* from London to Copenhagen

Knight's crew reported, after an inspection below, that the water was over the cabin sole, and the boat was leaking as badly as ever.

Now, this occurred in the spring of the Jubilee year (1887), and it was a spring of gales and continuous rain. A typical description in the book is ". . . It was blowing half a gale at least. The rain was falling in torrents, and the broad estuary of the Medway was white with breaking waves." Under such conditions, with a leaking boat, so that it was almost as wet below (including all the bedding) as on deck, Knight might have been forgiven for giving up the idea of his North Sea cruise, until he had made certain that his ship was sound. However, they took a philosophical view, deciding that since it appeared to be "beyond the power of man to remedy this mysterious evil" they must lump it and just make the best of it. Make the best of it they did, and the fun and enjoyment they had later more than justified their guts in "sticking to it".

But how that leak haunted them! Knight describes, too, how ashamed they were of it, and how they would take it in turns to pump her out at dead of night, so that nobody would guess their shameful secret. They were unable to disguise this malady from the Dutch pilot who took them into the Maas River, after their North Sea crossing, and the latter amused himself with some very sarcastic comments as they ran before a strong westerly towards the island of Voorne. Across the Voorne dikes, however, a great collection of windmills for pumping water off the land gave Knight his opportunity of observing to the pilot that although the *Falcon* leaked, the Dutchman's country leaked even more; where-upon the good-natured Hollander merely grinned and asked for a repeat of the glass of rum with which he had been provided.

Looking again at the chart, it will be seen that, from Rotterdam, Knight proceeded by canal to Amsterdam, up the coast to Hoorn and from there across the Zuider Zee. The trouble in this part of the cruise was not so much the weather, nor the leaky condition of the boat, but the small boys of Holland. This was especially the case in the island of Marken, where Knight says ". . . The Marken child . . . is the most terrible of the Zuider Zee . . ." These boys hurled not only stones at the boat, but bricks! The answer lay in mooring out of reach of even the strongest thrower!

From Moffel, on the eastern side of the Zuider Zee, they entered canals, once again re-emerging into the North Sea for a passage through the Frisian Islands. In an article in the "Yachting Monthly Magazine" of 1898, Erskine Childers describes a passage to the Baltic in a 7-tonner. It was this article which provided the basis for Childer's yachting classic "The Riddle of the Sands", and in it he mentions "Knight's *Falcon* cruise". There is little doubt that Knight's descrip-tion of cruising among the Frisian Islands not only appealed to Childers as "a

Falcon towing dinghy, passing Wangeroog Island (East Frisian Islands)

novel and amusing mode of getting . . . to the Baltic", but may well be said to
have laid the foundation of his immortal book.

Knight had to reach Kiel in the Baltic, by way of Tonning, the Eider River
and the Schleswig-Holstein Canal, but by 1898, when Erskine Childers's
"Drifted to the Baltic" was published, the then new "Kaiser Wilhelm Canal"
had been completed which shortens this part of the journey, since instead of
having to sail as far north as Tonning a yacht now only has to sail up the Elbe
River to Brunsbüttel. The chart will make this clear and will also show the course
followed by *Falcon* in the Baltic until she was left at Copenhagen to pass the
winter in Danish care. The following year Knight and some friends reversed
their outward passage, eventually mooring the *Falcon* (somewhat altered) safely
at Kingston-on-Thames on the 15th September.

Knight and his friends had two memorable cruises, but it was about the
passage out that he wrote, and we may be glad he did, so restless a soul was he;
so full his life with action; leaving, it would seem, little time for writing. In 1888
he sailed a vessel called the *Alerte*, of 56 tons, with a crew of four paid hands
and nine "gentlemen adventurers", to Trinidad on a treasure hunt. Back in
England in 1890 he got a job as "The Times" War Correspondent, which took
him to Kashui, Tibet and the Himalayas. In 1896 he covered the Sudan campaign. The early part of the following year saw him covering the Turko-Greek
war and the latter part of the year saw him in Cuba, when he tried to get ashore
in a dinghy (which capsized) and (once again) was arrested and imprisoned as a
spy.

About this time he wrote two sailing handbooks and a collective account of
cruises in small craft in Florida and the Nile! He lost his right arm, but this did
not stop him from sailing. Indeed, he was the sort of man that nothing stops
except the inevitability of death, which came to him on the 3rd of July 1925. He
was an interesting and lively personality. Above all, he enjoyed life, and his book,
"The *Falcon* on the Baltic", is a suitable epitaph.

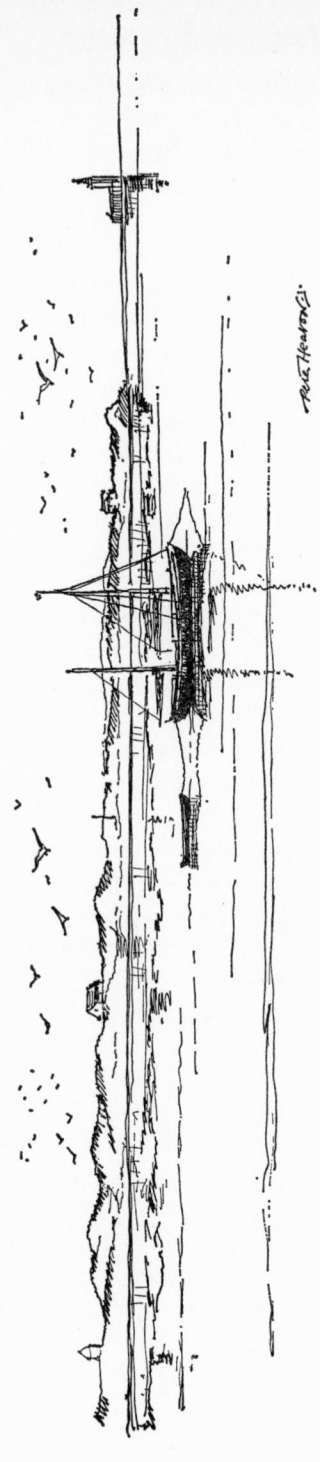

Anchored in flat calm, off Spiekeroog Island

9

The Riddle of
"THE RIDDLE OF THE SANDS"

In 1898 a clerk in the House of Commons with a taste for small-boat cruising made a voyage to the Baltic, following to some extent in the track of E. F. Knight in the *Falcon*. Five years later there appeared on the bookstalls the novel, using the same passage and cruising grounds as its background written by that same Commons' clerk. The name of the clerk was Robert Erskine Childers and the book was called "The Riddle of the Sands". From its first appearance in 1903, when it was published by Smith Elder and Company, it became a best-seller. It was reprinted over and over again. The eleventh impression was issued under the imprint of John Murray. In 1927 it became the property of Sidgwick and Jackson, who still control it, and continue to reprint it. It has appeared naturally in paperback form as a Penguin in 1952. It reads as true and as excitingly today as it did in 1903.

It is no exaggeration to say that "The Riddle of the Sands" is one of the greatest stories of its kind ever to be written. Briefly, the plot concerns the adventures of two young Englishmen of very different types. One a rough and ready fellow—Davies—who is only at home in a boat, and a boat at sea, not a boat in harbour—and the other a fop, idling his time away in the Foreign Office, by name, Carruthers. The impact of the character of Davies upon Carruthers and the subtle changes in the latter is not one of the least absorbing aspects of the story. Their adventures together in the converted lifeboat *Dulcibella*, sailing in the difficult tidal waters of the German Frisian Islands, are wonderfully described and the tension builds up steadily to the book's climax. It would spoil the book for the reader were I to say more, but there is an interesting point about this story that may not be so generally known that I would like to make. Although this book is fiction, the navigational details are taken from the cruise mentioned earlier, and the author wanted to be certain that his facts were correct. At the time when Childers was writing Germany was growing stronger and stronger, and this development naturally included not only her navy but her naval bases. Now, Germany had always suffered from lack of coastline and particularly of good ports opening into the North Sea. Childers was convinced that there was far more development going on on the German seaboard and behind the Frisian Islands than the British Admiralty realized. This book, a spy story, was intended as a warning, and the interesting thing is that it came to be regarded seriously and had a definite influence on naval policy at the time.

Now, it is frequently the case that a novelist will base a story upon some experience—but in this instance, the remarkable account of the navigation of the *Dulcibella* in that bleak, windswept area of shoals and banks and moaning winds rings so true that one is left in no doubt that this is, in fact, an account in the main of what happened taken from a log-book, making allowance for the addition of certain adventures for the purpose of the narrative. It is this fidelity, however, that gives this book its unique and universal appeal. Nowhere have the bleak wastes of the North Sea been so faithfully painted. What lover of this wild type of scenery can fail to react to, for example, this description by Carruthers? (It is Carruthers, incidentally, who tells the story.)

"The yacht lay with a very slight heel (thanks to a pair of small bilge-keels on her bottom) in a sort of trough she had dug for herself, so that she was still ringed with a few inches of water, as it were with a moat.

"For miles in every direction lay a desert of sand. To the north it touched the horizon, and was only broken by the blue dot of Neuerk Island and its light-house. To the east it seemed also to stretch to infinity, but the smoke of a steamer showed where it was pierced by the stream of the Elbe. To the south it ran up to the pencil-line of the Hanover shore. Only to the west was its outline broken by any vestiges of the sea it had risen from. There it was astir with crawling white filaments, knotted confusedly at one spot in the north-west, whence came a sibilant murmur like the hissing of many snakes. Desert as I call it, it was not entirely featureless. Its colour varied from light fawn, where the highest levels had dried in the wind, to brown or deep violet, where it was still wet, and slate-grey where patches of mud soiled its clean bosom. Here and there were pools of water, smitten into ripples by the impotent wind; here and there it was speckled by shells and seaweed. And close to us, beginning to bend away towards that hissing knot in the north-west, wound our poor little channel, mercilessly exposed as a stagnant, muddy ditch with scarcely a foot of water, not deep enough to hide our small kedge-anchor, which perked up one fluke in impudent mockery. The dull, hard sky, the wind moaning in the rigging as though crying in despair for a prey that had escaped it, made the scene in-expressibly forlorn."

Robert Erskine Childers was born in 1870. He was thus 28 years of age when he made his cruise to the Baltic and was 33 when this book was published. He was educated at Haileybury and at Trinity College, Cambridge. In 1895 he joined the staff of the clerk of the House of Commons, remaining in that office until 1910. He used the Parliamentary recesses (which in those days were longer than they are now) for sailing. He also travelled extensively by more conventional means, and it was as a result of a visit to Boston he met Mary Alden, whom he married in 1904.

He was partly Irish by birth, and was passionately keen on the "Irish Cause". So much so that he resigned his clerkship in the House of Commons in 1910, so that he could work for that "Cause". In 1911 he published "The Framework of Home Rule", a work of propaganda for Dominion status in the country he loved.

In 1914 came the First World War and Childers joined up, serving in both the R.N.V.R. and what was then known as the Royal Naval Air Service. He was awarded the D.S.C., a decoration which, as everyone knows, is not easily come by. When the war ended he went back, having "done his bit for England", to work for Irish independence. No believer in half measures, he joined the Republican Army when the Free State was established. In the civil war he was arrested and shot. The best epitaph on this remarkable man came from the pen of John Buchan, who wrote "No revolution ever produced a nobler or purer spirit".

The "Riddle of the Sands" and the "Home Rule" treatise were not the only books that Erskine Childers wrote. When the South African War broke out he volunteered, and afterwards contributed "In the Ranks of the C.I.V.", the fifth volume of "The Times History of the War". It is interesting, too, that this period produced two books on the use of cavalry against up-to-date weapons. Shades of Davies's long tirades in the *Dulcibella*'s cabin against the outmoded policy of the British Admiralty and their failure to build up a real reserve fleet, This "Reserve fleet of yachtsman" was one of Davies's (and, of course, Childers's) pet dreams; a body of men, easily mobilized, with special local knowledge of tidal streams and depths, etc. It must have been some satisfaction to Childers when the Manning Committee of 1903 reported in favour of a Volunteer Reserve. In the postscript to the book in commenting on this, it says "there is no means of knowing what this recommendation will lead to . . ." It is doubtful if even Childers could have visualized the tremendous contribution made by the R.N.V.R. in the last war.

But this aspect of the book, the "defence propaganda" side, interesting as it is, is of little account beside the pleasure to be derived from this exquisitely told sea/spy story. Let us now join Carruthers in his London club. He has just received a letter from Davies from Flensburg in Schleswig-Holstein, suggesting that Carruthers join him for "a little yachting". In this early part of the book Childers is at pains to emphasize the foppish, self-centred side of Carruthers's character, and the following extract will show how well he succeeded.

"This letter marked an epoch for me; but I little suspected the fact as I crumpled it into my pocket and started languidly on the *voie douloureuse* which

I nightly followed to the club. In Pall Mall there were no dignified greetings to be exchanged now with well-groomed acquaintances. The only people to be seen were some late stragglers from the park, with a perambulator and some hot and dusty children lagging fretfully behind; some rustic sightseers draining the last dregs of the daylight in an effort to make out from their guide-books which of these reverend piles was which; a policeman and a builder's cart. Of course the club was a strange one, both of my own being closed for cleaning, a coincidence expressly planned by Providence for my inconvenience. The club which you are 'permitted to make use of' on these occasions always irritates with its strangeness and discomfort. The few occupants seem odd and oddly dressed, and you wonder how they got there. The particular weekly that you want is not taken in; the dinner is execrable, and the ventilation a farce. All these evils oppressed me to-night. And yet I was puzzled to find that somewhere within me there was a faint lightening of the spirits; causeless, as far as I could discover. It could not be Davies's letter. Yachting in the Baltic at the end of September! The very idea made one shudder. Cowes, with a pleasant party and hotels handy, was all very well. An August cruise on a steam yacht in French waters or the Highlands was all very well; but what kind of a yacht was this? It must be of a certain size to have got so far, but I thought I remembered enough of Davies's means to know that he had no money to waste on luxuries. That brought me to the man himself. I had known him at Oxford—not as one of my immediate set; but we were a sociable college, and I had seen a good deal of him, liking him for his physical energy combined with a certain simplicity and modesty, though indeed, he had nothing to be conceited about; liked him, in fact, in the way that at that receptive period one likes many men whom one never keeps up with later. We had both gone down in the same year—three years ago now. I had gone to France and Germany for two years to learn the languages; he had failed for the Indian Civil, and then had gone into a solicitor's office. I had only seen him since at rare intervals, though I admitted to myself that for his part he had clung loyally to what ties of friendship there were between us. But the truth was that we had drifted apart from the nature of things. I had passed brilliantly into my profession, and on the few occasions I had met him since I made my triumphant *debut* in society I had found nothing left in common between us. He seemed to know none of my friends, he dressed indifferently, and I thought him dull. I had always connected him with boats and the sea, but never with yachting, in the sense that I understood it. In college days he had nearly persuaded me into sharing a squalid week in some open boat he had picked up, and was going to sail among some dreary mud-flats somewhere on the east coast. There was nothing else, and the funereal function of dinner drifted on. But I found myself remembering at the *entree* that I had recently heard, at second or third hand, of something else about him—exactly what I could not recall. When I reached the savoury, I had concluded, so far as I had centred my mind on it at all, that the whole thing was a culminating irony, as, indeed, was the savoury in its way. After the wreck of my pleasant plans and the fiasco of my martyrdom, to be asked as consolation to spend October freezing in the Baltic with an eccentric nonentity who bored me! Yet, as I smoked my cigar in the ghastly splendour of the empty smoking room, the subject came up again. Was there anything in it? There were certainly no alternatives at hand. And to bury myself in the Baltic at this unearthly time of year had at least a smack of tragic thoroughness about it.

"I pulled out the letter again, and ran down its impulsive staccato sentences, affecting to ignore what a gust of fresh air, high spirits, and good fellowship this flimsy bit of paper wafted into the jaded club-room. On reperusal, it was full of evil presage—'A1 scenery'—but what of equinoctial storms and October fogs? Every sane yachtsman was paying off his crew now. 'There ought to be duck'— vague, very vague. 'If it gets cold enough' . . . cold and yachting seemed to be a gratuitously monstrous union. His pals had left him; why? 'Not the "yachting" brand'; and why not? As to the size, comfort, and crew of the yacht—all cheerfully ignored; so many maddening blanks. And, by the way, why in Heaven's name a 'prismatic compass'? I fingered a few magazines, played a game of fifty with a friendly old fogey, too importunate to be worth the labour of resisting, and went back to my chambers to bed, ignorant that a friendly Providence had come to my rescue; and, indeed, rather resenting any clumsy attempt at such friendliness."

Of course, Carruthers *does* go to Flensburg and his initiation slowly begins. He is surprised to discover that the life, though hard, is actually very pleasant; as he puts it, "There was another charm in the scene, due to the way in which I was viewing it—not as a pampered passenger on a 'fine steam yacht', or even on a 'powerful modern schooner', as the yacht agents advertise, but from the deck of a scrubby little craft of doubtful build and distressing plainness, which yet had smelt her persistent way to this distant fiord through I knew not what of difficulty and danger, with no apparent motive in her single occupant, who talked as vaguely and unconcernedly about his adventurous cruise as though it were all a protracted afternoon on Southampton Water."

Friendship between the two men is slow to ripen, however. There is something wrong, some unspoken thing coming between them. To give an indication here of what that something was, and of how it was resolved, would not only ruin the book for the reader, since it depends so much on its capacity for a gradual building up of tension, but it would also be presumptuous. Let me finish, however, with an example of Childers's descriptive writing at its best. It is where he is following another yacht, the *Medusa*, and losing sight of her, is driven ashore in a north-east gale; Davies is telling the story to Carruthers: " 'We went next morning at six. It was a dirty-looking day, wind W.N.W., but his sails were going up and mine followed. I took two reefs in, and we sailed out into the open and steered E.N.E. along the coast for the Outer Elbe Lightship about fifty knots off. Here it all is, you see.' (He showed me the course on the chart.) 'The trip was nothing for his boat, of course, a safe, powerful old tub, forging through the sea as steady as a house. I kept up with her easily at first. My hands were pretty full, for there was a hard wind on my quarter and a troublesome sea; but as long as nothing worse came I knew I should be all right, though I also knew that I was a fool to have come.

" 'All went well till we were off Wangeroog, the last of the islands—*here*—and then it began to blow really hard. I had half a mind to chuck it and cut into the Jade River, *down there*; but I hadn't the face to, so I hove to and took in my last reef.' (Simple words, simply uttered; but I had seen the operation in calm water and shuddered at the present picture.) 'We had been about level till then, but with my shortened canvas I fell behind. Not that that mattered in the least. I knew my course, had read up my tides, and, thick as the weather was, I had no doubt of being able to pick up the lightship. No change of plan was possible now. The Weser estuary was on my starboard hand, but the whole place was a lee-shore and a mass of unknown banks—just look at them. I ran on, the *Dulcibella* doing her level best, but we had some narrow shaves of being pooped. I was about *here*, say six miles south-west of the lightship, when I suddenly saw that the *Medusa* had hove to right ahead, as though waiting till I came up. She wore round again on the course as I drew level, and we were alongside for a bit. Dollmann lashed the wheel, leaned over her quarter, and shouted, very slowly and distinctly so that I could understand: "Follow me—sea too bad for you outside—short cut through sands—save six miles."

" 'It was taking me all my time to manage the tiller, but I knew what he meant at once, for I had been over the chart carefully the night before. You see, the whole bay between Wangeroog and the Elbe is encumbered with sand. A great jagged chunk of it runs out from Cuxhaven in a north-westerly direction for fifteen miles or so, ending in a pointed spit, called the *Scharhorn*. To reach the Elbe from the west you have to go right outside this, round the lightship, which is off the Scharhorn, and double back. Of course, that's what all big vessels do. But, as you see, these sands are intersected here and there by channels, very shallow and winding, exactly like those behind the Frisian Islands. Now look at this one, which cuts right through the big chunk of sand and comes out near

Cuxhaven. The *Telte* it's called. It's miles wide, you see, at the entrance, but later on it is split into two by the Hohenhörn bank; then it gets shallow and very complicated, and ends in a mere tidal driblet with another name. It's just the sort of channel I should like to worry into on a fine day or with an off-shore wind. Alone, in thick weather and a heavy sea, it would have been folly to attempt it, except as a desperate resource. But, as I said, I knew at once that Dollmann was proposing to run for it and guide me in.

" 'I didn't like the idea, because I like doing things for myself, and, silly as it sounds, I believe I resented being told the sea was too bad for me, which it certainly was. Yet the short cut did save several miles and a devil of a tumble off the Scharhorn, where two tides meet. I had complete faith in Dollmann, and I suppose I decided that I should be a fool not to take a good chance. I hesitated, I know; but in the end I nodded, and held up my arm as she forged ahead again. Soon after, she shifted her course and I followed. You asked me once if I ever took a pilot. That was the only time.'

"He spoke with bitter gravity, flung himself back, and felt his pocket for his pipe. It was not meant for a dramatic pause, but it certainly was one. I had just a glimpse of still another Davies—a Davies five years older throbbing with deep emotions, scorn, passion, and stubborn purpose; a being above my plane, of sterner stuff, wider scope. Intense as my interest had become, I waited almost timidly while he mechanically rammed tobacco into his pipe and struck ineffectual matches. I felt that whatever the riddle to be solved, it was no mean one. He repressed himself with an effort, half rose, and made his circular glance at the clock, barometer, and skylight, and then resumed.

" 'We soon came to what I knew must be the beginning of the Telte channel. All round you could hear the breakers on the sands, though it was too thick to see them yet. As the water shoaled, the sea, of course, got shorter and steeper. There was more wind—a whole gale I should say.

" 'I kept dead in the wake of the *Medusa*, but to my disgust I found she was gaining on me very fast. Of course I had taken for granted, when he said he would lead me in, that he would slow down and keep close to me. He could easily have done so by getting his men up to check his sheets or drop his peak. Instead of that he was busting on for all he was worth. Once, in a rain-squall, I lost sight of him altogether; got him faintly again, but had enough to do with my own tiller not to want to be peering through the scud after a runaway pilot. I was all right so far, but we were fast approaching the worst part of the whole passage, where the Hohenhörn bank blocks the road, and the channel divides. I don't know what it looks like to you on the chart—perhaps fairly simple, because you can follow the twists of the channels, as on a ground-plan; but a stranger coming to a place like that (where there are no buoys, mind you) can tell nothing certain by the eye—unless perhaps at dead low water, when the banks are high and dry, and in very clear weather—he must trust to the lead and the compass, and feel his way step by step. I knew perfectly well that what I should soon see would be a wall of surf stretching right across and on both sides. To *feel* one's way in that sort of weather is impossible. You must *know* your way, or else have a pilot. I had one, but he was playing his own game.

" 'With a second hand on board to steer while I conned I should have felt less of an ass. As it was, I knew I ought to be facing the music in the offing, and cursed myself for having broken my rule and gone blundering into this confounded short cut. It was giving myself away, doing just the very thing that you can't do in single-handed sailing.

" 'By the time I realized the danger it was far too late to turn and hammer out to the open. I was deep in the bottle-neck bight of the sands, jammed on a lee shore, and a strong flood tide sweeping me on. That tide, by the way, gave just the ghost of a chance. I had the hours in my head, and knew it was about two-thirds flood, with two hours more of rising water. That meant the banks would be all covering when I reached them, and harder than ever to locate; but it also meant that I *might* float right over the worst of them if I hit off a lucky place.' Davies thumped the table in disgust. 'Pah! It makes me sick to think of having to trust to an accident like that, like a lubberly cockney out for a boozy Bank Holiday sail. Well, just as I foresaw, the wall of surf appeared clean across the horizon, and curling back to shut me in, booming like thunder. When I last saw the *Medusa* she seemed to be charging it like a horse at a fence, and I took a rough bearing of her position by a hurried glance at the compass. At that very moment I *thought* she seemed to luff and show some of her broadside; but a squall blotted her out and gave me hell with the tiller. After that she was lost in the white mist that hung over the line of breakers. I kept on my bearing as well as I could, but I was already out of the channel. I knew that by the look of the water, and as we neared the bank I saw it was all awash and without the vestige of an opening. I wasn't going to chuck her on to it without an effort; so, more by instinct than with any particular hope, I put the helm down, meaning to work her along the edge on the chance of spotting a way over. She was buried at once by the beam sea, and the jib flew to blazes; but the reefed stays'l stood, she recovered gamely, and I held on, though I knew it could only be for a few minutes, as the centre-plate was up, and she made frightful leeway towards the bank.

" 'I was half-blinded by scud, but suddenly I noticed what looked like a gap, behind a spit which curled out right ahead. I luffed still more to clear this spit, but she couldn't weather it. Before you could say knife she was driving across it, bumped heavily, bucked forward again, bumped again, and—ripped on in deeper water! I can't describe the next few minutes. I was in some sort of channel, but a very narrow one, and the sea broke everywhere. I hadn't proper command either; for the rudder had crocked up somehow at the last bump. I was like a drunken man running for his life down a dark alley, barking himself at every corner. It couldn't last long, and finally we went crash on to something and stopped there, grinding and banging. So ended that little trip under a pilot.

" 'Well, it was like this—there was really no danger'—I opened my eyes at the characteristic phrase. 'I mean, that lucky stumble into a channel was my salvation. Since then I had struggled through a mile of sands, all of which lay behind me like a breakwater against the gale. They were covered, of course, and seething like soapsuds; but the force of the sea was deadened. The *Dulce* was bumping, but not too heavily. It was nearing high tide, and at half ebb she would be high and dry.

"In the ordinary way I should have run out a kedge with the dinghy, and at the next high water sailed farther in and anchored where I could lie afloat. The trouble was now that my hand was hurt and my dinghy stove in, not to mention the rudder business. It was the first bump on the outer edge that did the damage. There was a heavy swell there, and when we struck, the dinghy, which was towing astern, came home on her painter and down with a crash on the yacht's weather quarter. I stuck out one hand to ward it off and got it nipped on the gunwale. She was badly stove in and useless, so I couldn't run out the kedge' —this was Greek to me, but I let him go on—'and for the present my hand was too painful even to stow the boom and sails, which were whipping and racketing about anyhow. There was the rudder, too, to be mended; and we were several miles from the nearest land. Of course, if the wind fell, it was all easy enough; but if it held or increased it was a poor look-out. There's a limit to strain of that sort—and other things might have happened.

" 'In fact, it was precious lucky that Bartels turned up. His galliot was at anchor a mile away, up a branch of the channel. In a clear between squalls he saw us, and, like a brick, rowed his boat out—he and his boy, and a devil of a pull they must have had. I was glad enough to see them—no, that's not true; I was in such a fury of disgust and shame that I believe I should have been idiot enough to say I didn't want help, if he hadn't just nipped on board and started work. He's a terror to work, that little mouse of a chap. In half an hour he had stowed the sails, unshackled the big anchor, run out fifty fathoms of warp, and hauled her off there and then into deep water. Then they towed her up the channel—it was dead to leeward and an easy job—and berthed her near their own vessel. It was dark by that time, so I gave them a drink, and said good night. It blew a howling gale that night, but the place was safe enough, with good ground-tackle.

" 'The whole affair was over; and after supper I thought hard about it all.' "

The mention of Bartels in that last quotation from "The Riddle of the Sands" brings me back to the article Childers wrote in 1898, and mentioned at the beginning of this chapter. In this a skipper called Bartels is mentioned, as is also his galliot (a barge type of vessel) the *Johannes*. As I mentioned in Chapter 8, the article appeared in a paper called the *Yachting Monthly Magazine*, Volume 1, 1898, of which only two issues ever appeared. It was called "How we Drifted to the Baltic in a Seven-tonner". I do not propose to quote from it at length, but the following extract is enough to leave one in no doubt as to the source, not only of the inspiration for Childers's book, but of the all-round accuracy that gives this book its reality and its immortality.

"Suddenly the huge lock-gates loomed high above us, we rounded up sharply, and slid alongside a floating stage below a towering wall, made fast and stowed our canvas.

"A profound silence reigned, and there was not a soul in sight. We had no idea when and for how long the gates were opened, and a growing and gloomy impression of our own insignificance at the threshold of these gigantic works gave us a feeling that we should never get through till something else more worth notice came along. So we were preparing to spend the night where we were—and a most comfortless berth it would have been, with the wind blowing right in and bad weather blowing up—when we noticed a kaleidoscopic shifting of lights ahead, and saw that the gates of one of the great locks were slowly opening. We were just hoisting the fore-sail to run in, when a sleepy voice from a shadowy ulster, which had silently appeared in the gloom of the quay-wall high overhead, bade us, in excellent English, desist. How it knew we were English I do not know. Sailing was forbidden, it seemed, so I mounted the wall by a ladder and towed *Vixen* through into the lock, in a corner of which she lay, her tiny hull scarcely visible in the blackness below. Though locks and canals, and all connected therewith, are generally the most prosaic and tedious of things, there was something strangely impressive in this night's episode. The contrast of our insignificance with the mighty works—designed to receive the largest battleships —whose ponderous machinery had opened to admit us; this, with a certain mystery born of the silence, the darkness, the desertion, will always make this scene memorable to us.

"The overcoat concealed a polite official who conducted me to a palatial structure hard by. I passed through silent, lighted corridors, and, under the eye of two more officers, was soon grappling with a comprehensive printed form, which, being equally intended for steamers and sailing-vessels of every tonnage and description, contained multitudes of questions, which, for a 7-ton yacht manned by two amateurs, had no answer. It took more than an hour to adjust a hitch, whose nature I did not understand, but which kept me tramping between this and another office, till I was tired enough. At last all was settled, and I was given a receipt for 14 marks, which included the ridiculously small sum of 3s. for towage through the sixty miles of canal by a Government tug. I was then courteously re-conducted to the yacht, and helped to tow her through to the inner basin; but it was close on midnight before we were moored and snug in company with half-a-dozen small sailing-vessels, which were to form the flotilla for towing on the morrow. When we thought all was over, a garrulous gentleman appeared and took copious notes of us, all over again, in a large note-book. I suppose it was official, but he seemed rather to be investigating a curious phenomenon in natural history.

"*October 8th.*—A wild wet morning, with half a gale blowing from the south-west, and very cold. Our flotilla started about midday, and we made fast along-side a barge-like cutter-rigged vessel of about 60 tons, loaded to her gunwale, a craft typical of the class of local trading boats, very like Thames barges, but without the sprit-rig, carrying far less canvas, and smarter and cleaner. The crew is two men. In the course of our cruise we made many friends among the skippers of these craft, and most friendly hospitable fellows we found them. We made great friends with this skipper, an excellent fellow, by name Bartels, and had many a pleasant chat in our respective cabins, while his boy did the steering for both boats through the long grey reaches of the canal. We only covered 20 miles this day, going at barely 4 knots, and moored for the night along a row of piles, which flanked one of the passing-stations. Nothing struck us more about this magnificent water-way than the lighting, which is by electric lamps at short intervals on both sides, mounted on gracefully-designed iron uprights; and can bear favourable comparison with many a London street.

"*October 9th.*—Our flotilla started at 6, but before long had to lie by at a passing-station for some hours, to make way for some mercantile leviathan which required the whole road to itself—had 'bought the street, Bill', so to speak. We visited a farm ashore, and bought a rye-loaf of extraordinary durability. It lasted three weeks and a day, by the log, and—I was going to say, died hard—but on the contrary, it was fresh up to the moment of evanescence. We used always to have one of these loaves in reserve, for occasions when *weiss-brod* was un-attainable.

"At last the cry of '*los*' ran along the line, and again we were gliding through a raw windless mist, with our little tug panting and groaning ahead. We met few steamers, but many flotillas, like our own, of small sailing-vessels. Hitherto the country had been invisible, above the embankments of the canal, but soon after passing Rendsbury, with its mighty twin suspension bridges, we were privileged to gaze with wonder on a distant mist-mantled *hill*—the first we had seen since Boulogne! Then the darkness came down, and we were stealing—so one might imagine—down the silent highway of some great deserted city, endless vistas of lights blurring into inky gloom ahead. Sometimes we would slow down and a wailing antiphony of steam-speech would begin between our little querulous tug and an unseen traveller on the same highway, whose graver deeper note prepared us for the towering hull of a big ocean liner. About 8 o'clock we were approaching a misty electric glow, which was Holtenau, the Baltic terminus, in Kiel fiord. Here we cast off from the *Johannes* and made fast alongside another boat similar to her, and bound, like ourselves, for Kiel. She was going to anchor outside for the night, and her skipper, on the introduction of Bartels, invited us to remain as we were, and so save ourselves the trouble of dropping our own anchor. Both lock gates were already open, so, after a few minutes for delivery of papers, the tug took us out to open water, where tow-ropes were let go one by one, and the flotilla dispersed into the gloom of a still foggy night. Our skipper dropped his anchor in four fathoms, and when all was snug we rowed off for a farewell chat with Bartels, who was anchored not far away, bound north at daybreak. We thought it was a final adieu, but we met him again in a Schleswig fiord in November.

"*October 10th.*—It was only four miles south-west to Kiel, but the wind also was south-west and very light. When we cast off from our companion with 'mutual expressions of good will,' we could just see the eastern shore of the fiord through shifting masses of creamy fog. But presently the sun burst through and, unreal as a dream, after the silent expanses of the North Sea and the lonely levels of Friesland, there came the vision of a noble fiord, green hills and richly wooded banks sloping to the blue, deep, tideless water, where, in a long majestic curve, lay moored a line of battleships. At the head of the bay lay Kiel, its wet roofs and spires sparkling through a shining haze. We tacked in and out of the battleships and along the western shore, which was gay with villas and gardens, set in deeply wooded slopes. Yet to yachtsmen, coming to the great German yachting centre, the scene had a desolation of its own, for of the many yachts which we passed, moored under the western shore, not one was in commission. A ghostly fleet of dinghy and mastless hulls were an eloquent reminder that the yachting season was over, and that it was time all self-respecting 7-tonners were in winter quarters. We sailed on till the town was abreast of us, and then anchored on the east shore, near a silent and lugubrious assemblage of boats like our own, only dead. It certainly seemed like the end of all things, and, to accentuate the feeling, the sun had disappeared, and rain was beginning to fall from a lurid stormy sky.

"Nothing seemed less likely than that a week later the *Vixen* would be sailing under warm sunny skies through one of the most beautiful regions of Northern Europe."

The *Vixen*, of course, became the *Dulcibella* and was transmuted from the drab little vessel of an obscure article in a yachting paper that only survived two issues into the heroine of one of the world's immortal books.

10

ALAIN GERBAULT

Real "Sea Fever"?

In the Mariner's Library of Rupert Hart-Davis Ltd there is published a book called "The Fight of the *Firecrest*". The book is by a Frenchman, Alain Gerbault. It describes a voyage from east to west across the Atlantic. I mention this because Gerbault was the first yachtsman to sail the Atlantic from east to west by the intermediate route. He made his voyage in 1924. The earliest southern-route crossing was made in 1928 by Franz Rower, a German. The northern east-west route was made much earlier, the first yacht being the *City of Ragusa*, a ship's lifeboat converted to a gaff-rigged ketch. She was sailed by John C. Buckley, an American, as far back as 1870. For the two southern routes, however, Gerbault holds the record.

It is not, however, for this reason that I include him in this collection. Indeed, he has what seems a better claim by reason of the fact that he sailed round the world in *Firecrest* single-handed and wrote a very fine book. But it is not, as will be clear by now, my intention to include only those who have made circumnavigations. It is in Gerbault's first book—"The Fight of the *Firecrest*" that we find his finest writing. He was newer to the game then. He made mistakes. Above all, he was wonderfully enthusiastic; he was febrile with "sea fever".

Later he became involved in a violent defence of the native cause in the South Sea islands. His grave is in the island of Bora Bora, one of the leeward group of islands. We have already had a good deal in this book about the fate of the Polynesians and others, and I think Gerbault's other book can therefore wait for a second similar volume to this (assuming that the publishers can be persuaded at gun point to risk one!)

No, it is in that first book that this man's love of the sea is so fascinatingly manifest on every page. I propose therefore to give a brief outline of the voyage, a description of the vessel herself, and then let Gerbault illuminate these facts with quotations from his own vivid writings.

Firstly, the man. Alain Gerbault spent most of his youth at Dinard on the north coast of France. His father was a yachtsman, and Gerbault learnt about the ways of a ship at sea at an early age. Moreover, when not sailing with his father he was making friends with local Breton fishermen and persuading them to take him to sea.

Eventually his idyllic life at Dinard came to an end and he was sent to Paris to study. He was not happy, confined between walls, and he admits that while in Paris, at the Stanislaus College, ". . . I spent the most unhappy years of my life".

The year 1914 and the First World War brought adventure in the shape of the Flying Corps, in which Gerbault immediately enlisted. It was during this period that a member of his squadron, an American, lent him some of Jack London's books to read. One in particular, "The Cruise of the *Shark*", fired his imagination. From then on, it appears, all he wanted to do was to ". . . cross the ocean in a small boat".

The war ended, and Gerbault found himself, like so many in the same position after both world wars, quite unable to settle down and get a "steady job". In 1921, while visiting a yachtsman friend, Ralph Stock (who wrote "The Cruise of the Dream Ship") aboard the latter's boat, he noticed a vessel for sale lying near by. That vessel was *Firecrest*.

Firecrest was designed by Dixon Kemp, and built by P. T. Harris at Row-hedge in Essex, in 1892. She was thus a lady of some twenty-nine summers when Alain Gerbault bought her. She was 39 feet in length overall, 30 feet on the waterline. Her beam measured 8 feet 6 inches and she drew 7 feet of water. She will be seen from my drawing to be narrow and deep, with a long counter and a short rounded bow. She was, in point of fact, a typical English cutter of the period, designed for racing and some cruising. She was, in the fashion of those days, strongly built of teak and oak.

No sooner did Gerbault see her than he decided to buy her. He sailed her to the South of France via the Bay of Biscay, which tested man and ship in its customary fashion. For over a year Gerbault cruised about the south coast of France, with a young English friend as crew. He was a tennis player of considerable ability and he managed to include tennis-tournament playing with his cruising. But if playing is the word for tennis, he was certainly not playing at sea; he was deadly serious. All this cruising had but one purpose, to assure himself that he could stand the physical discomfort and strain of an Atlantic crossing and that he could handle *Firecrest* in all normal conditions.

It was not for any reason other than pleasure, however, that he made his Atlantic crossing. In his book he says: ". . . It was only for the fun of the thing and to prove to myself that I could do it all alone . . ."

Nevertheless his solo passage made him a national hero. The French papers were full of him. Later, of course, his trip round the world produced much more startling results. He was given the Legion of Honour on board a destroyer. French newspapermen told their readers that France was a great maritime nation and that Alain Gerbault had proved this.

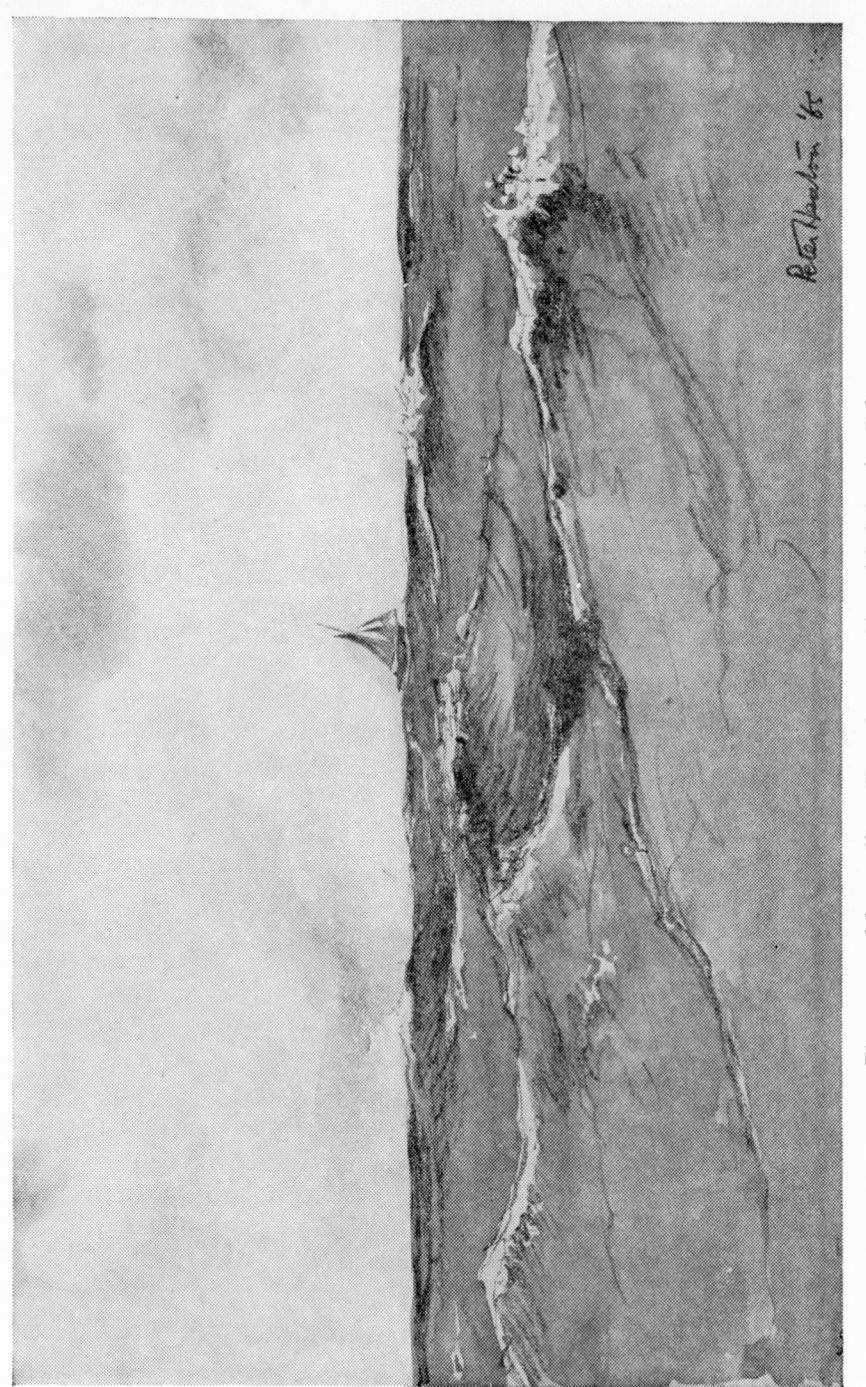

Firecrest and her gallant French owner in mid-Atlantic, July 1924

He left Cannes harbour, basking in spring sunshine, on the 5th April 1924. He arrived in Gibraltar a week later. On June the 6th he sailed for New York. His crossing took him 101 days. Much of this time was spent in making repairs to sails and running rigging. This in spite of his period of preparation and determination to see that all was sound before he left. He was either not know-ledgeable enough or—too broke! Nevertheless, on that long passage he was deck-hand, cook, carpenter, rigger, navigator and skipper, and he acquitted himself like a champion. It was while in New York that he changed the rig of *Firecrest* from gaff to Bermudan. With this new rig he made his world cruise, arriving back at Le Havre in July 1929 to a tremendous ovation. His circum-navigation took him four and a half years. His book about it is called "In Quest of the Sun".

Let us join him, on the 1st of May, having left Cannes just under a week earlier:

"The 1st of May, sixth day out from Cannes, was a very exciting one. After some days between sea and sky, when observations and calculations tell one land is near, it is always a source of breathless wonder to discover land exactly where it ought to be.

"In going aloft at noon I was able to discern a small cone rise from the water. That was land exactly where it ought to be. I felt proud of my navigation, although the navigator's work is nothing compared with the sailor's work. Soon many other cones appeared on my port bow. To the eyes of an inexperienced sailor they would have seemed to be many different islands, but I knew they were peaks a thousand to three thousand feet high whose bases were joined under the horizon. There, at least forty miles away, was Minorca, the second in size of the Balearic Islands.

"The next day many more peaks appeared, this time ahead, and towards evening the whole island of Majorca rose from the sea."

He sailed but slowly past the Balearic Islands, Majorca, Dragonera, Iviza, Formentera, in very light airs, and it was not until the 15th of May that Gib-ralta's towering eastern side came into view. He told no one in Gibraltar that he was intending to make a solo Atlantic crossing, although he must have at times been tempted, for he was there for two weeks, during which time he was given a great deal of help in fitting out. "The authorities", he writes, "were very kind to me." He records also that he took on board a very great deal of food and water (naturally), and one wonders if he was not perhaps being a little naïve in thinking the "authorities" to be unaware that a long passage to "somewhere" was intended. Moreover, since he had had a squaresail rigged, that somewhere must surely have been at the Western Atlantic limit of the trade winds? Perhaps not; he was, after all, the first man to try this east-west crossing. At all events, according to Gerbault, only two friends were "in the know".

In Chapter Four of his book he starts the Atlantic passage:

"It was the 6th of June at twelve that I left Gibraltar singing gaily—Hurrah, I am outward bound. The great adventure was only beginning.

"Before leaving France I had purchased a wind chart. This purported to show the direction of the prevailing winds on the Atlantic. It indicated that a boat sailing south-west from the Strait of Gibraltar would soon strike the north-east trade winds, which would carry him with fair winds south of the Tropic of Cancer, which is at the twenty-third parallel and south of the Sargasso Sea. Thence he would have to sail west, and wait to be south of Bermuda before going north towards New York.

"Although that course would carry me far to the south of a direct course to New York, and add many hundreds of miles to the distance to be sailed, I determined to follow it rather than to try to beat my way straight across the Atlantic against prevalent head winds. A straight line is the shortest distance for a steamer, but not the fastest course for a sailing-boat.

"A boat sailing from New York towards Gibraltar will meet westerly winds most of the way, and will have to cover just a little over three thousand miles. From Gibraltar to New York one has to sail at least four thousand five hundred miles. This explains the difficulty of the passage from east to west. Joshua Slocum, in 1895, and Blackburne, in 1902, crossed the Atlantic single-handed, from west to east, stopping at the Azores. The longest distance, covered without landing, was two thousand miles.

"Nobody had ever attempted to cross the North Atlantic alone from east to west. Slocum had accomplished a remarkable feat in staying seventy-two days alone at sea in the Indian Ocean. I always had a great admiration for this famous navigator. I knew that my passage would last much longer than any of his, but I was happy at the thought of the difficulties to be overcome.

"Aboard a sailing-boat you never know when you will arrive, and it was this reason that made me carry four months' food. The winds eventually proved anything but fair, so that many times during the passage I congratulated myself on my foresight.

"I left Gibraltar on the 6th of June, and it was an auspicious start, for the day was beautiful. When leaving the harbour the wind was very light, and I lay on deck basking in the sun, and dreaming of the days that were to come—of the joys, and possible hardships, that lay ahead.

"I had unbounded faith in my gallant boat, and a good deal of confidence in my navigation. I felt supremely fit, absolutely without anxiety, and with pleasant anticipation of a sunny run down the trade winds to the tropics, where I would find abundant sunshine, flying fish and possibly adventure.

"So I took a last glimpse of the land, and of the noble rock of Gibraltar shining in the spring sun.

"The light wind increased, so I trimmed in the sheets and laid my course from Algeciras Bay towards the Strait and the North African coast, and soon I was in the Strait rounding Carnero Point.

"The fish were so plentiful that they seemed to be making the water boil. Porpoises gambolled about the boat, and sea-gulls dived in the midst of their schools. I should have been glad to have hooked a fish, but was sailing too fast to make the attempt worth while.'

All, so far, was going swimmingly, but the next chapter is called "Alarming Discoveries", and is well named. The first "discovery" was that the sails started to chafe. His log for the 23rd June notes that he has doubts whether his sail twine will last the passage, so constantly is he having to repair sails.

The next discovery was far more alarming; most of his fresh-water supply had gone bad. Before he left Gibraltar he took aboard eighty gallons. Thirty gallons were in galvanized tanks beneath the cabin sole, and fifty were in two casks; one stowed in the forecastle and one on deck. The majority of his water was thus in the casks, and it was this which had gone bad. The casks had been bought new in Gibraltar. On examination, Gerbault found that the water in them had turned red, and tasted "too sour to use".

Thirst was thus to be a problem for him, and his other problem of rotten sail stitching increased in importance as the voyages lasted. This is clear as we join him in Chapter Seven of his book:

"It was always very hot, and I was always thirsty whilst the sun beat down, but I had to get along on that one cup of water a day, not a drop more. It was more than two weeks after I had found that I was short of drinking water before I managed to catch rain water in my sails, and on the night of July 17th a rain squall blew up, enabling me to collect about two more pints of water to add to the small supply. I sat naked in the rain, and enjoyed its refreshing coolness. I also found relief during the day in the form of frequent baths on deck by dousing myself with sea water from a canvas bucket. It was refreshing, but unluckily the effect soon passed, and I would be as hot and thirsty as ever.

"I had just finished repairing the forestaysail when the mainsail ripped for fifteen feet along a seam. There was therefore nothing to do but haul it down, get to repairing and set the trysail in its place. This meant twenty-four hours' work with needle and twine. To make matters worse, I now began to develop a sore throat, and by the following day it was so badly swollen that I could swallow nothing but a little condensed milk and water. For four days this continued. By July 28th I was so weak from fever that I lowered all but the headsails, and went below and turned in, leaving the *Firecrest* to take care of herself.

"Flying fish occasionally landed on deck, but I could take but little interest in them, for my throat was too sore to allow of eating anything solid. The tropical light, too, began to dazzle me. Many times, on looking towards the horizon, it seemed that land was ahead, but the delusion never lasted very long.

"Sometimes, towards evening, small clouds would appear and take the fallacious appearance of white sails: whilst the inflammation of my throat seemed to sharpen thirst till it became hard to keep within the allowance of one cup of water a day.

"By the morning of the 29th of July I was feeling a little better, but extremely weak after four days of milk diet. The handling of the sails in consequence took four times as long. I, however, steered due west all that day, and at night got a restful sleep, for the wind had died down and the sea was smooth again. This calm weather lasted for a week, and it seemed as though the *Firecrest* had been caught in the doldrums. One calm and blistering day succeeded another, until it seemed as though the very brain was burning in the scorching heat of the tropic sun.

"My conditions at this stage were anything but enviable. Rotten sails which required constant sewing and patching; a little bad water; fever and no wind. It gave no joyful feeling, but a certain sense of satisfaction in meeting and surmounting these obstacles. Perhaps I was over confident, but I knew that before I reached the American coast I would get wind enough—an anticipation which was more than abundantly fulfilled. An entry in my log at that time reads:

" 'Very hot, terribly thirsty. Should like to take a swim, but throat still so sore had better not.

" 'Have certainly lost the trade winds. This is the second time wind chart has lied. It promises fair winds to the 34th degree of north latitude. Only at the 29th degree and *Firecrest* lolling about in a greasy swell; sails idly flapping when set to catch the vagrant airs. If it had not been for the false promises of the wind chart would have gone farther south, and probably caught south-east winds.'

"However, everything seemed unusual on this cruise. And, anyway, very few forecasts are ever fulfilled.

" 'Have had to throw overboard that cask of salt beef. The tropics are too hot for it, and I can no longer stand either the taste or smell.' "

Like Slocum, Gerbault found the loneliness disturbing at first, but, like Slocum, he very soon got used to it. It appears that both men were well able to live with themselves over long periods of solitude and this is true of every successful lone voyager. He does mention having "strange dreams", however, and like many another solo sailor he suffered from the difficulty of keeping awake when it was necessary to be at the helm at night.

He had his fair share of dirty weather, too, but he seems quite to have enjoyed the test of his endurance and skill, although there were "*other*" moments! Here is a graphic description of being in a small boat in an Atlantic gale:

"During the forenoon she lay practically hove to under forestaysail while I repaired several rips in the mainsail, but by the afternoon, when I was ready to set it again, the wind had increased to a gale.

"The seas were running high and broke on board frequently throughout the afternoon. The deck seemed constantly under water. The narrow little cutter lay heeled over before the blast as she drove into the seas, burying her lee rail at times several feet under water.

"The deck sloped like the roof of a house, and I had to be careful in moving about. One slip and I should have gone overboard to leeward, and the cutter, with no one on board, would have gone on her way leaving me food for sharks and bonitos.

"The deck was so badly awash that I had to keep the skylights and hatchways closed. This made it hot and uncomfortable below decks. Cooking under such conditions was a difficult task. My forecastle was just wide enough to stand in, between the stove on the starboard side and the water-casks and the galley on the other.

"If, in a thoughtless moment, I set down a cup or dish, it was likely to be hurled spinning across the forecastle on to the opposite locker or the floor. My stove, too, had a habit of tossing a kettle of water, or a dishful of hot food, on my bare legs and feet; so I had to watch it carefully when the cutter was pitching about."

He was unlucky in his use of a sea anchor. He seems to have used a small jib with it, which, unless he had streamed it from the stern, and he does not say so, is against usual practice and likely to prevent the boat lying as near the wind as she should. He states that the sea anchor made no difference to the boat's action, and with a headsail set this could well be true.

It is really extraordinary that he remained so cheerful (and extracts from his log attest this) under the circumstances. He suffered from thirst and fever and fatigue, and was constantly repairing rotten sails. His passage took him 101 days. The long crossing of the Pacific from Balboa to the Marquesas, about 4,000 miles at sea, has taken most of the circumnavigators about thirty-seven days. The Hiscocks took twenty-six days to sail from Madeira to the West Indies, a distance of 2,662 miles. So it will be clear that Gerbault was at sea for

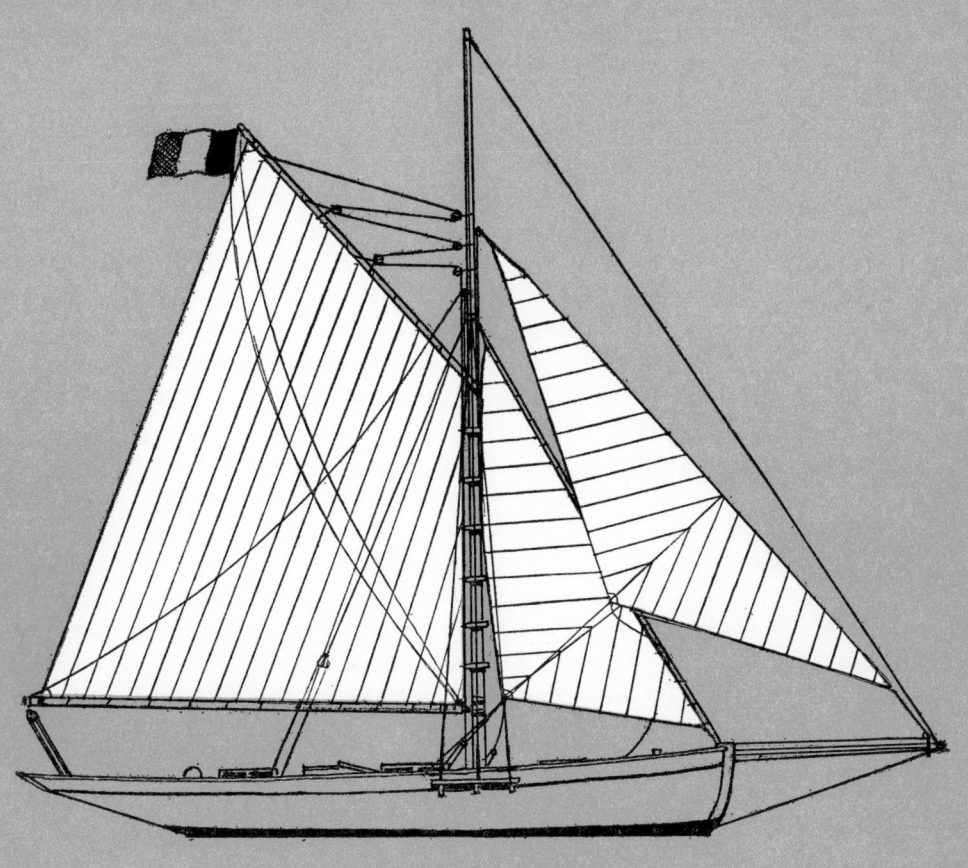

FIRECREST

Length overall: 39 feet
Length water-line: 30 feet
Beam: 8 feet 6 inches. Draught: 7 feet
Designed by Dixon Kemp
Built by P. T. Harris, at Rowhedge, Essex, in 1892
(After her Atlantic crossing she was converted to Bermudan rig)

a very long time in *Firecrest*, and when one visualizes being alone in a small boat
in very uncomfortable conditions for even two months—say sixty days—some
idea of Gerbault's power of endurance begins to shape in one's mind!

It was on the 20th of August that *Firecrest* had her most severe testing. It
came in the form of a monster wave. "I could hardly believe my eyes," wrote
Gerbault. "It was a thing of beauty as well as of awe as it came roaring down
upon us." This was what happened then:

"Knowing that if I stayed on deck I would meet death by being washed overboard, I had just time to climb into the rigging, and was about half-way to the
masthead when it burst upon the *Firecrest* in fury, burying her from my sight
under tons of solid water and lather of foam. The gallant little boat staggered
and reeled under the blow, until I began to wonder anxiously whether she was
going to founder or fight her way back to the surface.

"Slowly she came out of the smother of it, and the great wave roared away
to leeward. I slid down from my perch in the rigging to discover that it had
broken off the outboard part of the bowsprit. Held by the jibstay, it lay in a
maze of rigging and sail under the lee rail, where every sea used it as a battering

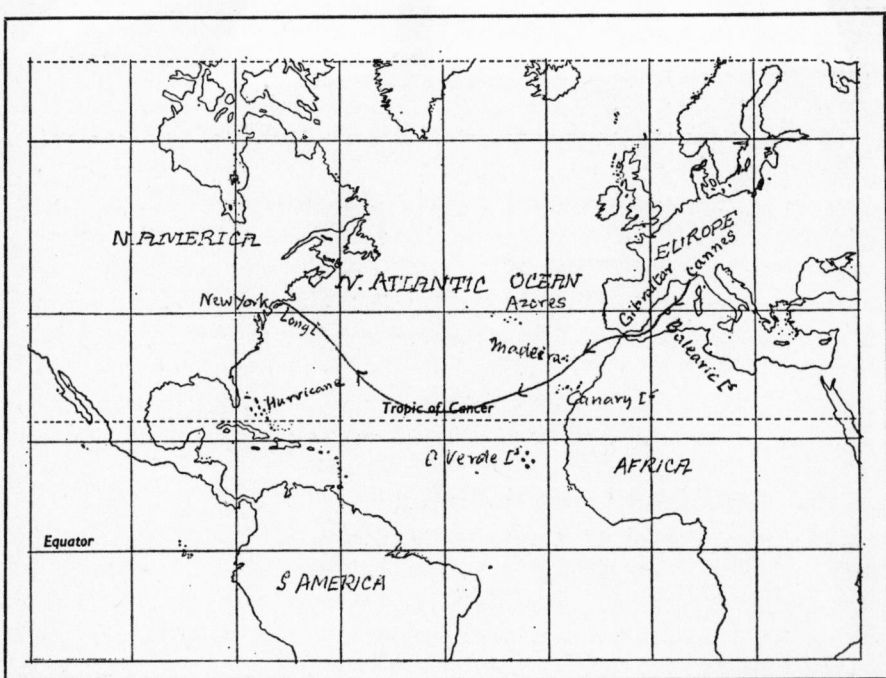

Firecrest in Trouville

ram against the planking, threatening, at every blow, to stave a hole in the hull.

"The mast was also swaying dangerously as the *Firecrest* rolled. Somehow the shrouds had become loose at the masthead. There was now a fair prospect that the cutter would roll the mast out of her, even if the broken bowsprit failed to stave the hole it seemed trying for. The wind cut my face with stinging force, and the deck was, most of the time, awash with breaking seas.

"But I was obliged to jump to work to save both boat and life. First I had to get the mainsail off her, and, in trying to do so, found the hurricane held the sail so hard against the lee topping lift that I had to rig a purchase to haul it down with the downhaul; but I finally managed to get it stowed.

"It proved a tremendous job to haul the wreckage aboard. The deck was like a slide, and the gale so violent that I had to crouch down in order to keep from being wrenched off the deck and hurled bodily into the sea. I clung desperately to the shrouds at intervals. The broken part of the bowsprit was terrifically heavy, and I had to lash a rope round it while it was tossing about and buffeting the side. Several times it nearly jerked me overboard.

"At last I had the jib in, and the bowsprit safely lashed on deck; but it was nearly dusk and I felt worn out."

Crippled as she was, with the marks of Gerbault's repair handiwork all over her, *Firecrest* struggled on, across the Gulf Stream, and into the foggy waters of the eastern seaboard of the United States. Signs of the nearness of land slowly showed themselves. The colour of the water changed as it shoaled. Dead butterflies floated on it. But most of the time fog enveloped the game little cutter and she crept slowly westward. The last phase of the voyage is described by Gerbault as follows:

"It was on the morning of the 10th of September that I sighted land, Nantucket, for the first time since leaving the African coast, a few days out from Gibraltar. But I cannot say that I gave a cheery cry of 'land-ho'. On the contrary, I felt a little sad, for I realized that it stood out there forecasting the end of my cruise; that it meant that all the happy and strenuous days I had spent on the open seas would soon be over, and that I should be obliged to stay ashore for several months. No longer would I be king of all I surveyed, but amongst human beings and a sharer in civilization once more.

"On the following day I sighted the Island of No Man's Land, and sailed through a fleet of innumerable small motor fishing boats. On Wednesday, the 12th of September, I had the pleasure of meeting at sea part of the United States' naval fleet manoeuvring off Newport. It was a wonderful sight, and I watched with the keenest interest the swift destroyers moving in line at a speed of more than thirty knots.

"I had decided to approach New York through Long Island Sound, as I did not want to pass through the Hudson River.

"For the first time in three weeks I found a good sailing breeze off Block Island, and by evening had entered the Sound, passing through the Race. So I sadly bade good-bye to the old ocean.

"There were plenty of passing steamers now. The Sound liners, all ablaze with lighted windows, and electric lamps on deck, tore past all night, often with strains of music that came to me sweetly across the star-lit waters. After a lone cruise such as this had been these lighted steamers at night possessed a certain fascination.

"No longer could I allow the *Firecrest* a free helm to steer herself with at night. We were too near land, and I had a course marked by buoys and lights to follow. So near the goal, I was afraid to fail.

"From now onward for two days I sailed along the beautiful north shore of Long Island, admiring the stately country houses and their green lawns. Then the Sound shores come closer together, and I was opposite the mouth of the East River.

"So, at two o'clock on the morning of September 15th, I dropped anchor off Fort Totten. I had neither left the tiller, nor slept, for the last seventy-two hours, but the cruise of the *Firecrest* was ended, and just one hundred and one days after she had sailed out of Gibraltar harbour."

Alain Gerbault was given a great reception in New York, and he was deluged with letters from people who wanted to sail with him on his next voyage. At the end of his book he describes how he had her repaired and many improvements made. All this took some time, but the last paragraph finds him ready for sea once more. I cannot do better than end this chapter by quoting it:

"I have been ashore nearly a year. I have had many difficulties to overcome, but I have won, and I am ready to sail again. Now, every minute of the day, I am thinking of departure, and of the great joy called living, when I shall be again alone on the sea."

11

THE "CRUISE" OF GEORGE MULHAUSER
IN THE "AMARYLLIS"

"On a beautiful, still day in early September 1920, the Deputy-Assistant Harbour Master, resplendent in a blue uniform with much gold lace on it, stood at the dock head at Plymouth, and watched a small yawl-rigged yacht leaving the dock under power.

" 'What ship is that?' the D.A.H.M. asked.

" The *Amaryllis.*'

" 'Where are you bound?'

" 'Auckland, New Zealand.'

"As an afterthought he shouted: 'Good luck.'

"Such was our send-off.

"The weather conditions being favourable, i.e. there being no wind and an absolutely smooth sea, she was proceeding at 4 miles per hour, which was the maximum speed at which 'the power', a 12/15 h.p. motor, could drive her, even with all things in its favour."

Those words, with which George Muhlhauser opens his account of his world circumnavigation in the early 1920s, give us a good picture of the man; a man who, calmly setting off on a great undertaking, leaves port with as little concern as if he were off on a week-end cruise; is quietly amused at the Harbour Master's laconic "Good luck" coming as an afterthought. A seaman in the top class, he understated his achievements and belittled his talents. Muhlhauser served with the Navy during the war, and never were the traditions of the "silent service" better upheld than in the behaviour of this rugged, strange, withdrawn, but unquestionably sincere man.

George Muhlhauser was educated at Merchant Taylor's School. His first real taste of the sea came from trips aboard North Sea trawlers during the holidays. Although he was born in Surrey, he was really a product of the East Coast, and the North Sea, for it was in those grey, cold waters that his character was formed and his absorption with ships and sea began. Like many yachtsmen, he owned a number of small boats of modest tonnage in succession. In 1901 he had a little 3-tonner called *Camera*. He changed in 1905 to another small boat called *Vivid*, and in 1910 again (his boats seem to be changed in four-yearly intervals) he bought *Wilful*, which was the last ship he was to own before the outbreak of the First World War. During the war he served aboard a variety of ships, including a "Q" ship of which he became second-in-command. His war service was packed with exploits—not so much of wild and reckless daring in the face of the enemy, but rather of feats of remarkable seamanship, like, for example, the occasion when he brought back to the Firth of Forth the captured German ore-carrier *Düsseldorf*, a vessel of 1,200 tons.

The enemy here was not the Germans, but the weather. With no sextant, a faulty compass, inadequate charts, to have carried out this task quietly and efficiently, with but a handful of men—and in a North Sea gale, too—was typical of the man.

The heroine of Muhlhauser's book, *Amaryllis*, was a yawl of 36 tons, Thames measurement. The drawing will give an idea of her—sturdy, gaff-rigged; a yacht in the fishing-boat style, straight stem, deep draught, long keel, bowsprit, dead-eyes and lanyards on her shrouds, etc., and miles of running rigging—a beautiful ship to draw or paint or just to look at, although maybe a trifle heavy in her gear for a very small crew.

Muhlhauser speaks of her as a "small" yacht, but with her 62-feet overall length she seems large by comparison with *Wanderer* or *Trekka*. With her great draught of 10 feet and her beam of 13 feet she must have offered a fair amount of comfort below decks. Of her draught, Muhlhauser wrote that it ". . . was rather too much for knocking about amongst coral reefs, though a very good feature from the point of keeping the sea".

She was forty years old, but had been well built and was perfectly sound. This was lucky for Muhlhauser, for there is always danger in buying a yacht that has been laid up for a long period. At the end of the Second World War in 1945 many yachts were found to be badly affected by rot because the conditions of their laying-up during the war had not allowed for sufficient ventilation—the one sure prevention against rot.

Because of strikes and difficulties of obtaining materials, it took Muhlhauser the best part of a year to fit *Amaryllis* for her voyage; but he was philosophical about the delay (not *nearly* so angry as Arthur Ransome with *Racundra*!) and, as he puts it, he ". . . derived much pleasure from planning voyages all over the world. The West Indies attracted me, and then, of course, there was South America, the South Sea Islands, and Australasia, to say nothing of the Mediterranean, India, and the East or even South Africa. In imagination I visited them all, but in the end came back to the practical things in life, and decided on making a fair wind of it, and going to the West Indies before the North East Trade Winds, through the Panama, and across the South Seas before the South East Trades, to Australasia. What I should do then I left time and the Fates to decide. . . ."

AMARYLLIS

Length overall 62 feet
Length water-line: 52 feet. Beam: 13 feet. Draught: 10 feet
Built in 1882 by A. E. Payne

Actually, he had an idea, rather like that of "George" and "J" in Weston Martyr's delightful book "The Southseaman", of selling *Amaryllis* at a "nice profit", returning home, buying another yacht, and repeating the manoeuvre. And, as with the two friends in "The Southseaman", it didn't work out like that.

Instead, Muhlhauser sailed home to England, taking, as the chart will show, a route from New Zealand northwards to Fiji, to the Coral Sea and Torres Strait via the New Hebrides and Solomon Islands. Then he departed from most other circumnavigators in that he sailed *north* of Timor, Lombok, Bali, Java and Sumatra. From there he sailed via Ceylon to the Red Sea, so northwards via the Suez Canal, westwards through the Mediterranean Sea, and back to England, after a stop in Vigo in North Spain.

It is in the account of the passage through Malaysia that we come upon a tragedy. Muhlhauser's narrative stops abruptly at Timor, and the rest of the book is compiled from his log and from letters. This has been skilfully done, but it is tragic that Muhlhauser was prevented by ill health from finishing the story of his great voyage. On arrival back in England he tried in vain to sell *Amaryllis*. His friends report that he was a worried man, and a sick man—a man "looking ten years older". He was operated on, but without success, and he died.

It was a sad end to such a very active and enthusiastic life. To have sunk to such depression and worry and ill health from the heights not so far back when he could write of the Western Pacific:

"Next morning Amedee Lighthouse showed up, and by 10 a.m. we had it on the right bearing and ran in through Bulari Pass, with a strong following wind from the N.W. which sent a heavy sea on to the coral. As the waves reached the shoal water they reared up, curled over, and broke on the reef with a roar in a welter of white foam, and with a suggestion of irresistible power. It was an awe-inspiring sight, and a beautiful one. The blue of the seas changed to a multitude of tints as they broke, while rainbows showed in the spindrift blown off the tops. In the gap through which we passed, with great seas thundering on either hand, there was no broken water, but a big swell ran in. As the waves overtook us, up would go the stern and the ship rushed forward, then down would sink the stern and the bows rose up. It was a most exhilarating time. We felt we really were alive."

Muhlhauser did not sail single-handed. He tried, with little success at first, to find like-minded friends, so he began advertising. He got many replies, but did not find the sort of man he was looking for. Too many of them wanted "to get something out of me". Others ". . . had no qualifications beyond a vague desire to be somewhere else". How many people like that there are! Eventually, however, he found his crew: "Charles", an ex-Lieutenant R.N.V.R., a first-class seaman, and his brother "John", who was odd-job man and cook. The fourth member of his ship's company was "David", an Irishman, who casually remarked on the first day of the voyage: "Of course, it is madness to take a small ship like this across the Atlantic in the autumn", a retired sea captain having convinced him of this fact. The prospect of imminent death by drowning did not seem to worry David in the least and Muhlhauser writes of him that he proved to be "a very agreeable, cheerful companion . . . all the time he was on board". Finally, to make the crew up to five, Muhlhauser signed on a young fisherman. David had "signed on" for Australasia, but it did not quite work out like that. David's wife and small son, thought to be in Egypt by Muhlhauser, turned up in Kingston, Jamaica, and so the *Amaryllis* left Kingston without David! John and the mate left the ship (by agreement) in the West Indies, and to replace them Muhlhauser signed on a lad of "about 90% white" called Stéphane, and for a while the ship was handled by the skipper, Stéphane and David, the smallness of the crew giving apparently much amusement to the harbour police wherever they went in the West Indies. After David left, Muhlhauser signed on another boy by name of Sam, like Stéphane, inexperienced.

Muhlhauser was at times lucky and at others unlucky in his crew. Sometimes he was desperately short-handed in that heavily sparred ship. But he was always in every respect in command. The circumnavigation was virtually a one-man show. As he got farther on his way round the world, so the calibre of his crews declined.

In a letter dated 3rd February 1922 Muhlhauser writes: ". . . You ask if I have a white man with me. Yes, I am giving a young Australian a passage home. The crew now consists of him, a Lascar, a Malay cook, and of course Stéphane and myself. The Lascar is a fairly useless person, very apt to tear off superfluous clothes and dance about the deck in emergencies. The Malay has the face of an angel, but is a very wily young man really."

This is an unusual tale, this story of Muhlhauser's world voyage, and woven through it is his laconic humour, his candour and lack of affectation.

The following extract from his book, with which I will close this chapter, is a fair sample of his style of writing. The scene is the Southern Pacific, sailing from the Galápagos Islands to the Marquesas—their longest passage at sea. Muhlhauser was, as usual, short-handed for his heavy vessel. His three friends having left him in the West Indies, he had the two boys Sam and Stéphane, both of them young and inexperienced . . .

"Life became very simple, and consisted mainly in eating, sleeping, and

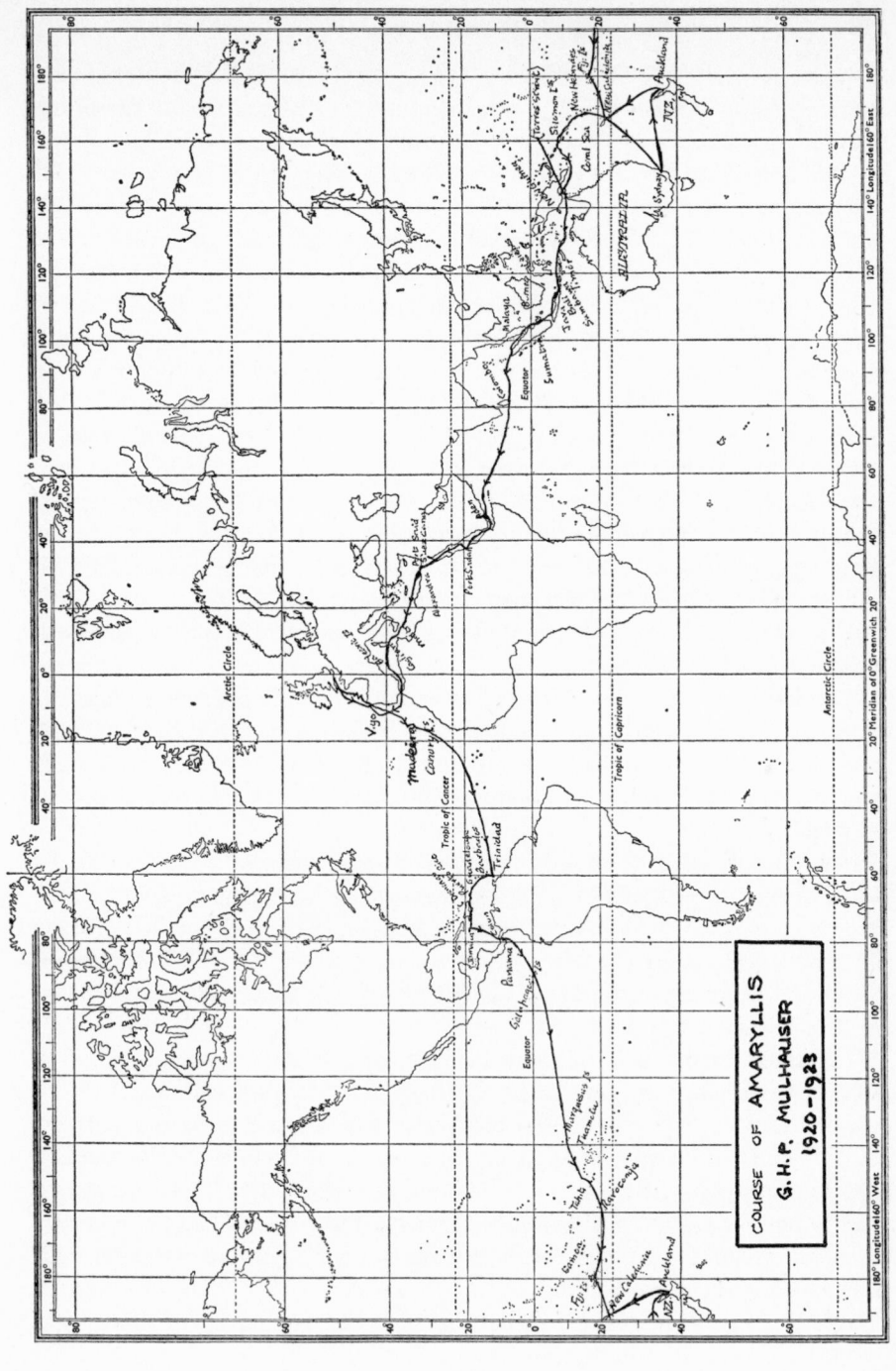

COURSE OF AMARYLLIS
G. H. P. MULHAUSER
1920 - 1923

steering. The ordinary routine was as follows: Breakfast at 7 a.m., dinner at noon, tea at 3.30 p.m., and supper at 7 p.m. These were the nominal hours, but, as Stéphane had the vaguest idea of time, meals often appeared an hour or so sooner or later. Between 7 a.m. and 8 a.m. I took a sight, while Sam steered, and another one at noon. After working out the first sight I steered while Sam slept. In the afternoon Sam steered, and I had a nap. Stéphane did the cooking and lamps, and work below, and did nothing much on deck during the day beyond helping to shift sails. The first night watch started after supper, until 10 p.m., when the helmsman was relieved and went below. At midnight the helmsman was again changed and also at 2 a.m. In this way each of us had two hours at the tiller and four hours off. Each was called twice each night, rather tiring work, but we usually had a nap during the day, and so managed to get enough sleep. The cooking was very plain. Breakfast consisted of eggs, while these lasted, coffee, bread or biscuit, butter, and jam. For dinner there were three standard dishes, pomme de terre, macaroni, or riz mélange. The potatoes, macaroni, or rice, according to which was to be used, were first boiled, onions were sliced and fried, and a tin of bully beef was minced. All these ingredients, together with a tin of tomatoes, a spoonful of Bovril, and two spoonfuls of Worcestershire sauce, were mixed together and warmed up, and the dish was ready. It served for dinner, supper, and at times breakfast next day. Occasionally dry hash, rissoles, or curry varied the menu, and at rare intervals fish, when we were lucky enough to hook or land one. A line was always towing astern, but we seldom caught anything.

"And so one day followed another in pleasing, uneventful monotony. The weather was mostly fine. Occasionally, however, there were days of continuous rain and squalls, varied by others when the wind was light and the ship rolled heavily in a very troublesome swell, with the boom, jerking to and fro, and shaking the ship. In one rain squall the spinnaker, which is made of light stuff, cotton and silk mixed, split in two, and it took me nearly two days to repair it with a table cloth cut into strips, as there was nothing else at all suitable on board. Time did not hang heavily on my hands. As a matter of fact, I was usually very busy and had no time for reading even. A small sailing-ship wants as much looking after as a harem, and there was always something to do about the decks. She was probably the most silent ship sailing the seas. I never spoke except to give an order, and the two lads quarrelled every now and then and would not speak to each other, or even feed together, for days at a time. Occasionally I had to intervene in these rows, and always found Sam in the wrong. He was a morose and uncouth person, a regular savage, and was inclined to bully Stéphane, who resented this hotly. In the intervals between quarrels the two were quite

Amaryllis—light airs and intense heat; many miles from land

friendly and chatted together in Spanish as if there had never been a cloud between them. In the main, however, she was a silent ship and forged ahead day and night to the soothing sound of water swishing past the bow, the creak of the gaff-jaws, a rope rattling on the sails, or the thud of a block, but rarely to the sound of the human voice.

"One day it occurred to me that if I fell over the side, or anything happened to me, the lads would be in rather a fix. Neither ever knew where he was, or where he was going, or how long it would probably take to get there. These matters they were content to leave to the white man, who would tell them what course to steer, what sails to set, and how to trim them, and they would eventually arrive at their port. So it had always been so far, and so, presumably, it it always would be. In order to provide for the chance of my being disabled I asked Sam what he would do if I fell overboard. He was steering at the time, and he continued steering for a minute or two without any expression at all on his heavy face. Then he smiled and spoke.

" 'Sir Cap, I go back.'

"He always addressed me as 'Sir Cap,' perhaps because he thought 'Sir' unsuitable when speaking to his skipper, while 'Cap' alone sounded a bit off-hand, so he combined the two.

"Going back would not, however, be an easy matter, as the wind would be dead ahead, and I told him to keep her away, full and bye, to the north-east, by so doing they would be sure to make the coast of North America, sooner or later. It would be safer for them to do so, than to try and find an island in the Pacific and possibly get involved amongst reefs. From that time I showed Stéphane, who is a very intelligent lad, the ship's position on the chart every two days, and also noted in the margin the course to aim for the homeward trip should it be necessary.

"When we were over 2,000 miles from the coast a white column appeared at dawn to the northward. It looked like a lighthouse, but proved to be a full-rigged ship following the sailing track from San Francisco to Cape Horn. She made a fine picture with all her towering mass of canvas showing white against the blue sky. The wind was light, and she was in sight all day. At dusk she passed under our stern two miles away. It is very pleasant to meet a ship at sea. It gives the feeling of companionship. She was, however, the only ship we met away from the land between Panama and Sydney.

"On 9th May the long trip was drawing to a close, and land was, by observations, due next morning. At dawn on the 10th, Hood Island—named after Lord Hood, then a midshipman in the *Resolution*, Captain Cook, who first sighted it in 1774—lay to port, with Ua Huka one point to starboard. A light breeze carried us slowly along and as the day drew on it became clear that we should not be able to make Nukuhiva, our port, which lies farther west, before dark, and I decided to anchor for the night under the lee of Ua Huka, in Shavay Bay. as we sailed along the south side of the island its beauty was very striking. In the centre is a line of high hills with ridges running down to the sea. The valleys between these ridges were a mass of luxuriant vegetation, very pleasing to the eye. We rounded Hemeni Islet, and stood on into Shavay Bay, but when the soundings should have been 10 fathoms, according to the chart, we were getting over 22 fathoms. It was impossible to anchor in such a depth, and I got the sails down and proceeded slowly along the coast under power, with Stéphane aloft to look out for rocks under water. On the north side of Tetutu Point a small bay with 7 fathoms was shown and we made for it and brought up."

The understatement in this quoted extract is typical: "It is very pleasant to meet a ship at sea"; "the valleys . . . were . . . very pleasing to the eye". If Muhlhauser sometimes seems a little remote and austere, his book is extraordinarily powerful and in its restraint and sincerity makes the same impression upon the reader as did the author upon all who met him.

12

ERLING TAMBS

A Happy Adventure that Ended in Tragedy

Of the book, first published in 1933, called "The Cruise of the *Teddy*" it can be truly said that it does not need a sailor to appreciate it. This is an account of three years of ocean sailing that has universal appeal as a book. It is really a chronicle of Norwegian life as lived aboard a small boat by Tambs, his wife, his son Tony, and a dog. To call the Tambs family happy-go-lucky sailors would be an understatement! They put to sea without a barometer, a sextant, a light list . . . indeed, Tambs himself is on record as saying "To be safe at sea . . . I think one should regard one's nautical calculations with a good deal of scepticism".

Yet it is this very amateurishness that gives the book so much of its charm. Tambs is at the very opposite end of the pole to those sailormen who never seem to make a mistake. While admiring their skill, we do not learn so much from them, and perhaps we may even find them at times a little boring. Tambs is never boring. He confesses freely the appalling messes into which he got and leaves one aghast not only at the mental picture but at the almost incredible forbearance of Mrs Tambs. In short, it is not so much feats of seamanship as honesty and humanity that this remarkable book has to offer. Simply as a good tale of seafaring it surely deserves a place in the library of that legion of human beings who like to read about the sea and ships.

Tambs put the name of his boat in the title of his book, and the *Teddy* is the hero, although some of the scenes are stolen by young Tony, his son. The family started on their voyage towards the end of August 1928. The *Teddy*, his vessel, was a 40-foot cutter built some thirty-eight years earlier, in Larvik, by the well-known designer and builder, Colin Archer. The drawing shows her attractive profile, typical of the kind of vessel. She was lovingly fitted out; indeed, she took all of Tambs's money; as he puts it ". . . my resources had run unmistakably dry, but the old boat was transformed into a trim yacht, and no writ was nailed to her mast".

I have emphasized earlier the amateurishness of Tambs's approach to his voyage, but it must be said that he was by no means unfamiliar with ships and the sea. His was not a gesture of quite such faith as that of John Caldwell, mentioned in Chapter 2. Tambs had, in fact, sailed in square-rigged ships and had also sailed a number of small vessels single-handed. It was the *Teddy* herself, an old boat, that caused the Arendal Harbour Master and the interested local authorities some uneasiness—that and a certain cheerful vagueness on the part of her skipper. Indeed, the authorities appear to have considered it to be their duty to prevent Tambs and his wife from setting out, as the following amusing extract from his book will show:

"When at anchor in this port, and while I was away on some business ashore, the Chief of Police came on board, apparently with instructions from the Marine Department, to prevent us from setting out on what they considered a foolhardy venture. My reception of these disquieting tidings can surely be imagined. My whole heart and my last penny had been devoted to the realization of my lifelong dream, was all doomed to frustration! For one brief moment I even entertained the desperate project of quietly slipping my cable and escaping under cover of night. Recollection of my wife's pledged word that I would not leave without the consent of the authorities rendered this solution impossible. I had to stay.

"On the following day, The Chief paid a second visit, accompanied on this occasion by an expert in the person of the Arendal Harbour Master. After a few pertinent questions, they announced their decision that they considered the *Teddy* unfitted for a long voyage.

"In vain I remonstrated with them, arguing against this assumption of a long voyage. Ah, didn't they know all about that! Hadn't they read the papers! And how could I explain my big fresh water tanks and the various other fittings, indicative surely of my ambitious intentions. Ambitious but foolhardy, they declared, including with a sweeping gesture the lack of spare sails, the absence of nautical instruments, books, tables, charts, etc., etc. In short, owing to the insufficiency of equipment and the shortcomings of the crew, they must condemn my *Teddy* as utterly unfit to cope with the difficulties of an ocean voyage, and they—the Authorities—were there to see that we did not enter upon an adventure that could not but end in disaster.

"What could I say, or do! I was no lawyer, and even if I had been, what chance would I have had in a dispute about enactments and amendments with a Government Department and its officials! I explained that I had been trained in square-rigged ships, that I had had experience in sailing small craft single-handed, and that I thought that my seamanship would surely counterbalance my shortcomings as a navigator. Oh, fiddlesticks! Was I conceited enough to think that unaided I could successfully handle a heavy boat like the *Teddy*.

"Say what I would, my visitors remained adamant. But suddenly I pricked up my ears. An unwary remark on the part of my main adversary gave me my

S.G.B.—M

cue. Though only a vague hint, it nevertheless gave me the impression that the Marine Department in their instructions to the Police had admitted the absence of a law which applied to my special case. I decided to make a bold move. I rose. 'Pardon me, gentlemen,' I said, 'but I must get busy.' 'Busy? What with?' 'Weighing my anchor,' I replied casually, 'the wind is fair.'

"The two officials looked at each other, then smiled.

" I suppose the game is up,' said the guardian of the law after a while. 'Unfortunately you are right in assuming that we have no legal grounds for stopping you. Although'—he continued musingly—'I dare say that if you would give me some little time to study the issue, I should eventually find a paragraph that would be applicable to your—hm—case.'

" 'I am afraid that I shall not have time to wait for the outcome of your researches, sir,' I retorted, 'and it would be lamentable if their thoroughness should suffer from the disadvantage of undue haste. You may let me know the result of your legal studies when I come back.'

"The old gentleman shook his finger at me. Then he offered me his hand and said earnestly: 'Well, I hope that you *will* come back, and—may neither of you ever repent of this foolishness. Meanwhile, Good luck and God speed you.'

" 'We have done our best to prevent you from going,' said the Harbour Master, when he shook hands with me, and then, lowering his voice, he startled me by adding rather wistfully, 'but if I were younger, I should have loved to go with you.'

"The Authorities departed. The old Chief kept waving us farewell, as the launch tore her way towards the town. I felt rather sorry for him. He had not achieved his aim."

So sail they did, all the way from Oslo, down through the English Channel, southwards along the coast of Portugal, to Madeira and the Canaries. The chart shows their course.

A refreshing thing about these writers is that there is so much variety in their writing and so much individuality. They may sail the same courses, but their accounts vary enormously. And yet when one considers the variety of moods of the sea itself, it is not so surprising. The most modest cruising yachtsman knows that the great joy of cruising lies in the fact that no two cruises are ever alike. Nowhere does one find such contrasts, such fears, followed so often by such unexpected delights, as in sailing. This earth of ours is three parts water and the scope for adventure while sailing in it is unlimited. You can never sit back and say "I know it all—I have seen it all", for there is always something new at sea.

There was certainly always something new for Erling Tambs. At Vigo there arrives the third member of the crew; an Alsatian dog, who Tambs named "Spare Provisions". A fourth member joins the crew at Las Palmas, in the person of Tony Tambs. He was born on the 10th May 1929, in the house of a friend of Tambs, and ". . . when three weeks old, he joined his ship".

Nowhere is Tambs's free and easy attitude to navigation more manifest than the passage in Chapter VII of his book when he describes his first attempt at taking his noon latitude and calculating the ship's position. He admits that "high seas and the rolling of our craft certainly interfered with the accuracy of my observations". He also admits that a great deal of his navigation was guess-work; and one wonders how many other people would admit that! He sights a steamer, the *Alegrete*, and assumes she is bound for the River Plate "or some other South American Port". He accordingly alters course so as to find more reassuring steamers by which to correct his position! However, he is unlucky in this, and as the *Teddy* approaches land on the western edge of the Atlantic Ocean Tambs grows, for him, quite worried.

He says he "climbed the rigging a dozen times but saw not a ship". He is aware that he may well be "a hundred or even two hundred miles west of our calculated position", and concludes the paragraph with two remarks of the "famous last words" variety: ". . . The situation threatened to become exciting. Where were we?"

But if Tambs throve on excitement, things at times must have seemed pretty exasperating for his wife. And yet there is no sign of any mutiny in that quarter! Not only that, it was his wife, who, spotting a light on the port quarter, saved their lives on that Atlantic crossing. They had both been staring into blackness when, his wife's sharp eyes detecting something, Tambs jumped into the rigging and climbed aloft. Sure enough, there was a light. It was one of the masthead lights of a steamer. Climbing still higher, the second light came into view, showing the steamer to be steering approximately a north-westerly course. Tambs writes:

"Acting on the impulse I clambered down, brought *Teddy* about, and let her come away on the other board until she headed NW. with the wind well abaft her beam.

"Then I went below and consulted my chart. It seemed as if my dead reckoning had been correct, after all.

"Working on this, I shaped a course for the straits, NW½N. Three hours later my confidence met a welcome support in the shape of a big liner steering a parallel course.

"At 2 a.m. we hove to: if my calculations were right, we ought to be just off

TEDDY

Length overall: 40 feet
Tambs does not give her other dimensions in his book; but
Teddy was a typical design by Colin Archer,
who having settled in Larvik, produced many
such craft of the 'Norwegian Pilot Cutter' type.
They were of moderate displacement, had
widely flaring sections at bow and stern, and
had a great deal of beam. Although slow
to windward, they were tough and could keep
the sea in all weathers.

the straits. That night we burnt our side lights for the first time since leaving Las Palmas.

"At daybreak, when the weather cleared up after a heavy squall, my wife suddenly put her arms around my neck and gave me a hug. The first rays of the sun had conjured forth the outlines of an island, high wooded mountains:
"TOBAGO!

"That was Friday, August 9th.

"But what a wonderful piece of luck it was that my wife chanced to espy that light. Five minutes later it would have been invisible even from the masthead, nor would any other lights have come our way. Before morning we should have been in the breakers on the banks off the river Orinoco. And yet, was it really the merest chance that prevented us from continuing our mad race to destruction?"

Yes, Mrs Tambs was a remarkable woman. Not a word of complaint escapes her when, sailing after a long hot spell in harbour, the waters of the ocean pour into the boat through seams opened by the heat. Not a word does she utter when exactly the same thing happens a bit later on. The only time she seems to have become distressed rather than upset was when Tambs, on falling ill at sea and thinking he might be going to die, issues detailed instructions to her on how to hoist his dead body out of the cabin with the fore-halyard, heave it over the ship's side, and let go!

The voyage of the Tambs family took them to places which have been described in this book. Of course, they had their own specific brand of adventure in each one. It stands out from every page that they all of them had the most exciting and wonderful time that can be imagined. Things were always happening to them and they not only enjoyed the good moments; they rose gloriously above the bad ones.

It seems, therefore, all the greater tragedy that this book should have to end with the loss of their ship.

The family had been staying at Auckland in New Zealand. It will be clear from the chart that after sailing across the Pacific, calling in at some of the Polynesian islands *en route*, Tambs took the yacht to New Zealand. Using this as their base, they took part in the Trans-Tasman Race to Sydney, afterwards battling back to Auckland against continuous easterly gales; but they also made a cruise northward to the Tonga (or Friendly) Islands and back. It was while in New Zealand that Mrs Tambs had ". . . done her part by dutifully adding a new member to the crew of an undermanned boat, a healthy little girl, on whom we later bestowed the New Zealand name of Tui". Auckland was their base for over thirteen months and, like all yachtsmen who have had similar experiences, they had grown so fond of the friendly and hospitable New Zealanders that when the time came to part the many farewells were sad indeed. What they did not know was that it was soon to be farewell to *Teddy* as well.

This is a sad way to end a chapter, especially since I have chronicled enough disasters in Chapter 2, but it is the way the book ends. I will leave it to Tambs to tell of the end of his boat in his own words:

"Now we were close against it. We felt the lift of the surge; cold breaths of a moisture-laden atmosphere chilled us. My heart shrank within me: *Teddy*'s end was near.

"We struck the first time. I felt how the rocks crunched beneath our keel. *Teddy* heeled over, hard, then, righting herself, was lifted again and carried onward, past the point, right into the breakers. . . .

"I shouted to my wife to fetch little Tui from out of her bunk in the cabin. The same instant *Teddy* was seized by an enormous wave, lifted high, and with one big sweep thrown sideways against the rugged rocks. Then everything seemed to happen at the same time. Planks crushed, spars splintered. Rumbling—crashing—shrieking—rushing waters—and above it all the thundering roar of ten thousand unfettered demons of the waves.

"Sometimes buried in foam so that we lost our breath, sometimes clinging to an almost perpendicular deck, when the sea was on the return, we needed all the presence of mind that we could muster. The main boom had come adrift. One of the topping lifts had jammed in a block sheave aloft, keeping the heavy spar suspended just over the cabin coamings and leaving it to sweep wildly from side to side, hardly twenty inches above the deck, whenever the boat rolled. The boom was like a huge club swung with deadly intent by a cunning giant hand. To dodge its shattering blows, we were continually forced to flatten out on the foam-swept deck.

"Tony in his canvas harness, tied by a short rope to the rail, was in immediate danger. I succeeded in undoing his rope and then, in that fraction of a second when the main boom hung still, while gathering momentum for another sweeping assault, I ventured to leap on to the rugged face of the rock. It was a desperate chance. For one terribly long moment I hung by one hand, with the other attempting to support Tony, whose grip around my neck was gradually loosening, while the rush of returning water seemed to load insufferable tons of weight on to us. The next moment I found a foothold and climbed on to the ledge, where I left Tony with strict orders to grab a hold and hang on. Then I returned to the boat. Somehow I contrived to bring Tui ashore. Hurriedly I handed her to Tony, instructing him to look after her and not to leave her, no matter what happened. I then hastened to the rescue of my Julie.

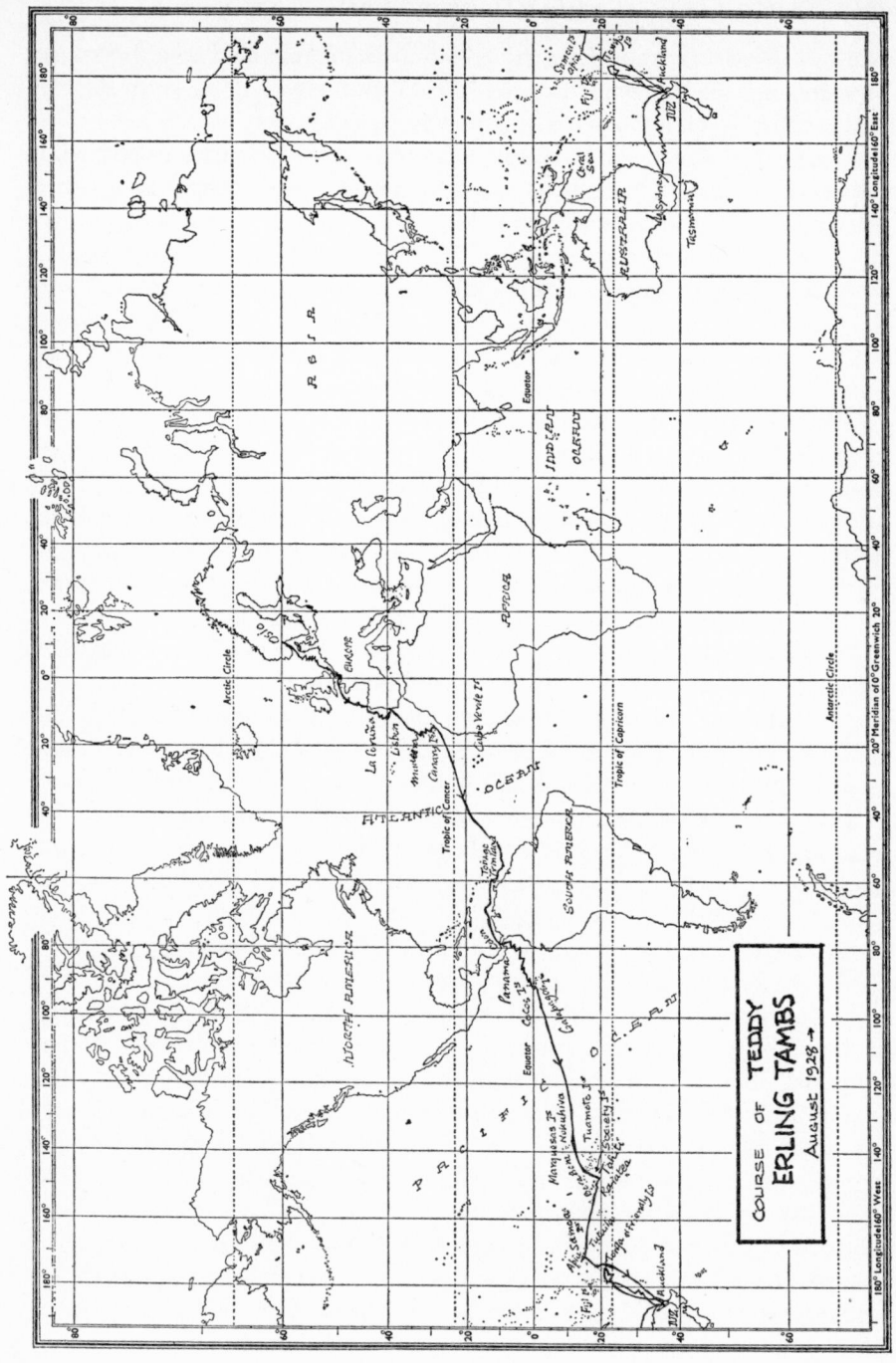

COURSE OF TEDDY
ERLING TAMBS
August 1928 →

"But in the meantime she had achieved the seemingly impossible feat of swimming clear of the surging breakers. With infinite relief I saw her making for a large piece of floating timber on the sheltered side of the point, meanwhile using the broken sweep for a support. A motor launch I had not previously noticed had put out a dinghy to go to her assistance. She called out to me in a voice which showed that she was very much alive. Well, she had certainly proved her mettle.

"Tony, too, had behaved like a hero. Without a word he had taken his duties like a man, sitting on the rocks where I had left him in charge of Tui. He never budged, even when the breakers washed over them occasionally. In all my misery, I could not help feeling proud of him.

"Spare Provisions had also been washed overboard. I had seen the poor dog fighting in the surf, but could do nothing for her. However, she had saved herself, limping and bleeding she joined our little group of castaways.

"The fishing launch brought us back to Kawau. When the family had been put up at the Mansion House, I returned to the wreck to see if anything could be salvaged. It proved impossible; the seas were continually sweeping over the hull, which was waterlogged and badly strained. Her flag, the proud ensign of the Norwegian Yacht Club, awarded her for her merits, was still flying, half mast, where it had jammed in the rush of events. 'As if *Teddy* bemoaned her own end!' said one of the fishermen. I felt differently. To me it seemed as if my noble boat mourned not only her own funeral but the end of a beautiful dream and the misfortune of the master who loved her.

"I turned away. I had seen her dear and pretty lines for the last time.

"When I returned on the following morning, *Teddy*—my kingdom—had vanished."

13

TREKKA

The Minute Circumnavigator

"On Saturday, 10 September 1955, I was all ready to leave. My few close friends had come to see me off from the dock near the Fishermen's Wharf. As they let go the lines and *Trekka* slowly gathered way, their voices carried clearly across the water. 'Good luck, *Trekka*! Don't forget to write, John.' It was a strangely sad moment, and I wondered when I would see them all again. I remembered the happy sailing we'd had together and how we'd gone over the charts planning the route for *Trekka*'s voyage; and now here I was actually starting. As if understanding my feelings, *Trekka* quickly drew away from the little group and headed out towards the breakwater and the open sea beyond."

Trekka was the name of a very small yacht of only 18 feet 6 inches on the water line, and "John" was John Guzzwell, a remarkable young man, who not only built her himself but sailed her round the world. When Guzzwell expressed his willingness to let me quote from his book I was delighted, for my own book would have been incomplete without reference to this heroic little vessel and her great achievement. Guzzwell calls his book "*Trekka* Round the World". It was published by Adlard Coles Ltd, in association with Rupert Hart-Davis Ltd of London, and John de Graff Inc. of New York.

The book starts with Guzzwell's account of how he came to build *Trekka*, and continues with his world voyage. Sandwiched between the chapters describing his voyage is an account (referred to earlier in this book) of how, while sailing with some friends by the name of Smeeton in a boat called *Tsu-Hang*, he twice experienced a capsize. The salvaging of this vessel and sailing to a port under jury rig occupy two chapters in the book. (The whole affair has been dealt with by Miles Smeeton himself in a book called "Once is Enough".)

John Guzzwell was born in England, but grew up in Jersey. His father came originally from the fishing port of Grimsby in England, and his grandfather was a trawler owner, whose red-sailed vessels sailed from that same port to the North Sea fishing grounds. His father after wandering about the world from "gold mining in the frozen wastes of Alaska to pearl fishing in the South Seas", eventually settled in Jersey. But "settle" does not appear to be quite the right word, because, to quote Guzzwell again, "I was only three years old when the call of the sea became too much for my father; shore life, though easy, was very unsatisfying to him and it was not long before he decided to have a small yacht built and make a long ocean voyage in her". The result of this yearning was *Our Boy*, a gaff-rigged ketch, 52 feet in length, in which Guzzwell's parents, another man, and the infant Guzzwell sailed to South Africa.

This is but one of a number of early adventures recounted by Guzzwell, all of which show that he spent his youth amongst boats. It is hardly surprising, from both an hereditary as well as environmental point of view, that he should eventually have made the great cruise which he did. What is more unusual is that, in the tradition of Harry Pidgeon and others, he himself built the boat in which he did it. It came about in this way.

Having left South Africa and returned to England, Guzzwell tried his hand at a number of things, including cycle-racing, a sport he had been keen on in South Africa. Nothing seemed to satisfy him, though, and it was while he was in Jersey that there grew on him the certainty that he would make a long sea voyage alone. He was a good joiner and was confident that he could build his own boat.

He then recalled his father's stories of the logging camps in British Columbia, and with, by this time, complete conviction of purpose, he emigrated to Canada. He settled in Victoria, British Columbia, arriving in March 1953. He got himself a job. The wages were good and his dream grew daily nearer as he saved money toward the cost of materials for his boat.

Sometimes he would go down to Thunderbird Park and look at *Tilikum*, Voss's old ship, but it was not his intention to sail the seas in any kind of "freak" vessel, but a well-found, sea-kindly little ship designed by an experienced naval architect. She would have to be small, because of the expense. He found the naval architect he sought in J. Laurent Giles of Lymington, England, a designer from whose board had come many a yacht that had made long voyages successfully.

He wrote to Giles, asking him to design him a small vessel that he could build himself and in which he would be sailing alone. Back came the reply in the affirmative, and *Trekka* was born. Giles designed for John Guzzwell a little yawl, of 18 feet 6 inches on the waterline. Her other measurements and her "hogged" sheerline will be seen on the drawing of her. (The orthodox "sheer" is higher at bow and stern than amidships.) Guzzwell writes that "there was a surprising amount of room inside the hull, with two bunks forward, and aft of them a chart table and a small galley where I could cook simple meals on a Primus kerosene stove".

We have mentioned Guzzwell's skill as a shipwright, and how eloquent of

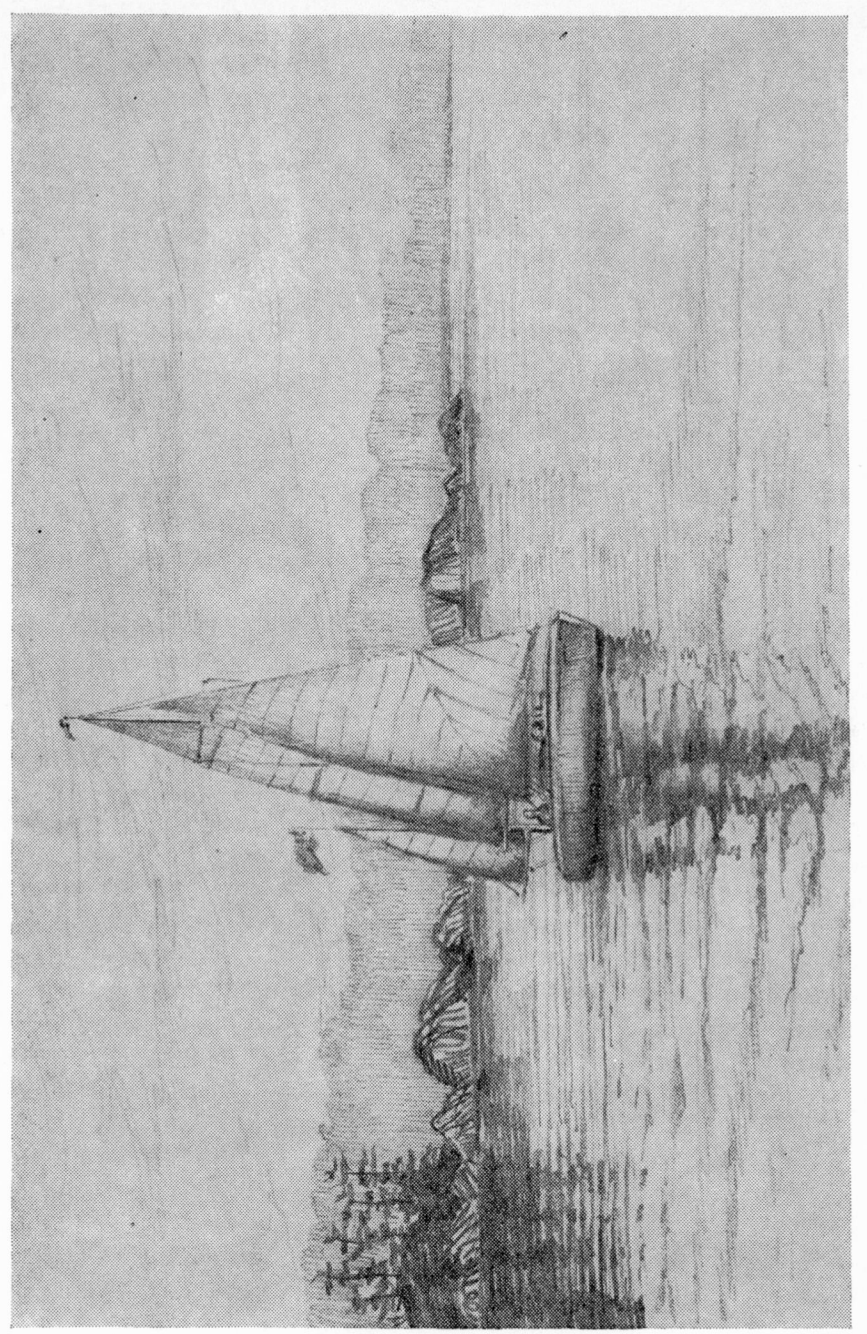

Trekka in light airs and idyllic surroundings

the love and care he put into his work is the paragraph in which he says:

"I feel there is something almost sacred about building a boat. It is a difficult thing to explain, but I have found that other boatbuilders have shared this feeling. It is almost like creating a living being, a boat seems to have a soul and character all of her own. Perhaps it is because of this that boats are usually thought of as being feminine."

It was neither an easy nor a quick job. For example, when the planking was finished Guzzwell had over 3,000 fastenings to rivet over. Nevertheless the latter part of August 1954 *Trekka* was ready for launching. There was too much work still to be done for Guzzwell to get a chance to sail his boat that year, and he waited impatiently for the winter of 1954 to pass. The early spring of the following year sees him stepping the masts and rigging them, until one long-awaited day . . . "I bent on the new suit of sails, let go the mooring lines and felt life in the tiller for the first time. It was a very satisfying moment. I realised that I had a fine little yacht, she was quite fast and stood up to her sail well in fresh conditions. I found that she would steer herself to windward quite easily and just as well as I could do."

He got to know his boat during the weeks that followed and one can picture what happy and exciting weeks those must have been! All the time he was laying in stores and preparing for his long voyage. And then one unforgettable day, he is off—the occasion quoted in the paragraph with which I opened this chapter; so let us sail with John Guzzwell by following the courses he shaped on the world chart, and by illustrating these courses with quotations from his book.

First the courses. His first sail from Victoria took him south to San Francisco. Although nothing particularly violent occurred he met with a sufficient variety of weather, including a full gale (which it might be argued was violent enough!), to test his little ship and give him confidence in her as well as in himself as skipper.

It was while Guzzwell was in San Francisco that he met Miles and Beryl Smeeton and their young daughter Clio. The Smeetons were cruising aboard a ketch called *Tzu Hang*, and they became very friendly with Guzzwell and eventually decided to cruise together, at least as far as Hawaii.

Actually Guzzwell himself sailed for the Hawaiian islands about a week ahead of *Tzu Hang*, considering the latter to be a faster ship, but in fact on arrival in Honolulu he found that *Tzu Hang* had not caught him up. This was largely because *Tzu Hang* had experienced light airs most of the way, while *Trekka*, sailing earlier, had had, at least for part of her passage, a good easterly wind to send her along.

It was while the two yachts were lying alongside one another in Hawaii that their owners decided on continuing their cruise in company.

John Guzzwell's voyage resembled that of Harry Pidgeon. Both sailed in vessels built by themselves, and both made a preliminary cruise to Hawaii. While at Hawaii, Guzwell and the Smeetons got to know each other well. Guzzwell made a new mast for *Tzu Hang* when some rot was discovered in the old one. They decided to continue cruising to the Southern Pacific in company.

It was later in *Tzu Hang* that Guzzwell had the distinctly uncongenial experience of turning turtle, which I mentioned in Chapter 2, and I will not elaborate further upon that. Interesting, indeed fascinating though it is, its account occupies a relatively small part of Guzzwell's book. Moreover, it is not just for disasters and mishaps that we read these books, but for the pleasure in sailing with the author in fair weather and foul, seeing and experiencing, with his eyes and thoughts. Nevertheless I would in passing recommend Smeeton's own book, "Once is Enough", in which the disaster is described in full.

Guzzwell started his world voyage, leaving San Francisco on the 26th of September 1955, arriving in the Hawaiian Islands on November the 3rd. His course southwards from there to New Zealand took him via Fanning Island, a small coral island, about 1,100 miles south of Honolulu, and Samoa, where, like so many before him, he walked to the top of the Mount overlooking Apia to pay homage to Robert Louis Stevenson, whose grave is there. His courses on his world voyage may be clearly seen from the chart.

All this time he was taking the same route as the Smeetons, although not, by any means, sailing in company with *Tzu Hang*.

On leaving Samoa he continued on a south-westerly course to Vavau, the northern group of the Tongan Islands, meeting unsettled squally weather *en route*, alternating with patches of calm and necessitating much sail-changing. In the calms he was also able to do some sail-repairing. *Trekka* had made the passage from Samoa a day quicker than *Tzu Hang*, but Smeeton said: "We weren't trying very hard!"

Guzzwell arrived in Russell, New Zealand, on the 30th of May 1956, and was not to leave until the 21st April 1958. His cruise in *Tzu Hang* from Australia to South America lasted from the 26th December 1956 to the 21st March 1957. (The accident occurred on the 14th February.)

After the *Tzu Hang* episode, he left the Smeetons at Chile, having helped them with the biggest repair jobs, and flew to South Africa to visit his mother in Natal. Here he found her in the process of returning to the Channel Islands, having sold her house. There was consequently a good deal of work once more for Guzzwell, arranging the sale of his mother's furniture and grappling with paper work. He accompanied her to Jersey, and was able to help her to settle down with old friends still living on the island, and finally took ship in London bound for Sydney (as he could not get a ship for New Zealand.)

On arrival in New Zealand he caught another ship immediately, bound for Auckland, and three days later stepped ashore. He had thus not only been away from his little ship for sixteen months, but had packed a deal of experiences and travel into those months.

There was no question about what he wanted, though, and that was first to see his boat, secondly to fit her out, and finally to get back to sea in her. On arrival at Russell, where *Trekka* was hauled out, he met two friends, Francis and Mille Arlidge, who, as he puts it, ". . . really made me feel that I had come home. . . .

" 'Go on, John,' said Mille. 'I know you won't be satisfied until you've seen *Trekka* again.'

"And they both laughed when they realised how true to the mark they were. I walked across the garden to the big shed and opened the door quietly. I am not ashamed to admit that my eyes were wet as I viewed the sweet little hull sitting in her cradle where she had waited patiently for my return."

Guzzwell had decided that *Trekka*'s fitting out was to include the fibre-glassing of her hull; that is to say, giving her a sheath of fibreglass-reinforced plastic. His description of this characteristically makes light of a skilful job, as also does it of other tricky pieces of shipwright's work.

One of the things that strike one particularly about John Guzzwell is his capacity for making friends everywhere he goes. The book is full of encounters, and re-encounters, and it somehow manages to convey an impression of youthful exuberance and enthusiasm coupled with a genuine liking of his fellow men. It is the likeability of the author that makes this book so refreshing in an age of suspicion, sick humour and "one-upmanship". There is no "Damn you, Jack— I'm all right!" about John Guzzwell.

Having crossed the Tasman Sea and reached Australia, Guzzwell's route for the remainder of his circumnavigation took him up through the Barrier Reef and so through Torres Strait and the Arafura Sea to the Cocos Islands, Rodriguez, Mauritius and so to South Africa. While only half-way through the Barrier Reef he became concerned at the way time was "slipping by". He wanted to get to South Africa, then the vast distance of over 7,000 miles away, by Christmas, and avoid the cyclones in the Indian Ocean. (The compiler of this book has been in an Indian Ocean cyclone and I fully sympathize with Guzzwell's concern!) He had met in Middle Island an Englishman called Norman

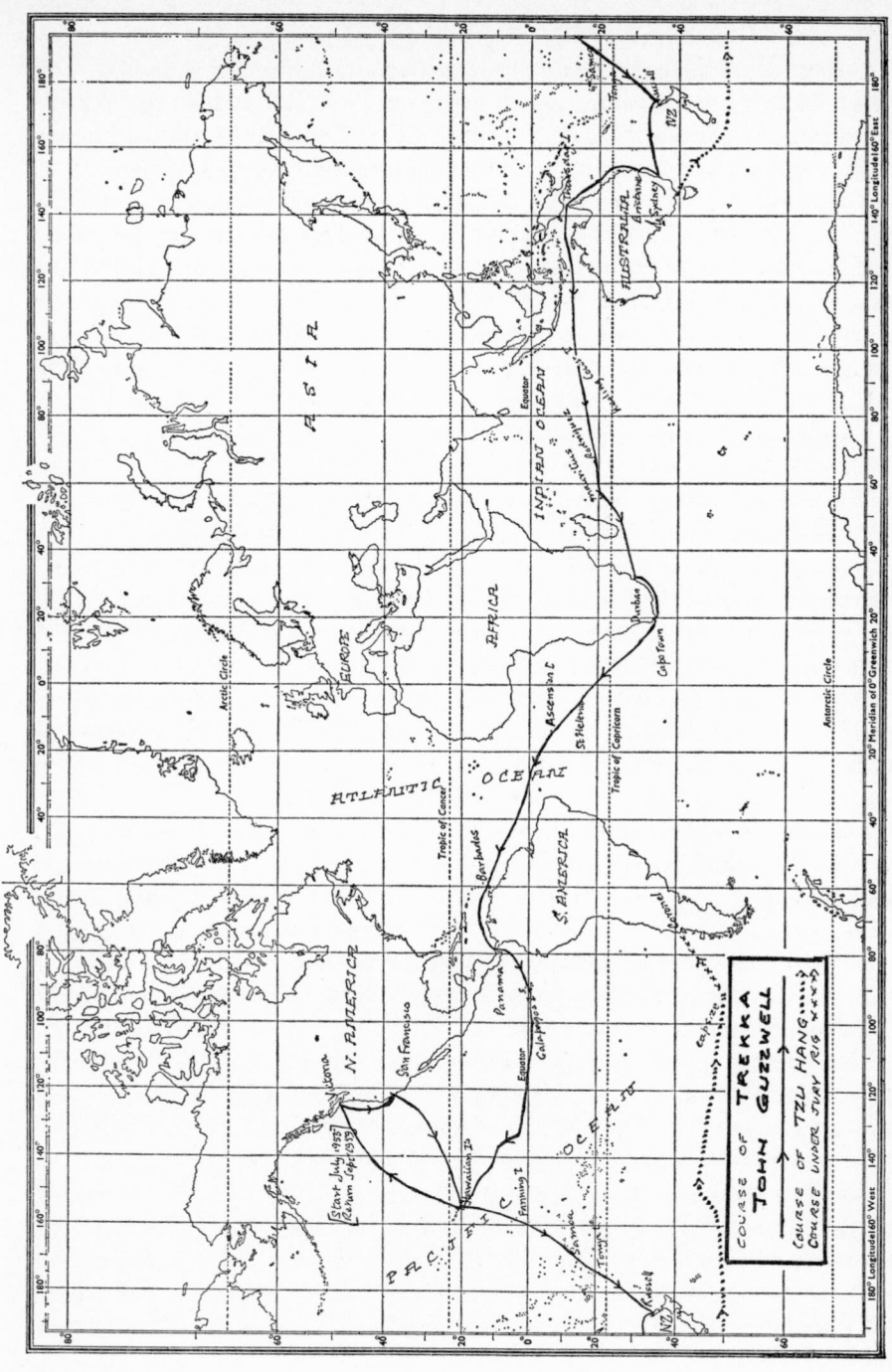

COURSE OF *TREKKA*

JOHN GUZZWELL

COURSE OF *TZU HANG* ·····>

COURSE UNDER JURY RIG ×××>

Young sailing a Falmouth quay punt called *Diana* with three other friends. They were bound for South Africa and the two boats sailed in company up through the Barrier Reef. He arrived at Thursday Island in the Torres Strait on the 4th September 1958, so that he spent the autumn and early winter months crossing the Indian Ocean, arriving at Durban on the 2nd December. It is interesting that he calls the Indian Ocean "kindly" in a chapter heading, when so many have called it (if only to themselves) by very different names. He was given a wonderful time in Durban, where he spent Christmas, all of which added to the fun. While in Durban he met a young South African who had not long returned from Canada. He told Guzzwell about a young man he had met while in Canada who was building a small boat. He, it turned out, was the young man! They had both forgotten each other.

As with many another yachtsman, Guzzwell had to listen to grim tales of the horrors of rounding the Cape of Storms. He writes as follows:

"There were many other tales of woe that set me thinking about the Cape. Was it always bad? Or were most of these other hectic voyages made at the wrong time of the year? On checking, I found that the more hectic passages had nearly always been made at the wrong time of the year or the boat had not been in the best condition. Even so, the crews of the other four visiting yachts that were due to sail for Cape Town eyed each other wondering who would be the first to stick their necks out. We all discussed the 900-mile passage and argued whether it was better to stay close in to the shore or well off. The Agulhas Current was the main bogey. This mass of water flows down the African coast towards the Cape at a rate of about fifty miles a day but it frequently attains double that speed. A gale from the south-west against the current kicks up a vicious short sea, and I think it is this that has caused most trouble to small craft."

He left on the 15th January 1959 under conditions that promised well. A light easterly breeze combined with the current soon took him 100 miles down the coast. He was about 30 miles offshore. Suddenly, during the night, the whole picture changed. The wind switched to south-west, and began to freshen rapidly. A steep sea soon got up, the wind being against a strong current, as was attested by the fact that although Guzzwell had had to heave-to for a few hours he made good over fifty miles to windward under the current alone!

He reached Cape Town without mishap, the biggest surprise coming when only a few miles from the harbour, and he had to sail in under his headsails. He tells the story as follows:

"I could see that Table Mountain was also wearing its 'tablecloth'. This is the sign that the south-easter is blowing, but here, in the lee off Seapoint, we were

TREKKA

Length overall: 20 feet 6 inches
Length water-line: 18 feet 6 inches
Beam: 6 feet 6 inches. Draught: 4 feet 6 inches
Designed by: J. Laurent Giles
of Lymington, and built by
her owner

just moving along very quietly. Darkness fell, and we drifted past the Green Point light towards the light on the end of Cape Town's long harbour break-water.

"The view of Cape Town at night from the sea is superb, lights from houses, street lamps and traffic climb high up the slopes of Table Mountain; and this scene seemed all the more unforgettable because I was so elated at having safely rounded the 'Cape of Storms'. Suddenly, a terrific blast of air hit us and *Trekka* staggered from the blow. I thought it must be just a willywaw from the mountains, but I soon realised that it was continuous. With *Trekka* heeled far over I crawled along the deck and got the mainsail down, then I went on beating with the staysail and mizzen towards the harbour entrance, now less than a mile away."

He took on stores and water while in Cape Town and comments that when he put to sea again *Trekka*'s motion felt very different because she was so low in the water owing to the extra weight on board. He left Cape Town on the 14th of February 1959, exactly two years after *Tzu Hang*'s capsize.

Just before midday on the 2nd of March the steep cliffs of St Helena appeared, about 30 miles distant. Guzzwell comments on the dismal aspect of the place saying: ". . . I can quite understand how the Emperor Napoleon Bonaparte felt when he first saw those cliffs." The relatively short passage to Ascension Island, on the north-westerly course for Barbados, took but a week. Of Ascension, Guzzwell comments that it was amusing to find everyone talking of "Snark guided missiles and rocket motors", while at St Helena talk had been about "Napoleon and the old days".

Now he was in the trade winds, and leaving Ascension on the 15th March at once picked up a fine, steady breeze to start him off at least on the long 3,000-mile passage. He crossed the Equator on the 30th of March, where he was becalmed and took the chance of observing the teeming fish life all round him, even going to the rescue of some of the smaller fish (who were being menaced by a shark) with a pole.

As he got farther west the radio stations of the West Indies and British Guiana grew stronger. On April the 20th at night he sighted the light on the most easterly point of Barbados, Ragged Point. He had taken just under thirty-seven days for the passage.

An amusing comment on how little regard can be paid to a yacht which has just made a formidable passage for her size is made here as Guzzwell recounts how the only thing the port officials were remotely interested in was that he had not remembered to hoist his yellow quarantine flag!

He stayed a week in Barbados and then sailed for Panama, arriving at

Cristobal just after daylight on the 12th of May, after a passage lasting fourteen days, and managed to navigate the Panama Canal without fuss. He secured against a banana boat, using car tyres as fenders. *Trekka*, although bounced about a good deal, bounced only against the fenders, and no damage was done.

Knowing the passage from the Panama Canal to be a very difficult one, because of contrary currents and headwinds, Guzzwell wisely decided to stand well out into the Pacific. In fact, he went one better; he sailed back to Hawaii, and completed his solo circumnavigation of the world in the smallest vessel to date. This passage was a very long one indeed, being some 5,400 miles. Guzzwell left Balboa on the afternoon of the 21st of May. She arrived sixty-two days later, having had to weather a severe gale which caused Guzzwell to lower all sail and wait for the wind to moderate. This long passage alone, in that small ship, would be a remarkable achievement. There is something so natural and unselfconscious about this book that one is inclined to forget what a very great voyage it was. Let me leave the last words, describing his homecoming to the Hawaiian Islands, to Guzzwell:

"On 20 July I had been at sea for sixty days and was looking out for the top of Mauna Kea, the 13,825-foot mountain on the island of Hawaii. We were still 60 miles off but had the horizon been clear I would have been able to see it, as I sighted it 85 miles away on the run down from San Francisco nearly four years before.

"A plane passed overhead going towards America, and a couple of hours later I saw a small tanker also bound for the States. She passed about a mile away.

"The night was a very special occasion, and I had my last can of Australian Christmas pudding to celebrate it, for *Trekka* had just crossed her outward track, and had completed her voyage round the world, the smallest vessel ever to do so. I felt very proud that she was mine.

"The next morning when I tumbled out of the hatch, there were Hawaii and Mauii peering out of the morning haze. *Trekka* closed the shore, and we romped along the northern coast of Mauii while I feasted my eyes on the lovely green slopes that swept down to meet the edge of the sea. Past Kahului, we went, where I had made *Tzu Hang*'s mainmast, and where her southern voyage had been planned, then on towards Molokai, lit by the last of a lovely sunset.

"I stayed at the helm that night, running along the coast of Molokai with a bright tropical moon to light the way. It was wonderful to be back in familiar waters again.

"With the first light of dawn, we were entering Molokai channel with about 50 miles left to Honolulu. The spinnaker was pulling steadily, and a couple of hours later the mountains on Oahu became clearer. The lighthouse on Makapuu Point came into view, and early that afternoon we passed it and sailed into more sheltered water.

"Towards late afternoon we rounded Diamond Head and came up to the entrance to the Ala Wai Yacht Basin. I tacked up the channel with just enough wind to fill the sails, and then moored against the gas dock, where I waited for the authorities to clear me. It had been a very long passage."

14

FRANCIS CHICHESTER

Not Only Single-handed but Racing as Well

All the yachtsman/authors in this book are individualists and Francis Chichester is no exception. He is a difficult person to write about, though, because he has become something of a legend; and it is very difficult to write about a legend who is still living. Moreover, the fact that he was diagnosed as having cancer, and having not only conquered that, but subsequently raced single-handed across the Atlantic Ocean, fills one with such respect for his guts and determination never to give in that one loses all objectivity about his achievements and tends to become overwhelmed by admiration for the man.

And as if all this were not enough, there is something else you find out about him after a very short time. He is modest. In his book he gives great credit to his wife, and rightly so. But one closes the last page of this book feeling that one has been in the presence of a big man, and that is a fine feeling for anyone.

For this alone I would recommend his book, called "The Lonely Sea and the Sky" and published by Hodder and Stoughton. For the tired, the downcast, the jaded or the ill, it is a tonic; more, it is hope.

This book is all about Chichester's adventurous life, particularly his exploits as a pioneer in aviation. It tells of how he went to New Zealand in 1919, took part in fortune-hunting; of how he learned to fly; of his famous flight of $180\frac{1}{2}$ hours from London to Sydney, a distance of 12,650 miles: of his solo east-west crossing of the Tasman Sea—the first time it had ever been done; of how his plane was wrecked, of his flight to China (here there is a fascinating chapter appropriately called "Triumph and Disaster"); of how he flew 21,000 miles with Frank Herrick in a Puss Moth from Sydney via China, back to England and of how eventually he became a map publisher—by accident! Having, I hope, said enough to convince the reader of the scope of this book and of its quality, I will now turn to what concerns us here in this book, namely, Chichester's Atlantic crossings, and his descriptions of them.

Chapter 24 in Chichester's book is entitled "Back to Sea", and in it he describes how he "signed on" as crew for a friend to the Baltic. He had, he writes "the keenest anticipation of cruising over the waters made famous by Erskine Childers's 'Riddle of the Sands', which I had re-read time after time. . . ."

Although they never reached the famous "sands", and the cruise was certainly "not a success", it did lead to Chichester becoming interested in ocean racing. He decided that "sailing would be a misery for me if I was going to worry about the weather all the time, about getting caught out in a gale and being fearful of my gear in a blow". He decided to race with the Royal Ocean Racing Club because they raced no matter what the weather was doing.

But although he tried to get taken on as a navigator, he was out of luck, and in the end was forced to buy a boat of his own. He describes how after much searching he acquired a boat ". . . with the horrible name of *Florence Edith*." There is a delightful account of an early sail which I quote here. Chichester had just bought *Florence Edith*.

"Then I had to break the news to Sheila, expecting a terrific rocket for my extravagance. Imagine my astonishment when she said 'Oh, I always wanted to sail. What an excellent idea!' I had no time to spend on navigating, charged sandbank after sandbank on the east coast, and when Sheila came up to have her first sail from Brightlingsea no one had seen or heard of the *Florence Edith*. At last an old fisherman said to her, 'Oh, you mean that there yellow boat? She be lying on Buxey Sands, and it's lucky 'tis fine weather, otherwise she'd be sunk where t'sea rises. What's more, there be thick fog coming up, and if she do get off the sands, it'll be a long time before you see her in Brightlingsea.' My wife was urged by the friend she was staying with to go home and get a divorce, but she decided to defer that, and left a message in case I should turn up. The fog did come up, as the fisherman forecast, but I had an amusing bit of navigation feeling the way along the channel into Brightlingsea by means of a hand lead. Sheila had her sail next morning, and enjoyed it. She joined in enthusiastically in redesigning the interior of the yacht. We rebuilt the cabin, making berths for six, which cost as much as the boat."

Chichester persevered and was soon an accomplished ocean-racing man. The rebuilt boat had been named *Gypsy Moth II* (the first Gypsy Moth was the aircraft), and in her Chichester raced hard and often. He also crewed aboard the crack American yacht *Figaro* in 1957, for a series of races presented by the Admiral of the Royal Ocean Racing Club for international competition by teams of three yachts. Inevitably the time came when he wanted a new boat, and the job of designing *Gypsy Moth III* went to Robert Clark, a well-known British designer, and of building her to Jack Tyrrell of Arklow, in Ireland.

But by now Chichester began to have worries. His map business was struggling, and, more sinister, he had become afflicted by pleurisy and related lung illnesses. Eventually X-rays revealed the fact that he had cancer of the lung. He was told his only hope was immediately to have one lung removed but his wife was set against this course, believing him to be too weak to stand such an operation. He took a second opinion, a third, a fourth and a fifth. The diagnosis was always the same, and the remedy the same also. He writes: "On leaving my house, I called in at the Royal Ocean Racing Club to have a farewell drink. Talking to some of my friends at the bar there I felt intensely lonely. The thought of being cut off from my friends, added, I suppose, to fear and dread, turned my bones to water and already I seemed isolated in unbridgeable space. I did not say where I was going; no one wants a spectre at a feast."

But then his wife took further action. She interviewed the head surgeon, and by sheer dogged determination persuaded him to examine her husband once more. Back came the electrifying report. The cancer was not active, and there was hope! Chichester did not need the operation. He was given a course of anti-biotics, but this caused him great distress and he suffered fearfully from fits of coughing. Again his wife intervened and persuaded him to go to Enton Hall for a "rest cure". There follows in his book a moving piece of writing when he describes the series of crises through which he passed, but all the time, desperately ill as he was, his lung cancer had not increased and was still inactive.

Gradually (but how gradually!) he began to think he was going to get better. He went for a holiday to the South of France, and then, wonder of wonders, he started ocean racing again. People criticized his wife for allowing him to sail in this way, but she was convinced that in such treatment lay the hope of his cure. And then one day, in the Royal Ocean Racing Club (which he thought he would never see again), he saw on the notice board Colonel Haslar's notice about a Solo Transatlantic Race. Chichester entered for it and he writes: ". . . I regard it as miraculous that within thirty-two months of being first taken ill . . . I was able to cross the starting line for the toughest yacht race that has ever taken place, and able to finish it in forty and a half days." This is true indeed, but at the beginning of his book is a charming and moving dedication to his wife Sheila, who made that miracle possible.

We now come to Part Five of the book, which deals with the solo race across the Atlantic. The proposed race would be no picnic! Only once before had there been a yacht race from east to west—the time the two great schooners, *Cambria* and *Dauntless*, sailed their great race in 1870. To sail this course means battling to windward against the prevailing westerly winds, and against the current of the Gulf Stream, as a reference to the relevant charts will show. At first people were shy of Haslar's proposal, thinking it unnecessarily risky and not in the best interests of racing, but finally the newspaper "The Observer" agreed to offer £250 each to any starter as option money for the winner's account of the race, for which a further sum of £750 would be forthcoming. It is interesting to note that

GIPSY MOTH III

Length overall: 39 feet 7 inches
Length water-line: 28 feet
Beam: 10 feet 1¾ inches; Draught: 6 feet 5 inches
Designed by Robert Clark
Built by Tyrell of Arklow, Ireland 1958/9

Chichester says: "Several good clubs were asked to start this race, but all turned it down." He mentions no names, but one wonders what on earth the objection could have been. However, the Royal Western Yacht Club of England came to the rescue and there could not have been a better choice. Plymouth was the obvious place both by tradition as well as convenience from which to sail for America! There were five entrants for the race. Haslar himself in a Folk-boat (but a Folk-boat rigged as a junk!) called *Jester*, another Folk-boat sailed by Val Howells called *Eira*, Jean Lacombe in a small French yacht called *Cap Horn*, David Lewis in a Vertue Class yacht called *Cardinal Vertue*, and Francis Chichester in *Gypsy Moth III*. Let us now take a look at *Gypsy Moth III*.

She was a good deal bigger than her predecessor, being some 39 feet 7 inches in overall length. Her draught was 6 feet 5 inches, and her Thames tonnage 13. Now, this is a fairly comfortable size of boat in which to go ocean racing, but not single-handed! Her mainsail had an area of 380 square feet, and when one remembers that Chichester was still far from well and was relatively weak, one marvels at his determination.

At the end of his book he gives a list of the number of sail changes he made in that first Solo Atlantic Race of 1960 and from it one can see that he set his full mainsail twenty-three times, and reefed mainsail six times, double-reefed mainsail four times and mainsail with three reefs in six times. He set his try-sail (the small heavier sail to replace the mainsail in very strong winds) no less than seven times. Now, these are merely changes of the mainsail. His No. 1 Genoa jib, for example, was set seventeen times—but this will be enough to show how active he was in continually getting the utmost speed possible out of his boat. He did not just sail the Atlantic; he really raced there, and the proof of that is that he won!

Now, there is one respect in which *Gypsy Moth III* differs from the other vessels in this book. Of late there has been a marked advance in the development of Vane self-steering gear for yachts, and Chichester was to use such a device on his race. This is Chichester's description of how he came to install it.

"I was hampered in my trials by having no self-steering gear until 5th May, only five weeks before the start of the race. It was clear that no yacht without a self-steering gear could have a chance against yachts equipped with them. One of the rules of the race was that no yacht could use an automatic pilot—or any other gear—driven by electricity or any other form of power. We were allowed only wind-powered or hand-operated gear.

"Every Sunday morning I took a bus to Kensington Gardens where I watched the model yachts being sailed across the Round Pond. I reckoned that if a model yacht can be sailed across the Round Pond without a helmsman, then my yacht could be sailed across the Atlantic in the same way. I bought an excellent book on model yacht sailing, and incidentally learned a lot about ocean racing from it though I dare say the author would be surprised to hear it. My new design was in principle a wind vane, which would always weathercock into wind. In fact it was a mast which could rotate in a socket at the stern of the yacht, with a flat sail instead of a metal vane. As soon as the yacht was sailing to my satisfaction I would lock the vane to the tiller. If the yacht came up into wind, the vane would be moved round with the yacht, and the wind would press on the side of it. This would pull on the tiller until the yacht had been steered back on to its original heading, when the vane would be weathercocked again, and do no work as long as the yacht kept on its original heading. The model yacht book told me that the area of the vane must be four and a half times that of the rudder, and so I designed my vane sail to be 45 square feet. The chief problem in design was to make all the parts, the stays, and the spars, strong enough to stand up to a gale, or even a storm without being so heavy that it would require too much wind to weathercock the vane. I cannot describe how ugly it looked on the beautiful *Gypsy Moth*.

"It was not till 7 May that the yard finished and installed the vane. I crossed the bar at the entrance to the Beaulieu River, headed the yacht across the Solent and locked the vane to the tiller. *Gypsy Moth* started tearing through the water, sailing herself entirely. Her wake was almost dead straight; it was fascinating to watch. That was one of the most thrilling moments of my life. Gradually I found out that 'Miranda', as I christened the self-steering device, required just as much skill to get the best out of her as does setting the sails of a yacht in a keen race. Also it gave me the same pleasure to succeed."

Eventually the day of the race dawned. Chichester and his wife had sailed *Gypsy Moth III* down to Plymouth on the 5th of June. There they had four days of Press and television interviews; of what Chichester calls "rushing about" and which he found "great sport". Less attractive was the day of the start:

"Dawn came cold, blustery and wet, and my spirits sank to their lowest ebb. Sheila and I went down early to move *Gypsy Moth* out of the tidal dock at high water. We tied up in a little basin outside, and I tried to eat something on board, but could not. My three rivals looked fairly bleak too. They were Blondie in his junk-rigged *Jester*, David Lewis in *Cardinal Vertue* and Val Howells in *Eira*.

"Several owners who had intended to start in the race did not come up to scratch; one American in a handsome yacht was prevented by his young wife; another American, Piver, on his way over from America in his trimaran with a full crew, had not yet arrived, and when he did he found he lacked enough time to chase after us and take part in the race. I met one of his crew in New York

The calm off Staten Island, New York, seems almost unbelievable to Chichester after the rigours of his forty-day crossing on the first single-handed Atlantic race in 1960

afterwards who told me that nothing would have induced him to try sailing it across alone. Piver had done well to sail it with a crew from west to east. Humphrey Barton had intended to start in his 12-ton *Rose of York* but withdrew because he could not make her sail herself. He had made a forty-seven day crossing in *Vertue* with O'Riordan as crew.

"In the tensed-up jockeying for position at the start I cursed one of my friends out alone in a yacht who baulked me. It was enough to keep clear of rivals, without having to dodge yachts, launches and a big trawler full of sightseers.

"The starting gun was fired. We were off! What a race! Instructions read 'Leave the Melampus Buoy to starboard and thence by any route to the Ambrose Light Vessel, New York.' The others got away ahead of me, but I began to catch them up as soon as I had set my big genoa. Then I slowed down as I pinched into the wind, to squeeze past the breakwater without tacking. As I drew away from the land the wind freshened and the seas got rougher, and I was soon wet through with sea water and sweat reefing the mainsail. The difficulty was to get the sail to roll easily on the boom without someone at the aft end to haul out the creases and folds. The last I saw of David Lewis, he had tacked inshore after the breakwater. He was well to windward of me, and not far behind. That must have been just before his mast broke in two; he rigged a jury sail and sailed back to Plymouth, where the Mashford brothers repaired his mast for him and got him away to sea again three days later. He is the only man I have heard of who has finished third in a race after breaking his mast at the start.

"For the first three days the weather was rough with gales. Heavy seas burst on the deck, and I reckoned that it took thirty seconds after a sea had broken on deck before the water finished running out of the lee scuppers. I had considered *Gypsy Moth* a dry boat apart from one or two minor leaks, and I had pumped no water out of her during the three months she had been afloat. After the first three days, however, all the cabin walls were streaked as if they had been in a slanting shower of rain, and everything was damp or wet. I can only imagine that the tremendous weight of seas bursting on deck opened the planking or seams for an instant to shoot spray through. The terrific crash of a sea several times started me out of my berth, thinking that the yacht had been struck by a steamer, or that the mast had snapped. While I was asleep one sea shot me into the air off the heavy wooden settee I was sleeping on and jumped it out of its fitting. The clothes I got wet stayed wet, and I did not get a chance to dry them out until thirty-seven days later. At the end of the first three days I had had nothing to eat except a few biscuits; I had been feeling seasick or queasy all the time. Reading through my log gives me an impatient longing to sail the race again. I see the mistakes I could have avoided, and how I could have made a faster pace. This is nonsense really, for the mistakes and errors are the price for the great romance of doing something for the first time.

"Miranda's antics cost me a lot of time. The lever which locked the wind vane to the tiller was periodically knocked free by the backstay, and I would be rousted out of my bunk to find the yacht headed the wrong way. I had a nightmare fear of the yacht's gybing herself to bring the wind vane against the backstay and snap its spars. Immediately I sensed the yacht's going off course—and I soon became sensitive to the least change in sailing conditions—I rushed out to the stern whatever I was doing, or however I was dressed."

Chichester got more and more skilful in handling his boat, and especially in trimming his sails to get the best out of her. He records how he awoke one morning to find the yacht had sailed herself 86 miles. This was in $12\frac{1}{4}$ hours, which meant she had averaged 7 knots, and all to windward. "That", he writes, "was what I had come for!"

At the end of two weeks Chichester had made good a distance of 1,264 miles from Plymouth, and Haslar had made good 1,038 miles. Howells, in his Folkboat, was the rival most feared by Chichester, but in fact he had only made good 900 miles after fourteen days. Lewis had had the bad luck to break a mast, but he had rigged a jury sail and put back to Plymouth, where he got his mast repaired by the brothers Mashford in time to get back in the race. So successfully did he achieve this that after fourteen days he was only 500 miles astern of *Gypsy Moth III*. Even allowing for the fact that his delay caused by the breaking mast meant that he missed the period of bad head-on weather at the start of the race, his achievement was notable. A formidable rival!

However, as most people know (for the race had wide publicity) Chichester won and won easily, beating Haslar, his nearest rival, by eight days. The rest of his book describes how he sailed back to England accompanied by his wife, and how, in 1962, he sailed *Gypsy Moth III* (with her altered sail plan and modified arrangements for the handling of gear) across the Atlantic for the second time. This was a solo effort and he managed to clip about seven days off his first time, but, great achievement that this was, it was not good enough to beat the target he had set himself of thirty days. Nevertheless, Chichester had had a wonderful sail across, had beaten his earlier record, and his illness was still not only at bay, but, it would appear, defeated. He had much to congratulate himself upon, and his cup must have been full indeed when he received two telegrams of congratulation, one from the late President Kennedy and one from Prince Philip.

It is not my purpose here to chronicle either of these crossings, but rather to give an idea of the scope of Chichester's great book, of his achievements as a sailorman, and of his style of writing. I will close this chapter with a wonderful section taken from his account of a storm in the Atlantic on the first race. There was a second Transatlantic race in 1964 but it is not included in Chichester's book. We join him sailing under twin headsails before the wind. He was below decks getting some rest when he noticed that the tell-tale compass attached to the cabin table was showing that the boat was sailing a very erratic course.

As soon as he was up on deck he realized not only that the wind had reached already about 60 m.p.h. but that it was still freshening and that he was ". . . in for big trouble.

"I realised that I had a serious storm on my hands. I spent five and a quarter hours on deck without a break, working hard. After lashing down the spinnaker poles, I next started on Miranda who was already breaking up. The topping lift had parted letting the spanker drop, and the halyard of the little topsail had gone. I could easily have got into a flap; it was now blowing great guns, and I had to stand on the stern pulpit while I worked with my hands at full stretch above my head at the wet ropes jammed tight. Miranda's mast was 14 feet high, and free to rotate with the wind. I was standing with stays and wires all round me, and could have been swept off the pulpit horribly easily if the wind had suddenly changed direction. I told myself that it would be much worse if I had iced-up ropes to deal with; not to fuss; and to get on with the job. There seemed fifty jobs to do, but I did them all in time. I lowered the mainsail boom to the deck, and treble-lashed it there. It was only after I had finished that I became aware of the appalling uproar, with a high-pitched shriek or scream dominating. I managed to strip off both Miranda's sails, and secure her boom with sail ties. I reckoned that the wind was now 80 m.p.h. (I still think of winds above 60 m.p.h. in terms of miles per hour instead of knots, because of getting used to the speeds of my seaplane propeller slip-stream in m.p.h.)

"The seas had been moderate when the storm broke, and by the time I got below at 4 o'clock in the afternoon I was still able to cook myself a breakfast, a fry-up of potatoes, onions and three eggs. I reckoned that the wind was now 90 m.p.h. I went to sleep reading Shakespeare's 'Tempest'. At 8.30 in the evening I woke to find the sea getting up, and the ship taking an awful pounding. Some seas, like bombs exploding, made the ship jump and shake; she was lying beam-on to the blast, which was from the north-north-east, and was moving pretty fast, about 3 knots. I knew that I must try to slow her down, so I dressed in my wet oilskins. First, I tried to head her into wind, but no matter where I set the tiller she refused to lie other than broadside to the wind. I had a big outer motor tyre for a sea anchor, and I shackled this on to the anchor chain, paying

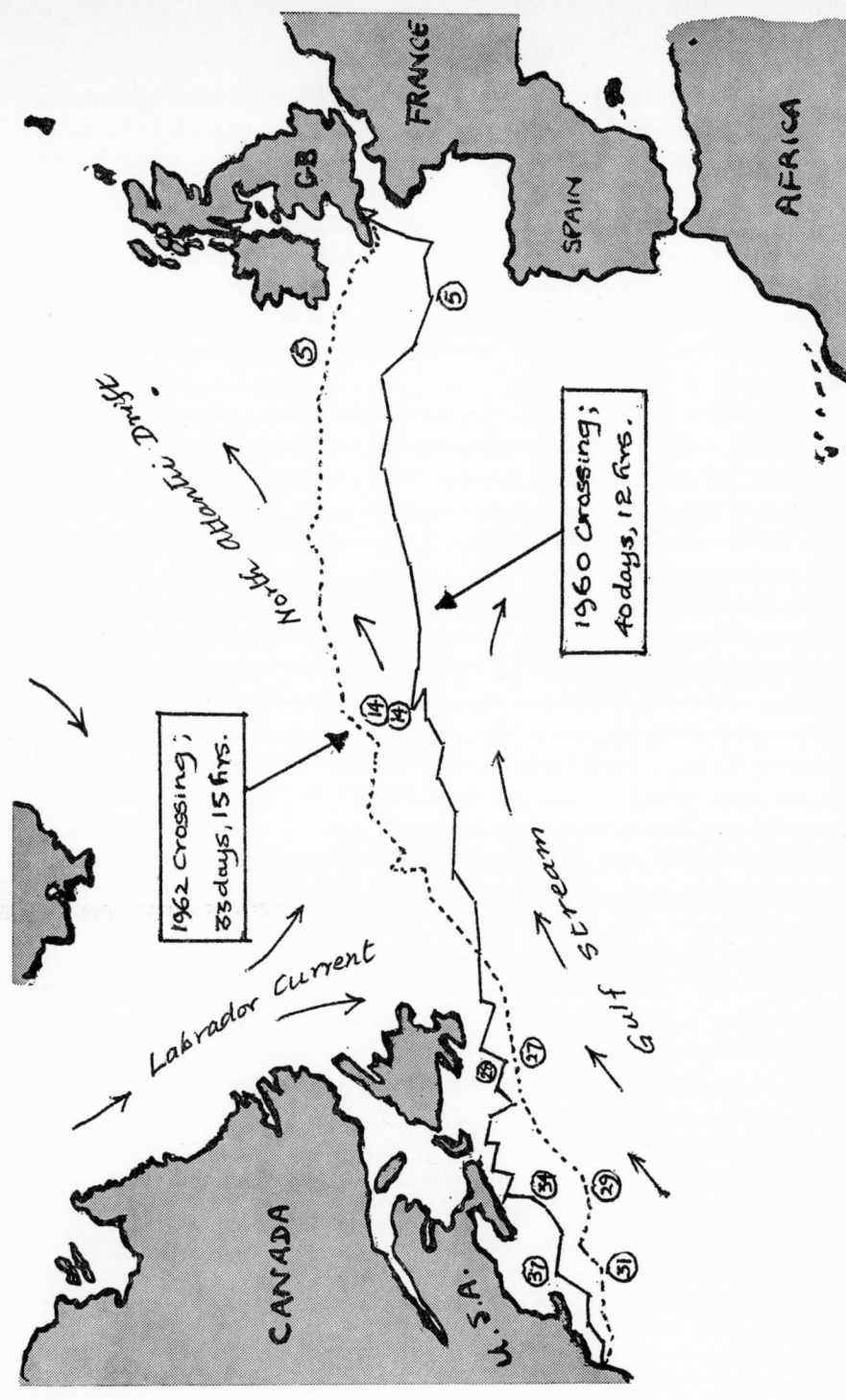

Courses, for comparison, of Chichester's two Atlantic crossings

out 10 fathoms of $\frac{5}{16}$-inch chain over the stern; I also paid out 20 fathoms of $2\frac{1}{2}$-inch warp over the stern. It did not seem to make the least difference to the speed.

"I put the wind speed now at 100 m.p.h. The noise was terrifying, and it seemed impossible that any small ship could survive. I told myself not to be weak—what was a 90- or 100-mile wind to a man on Everest? I filled a punctured tin with oil, and hung it over the side amidships in a piece of canvas, but it had no effect at all—the oil was too thick, and we were moving too fast. In any case, it was soon carried away.

"As night came on I tried to sleep, but waiting in the dark for the next crash made me tense, and I kept on bracing myself against being thrown out of the bunk. I was afraid; there was nothing I could do, and I think that the noise, the incredible din, was the chief cause of fear. The high-pitched shriek from the rigging was terrifying and uncanny. Two hours before midnight I came to think that we were headed into the eye of the storm. I dressed reluctantly, feeling dry in the mouth whenever I started to do anything, but better as soon as I began to do it. With difficulty, I climbed out into the cockpit. It took strength to hold the rudder full on, but slowly the ship gybed round. She seemed easier on the east-south-east tack.

"When I went below again I could not help laughing; all the same books, clothes, cushions and papers were back on the floor. I dozed, but could not sleep. I lay tense and rigid, waiting for the next sea to hit. Nothing mattered to me now except survival."

But survive he did, and having read as far as this, one realizes that one never would expect him to do anything else. The man is invincible.

15

BILL ROBINSON

Circumnavigator with an Enquiring Mind

"Svaap" means "Dream" in Sanskrit. It was the name of a yacht, ketch rigged, measuring 27 feet 6 inches on the waterline. She could not have been better named, for in her a young American named William Robinson made his dream cruise round the world. He was 25 years of age. His voyage of 32,000 miles took him three years and five and a half months and cost him £1,000. Afterwards he published a book about it all, called "Deep Water and Shoal", which first appeared in 1932, and which can now be obtained in an edition published by Rupert Hart-Davis Ltd.

His book became deservedly a good seller. But even had it not done so, and had he not made any money out of his adventure, Robinson would have still had the greatest bargain it is possible to conceive. For on his three-year voyage he saw far more of this world and had more and varied experiences than most of us know in a lifetime. He had adventures galore. On one occasion he dined with cannibals off human flesh, on another he was held to ransom by an Arab sheikh. He went in fear of water spouts and was chased by dragon lizards. He knew the exhilarating sailing in the trade winds and the violence of a hurricane in Nukualofa in the South Pacific islands, and he saw submarine volcanoes in action. This seems pretty cheap at the price of £300 a year!

But to our immeasurable gain he could, and wanted to, write and let us live again with him the really astounding adventures in this book and sail with him in that small yacht when he started from New York on the evening of June the 23rd, 1928.

Robinson had several friends aboard with him to start with, but they had to leave to return to college after *Svaap* had reached Bermuda. Here he found a Bermudan boy, Willoughby Wright, who agreed to ship as crew, and who sailed with him as far as Tahiti. From Bermuda *Svaap* sailed south-west, passing between the islands of Cuba and Haiti in the West Indies, and reached Cristobel at the eastern entrance to the Panama Canal by the afternoon of August 12th.

Robinson admits that his passage to Bermuda was a trial both of his own ability as a navigator and of the suitability of his ship for long-distance cruising. Both were severely tested.

Four hundred miles off Cape Hatteras they ran into a storm which was to

equal in ferocity most bad weather he subsequently met on the voyage. *Svaap*
and her crew came through with confidence increased. For a week they rode to
a sea anchor and Robinson admits that at first he ". . . hardly believed that
Svaap could . . . conquer those thundering avalanches that menaced her". But
she did, and on July 5th they made ". . . a perfect landfall on St David's Head.
Bermuda". Anyone who has sailed in the Bermudan Ocean Race knows that this
little island can be very elusive to the navigator, and to make so good a landfall
after such a storm proves that there was nothing wrong with Robinson's navigation.

In the prologue to his book Robinson writes that he hoped to make enough
money out of writing to continue his world cruise after his savings had run out.
He hoped, he writes ". . . to study, write, explore, do a bit of research, but
always enjoy the never-ending adventure with just enough uncertainty to flavour
it". How reminiscent of all youthful escapist dreams that sounds! I particularly
like ". . . do a bit of research". In these days of ultra-specialization this has a
pleasing ring of vagueness. But he wasn't, in actuality, in the least vague, this
American boy. He had this dream of a world cruise, and telling no one, not even
his parents about it, he set about making it all come true. His book is the
epitome of all young adventure stories of this kind.

His description of passing through the locks at Panama gives a vivid picture
of the way yachts were handled there at that time. Only two lines, a head rope
and a stern rope, were used, and neither Robinson nor his crew knew what to
expect.

"Suddenly *Svaap* shuddered and trembled, and we felt rather than heard the
disturbance of a tremendous volume of water in violent motion. The eight-foot
manholes which perforate the floor of the basin were starting to belch forth
their contents, and the placid waters about us now boiled and surged
angrily.

"*Svaap* was thrown about like a chip, the perpendicular lines affording hardly
any control. I had been warned that we would be practically helpless in the grasp
of the milling waters, but had never expected such a tempest. We were almost at
the mercy of the diabolical forces under us, and the pilot threw off his dignity
with his coat, and helped us in our struggle to get more fenders over the sides
coils of spare line, rolls of old canvas, anything to keep us from grinding away
our bulwarks and planking as we were thrown against the wall.

"One minute the bow would leap and strain on the line, and the men on the
other end would strive to keep it in place. Then another current would grip the
boat, and the bow would be thrown at the wall and the stern out.

"Our shouts to the men above the haul, to slack, and to hold fast, echoed and re-echoed from across the canyon. The pilot reiterated his statement that he would rather stay up all night every night for a week taking battleships through than take another 32-footer."

Robinson takes one, in his description, through the successive stages of the Canal. With him one gets a wonderful idea of this stage of the cruise, but it is not until the end of the Canal passage that one begins to get an inkling of the stubborn qualities of this young man. He had obtained his bill of health and French visa, and noted that the latter cost him $1.20. On being handed his Ecuadorian visa to call at the Galapágos Islands, he was asked for $60. There followed a violent argument. At the end of half an hour's shouting, the Ecuadorian official unbent so far as to admit that $30 of the $60 had been levied because the official closing time for the Consulate was three o'clock, and Robinson had arrived at five minutes past. But $30 to Robinson seemed almost as ridiculous as $60 for putting a stamp on a bill of health. So, leaving the Consulate, he betook himself to the Ecuadorian Legation, where he obtained a letter of introduction to the "Commandante" responsible for the Galapágos Islands, which, it appears, made a visa unnecessary.

Having navigated, in more ways than one, the locks and lakes of the Panama Canal, Robinson sailed *Svaap* to the little island of Tobago, just 10 miles off shore. He knew that there was a rise and fall of tide of from 12 to 16 feet there, and so in a little cove, ideally sheltered, they beached *Svaap* for painting the bottom. Here, too, they sewed and roped the great squaresail that was to be employed so effectively. They had one or two trial runs and made some alterations to the way they had rigged the sail. Eventually they were ready, and the first exciting stage of the Pacific journey lay before them.

"It was the morning of October 25th. We were off at last on the long Pacific cruise, our first stop to be the Pearl Islands. The boys of the Boston schooner *Chance* bound also for the South Seas, waved a last farewell. A large school of leaping dolphin escorted us out.

"It was a glorious start. Our new squaresail pulled like horses with a laughing breeze on our quarter, and I learned a new thrill. Never before had I seen such a sail in operation."

Bill Robinson was a most "un-ordinary" man. He obviously thought a great deal, and he was not afraid to put his conclusions, no matter how controversial, down on paper. Some of his remarks, like the outspoken condemnation of some South Sea missionaries that he met, in which he made accusations and addressed those he accused by name, no doubt caused both himself and his publisher a deal of bother. He had great gifts of observation, too, and was able to describe the things he saw; "unusual" things, because he was the kind of man who sees unusual things. Take, for example, this description of a water spout, seen in mid-Pacific two days after Christmas:

"As I sat below at the table plotting my noon position, I suddenly had a feeling that something was wrong. A glance through the companion-way quickly changed my uneasiness to alarm, for there, directly behind and coming rapidly up to us, still in the first throes of birth, hung the largest waterspout we had ever seen. Its long black tentacle, suspended from the lowering tumultuous mother cloud, writhed and groped half-way to the sea, like the arm of a Gargantuan octopus seeking a grip upon the enemy. Our eyes clung to it fascinated as it reached down and down, sometimes retreating but always growing again. There became audible the distant roaring or sighing sound that first warns of approach to a waterfall when travelling downstream in a canoe. Underneath, at the surface of the sea, the sympathetic disturbance suddenly became more intense as the incipient whirl revolved faster and faster, throwing off bits of foam and loose water. A distinct bulge in the surface appeared, as if sucked up by the parched column above, and rose higher every second. The spray and foam now begun to be snatched upward, and before our eyes was formed a vapoury connection with the descending tube, linking cloud and sea. The connection established, more and more loose water shot whirling aloft, and the disturbed area at the base grew larger and more violent as it received the too heavy particles thrown away from the column by centrifugal force. The noise and tumult grew as the hissing of the column, the cry of the wind, and the crashing of the waters blended to form a fearsome roar. Augmented by more and more water the lower half suddenly reached maturity and groped out to clasp hands with the upper, and the sea and sky were united by a spinning weaving pillar of water.

"The spout, moving slowly, reared itself higher and closer to our stern. Close enough now to be in the area of disturbed wind, our squaresail began to strain at its sheets, and we gathered speed momentarily and seemed to be holding our own with the black twisting column, contact with which would have been disaster.

"There has long been a somewhat superstitious belief among seamen that the firing of guns at a spout will break it up, and there have been cases where this has possibly proved efficacious. It is somewhat logical that the concussion of a heavy shot might break up the spout, but it is certainly almost impossible to expect a small gun to have any effect. Before I had finished loading my gun a sudden change occurred within the spout. The writhing increased and a weakening appeared half-way between cloud and sea, and this part became more and more tenuous, until there was a gap that grew larger as the lower half bored its way back into the sea and the upper part withdrew slowly to the boiling lower surface of the cloud.

SVAAP

Length overall: 32 feet 6 inches
Length water-line: 27 feet 6 inches
Beam: 9 feet 6 inches. Draught: 5 feet 6 inches
Designed by John Alden, Boston

"The black curtain was now directly overhead, and we were struck by a short-lived wind and rain squall of great intensity. We had been running under square-sail alone, and had held on to it in an effort to escape the spout. Now there was no time to get it off, and we tore through the water faster and faster, until the bow was high out of its proper element and the stern nearly under. *Svaap* travelled for a short time faster than I thought would have been possible, and water fell in such quantities that it was impossible to breathe without protecting the face. We held her before it and careered madly along for perhaps five minutes, expecting the sail to pull out of the bolt-ropes at any second. But everything held, and the wind shifted from east to north as it always did after squalls. Gradually it subsided and at last worked back to east again, and we jogged slowly along on our course as if nothing had happened."

Of all the descriptions of arrival at Papeete, in Tahiti, Robinson's must rank very near the top:

"We ghosted along within sound of the surf, looking for Papeete, and suddenly there it was—a crescent of tiny lights. Becalmed directly off the town we unshipped the squaresail yard, unbent the sail and stowed it below. For a month this sail had been off but once, and then only thirty hours. It was worn. The yard lacing was temporarily patched in many places. The sail itself was practically blown out of the bold-ropes half the way round. It would have to be almost remade before it could be used again. But if anyone should ask me I should say it was SOME sail.

"Tahiti is entirely surrounded by a barrier of reef which lies anywhere from a few yards to a half-mile or so from shore, upon which the sea almost always breaks heavily. There are passes here and there through which vessels may enter, but strong currents make caution necessary.

"The Pilot Book says of the Papeete pass that one must take a pilot and enter by day. But there are two red range lights on shore that make it possible to come in at night, and I had a good chart of the harbour. We had been at sea just a month and had sailed 3,700 miles. The twinkling lights were a magnet that was irresistible.

"So just after midnight we found the pass through the reef, brought the red lights to bear in a straight line, and ran in with the thunder of the surf on both sides. Once in the fairway along the shore we turned sharp east and slowly glided along the famous Papeete water-front, to tie up to a buoy in the inner harbour just off the government dock.

"The air was heavy with the scent of lovely flowers, and there were strange land noises. We could hear a milkman making his way about town, and soon all the sounds of a community awakening. Birds, dogs, cattle—it was all so strange to us. I put up the quarantine flag and gave myself over to the ecstasy of it all—the glorious feeling that comes only at the end of such a voyage—a feeling of utter relaxation and peace, and of accomplishment."

Robinson loved Tahiti. He stayed there long enough to feel thoroughly at home there, as this extract shows:

"When the last transient had gulped the final Rainbow cocktail and fled, the Club resumed its customary quiet and the little cliques found their accustomed tables on the wide veranda, and, disdaining the crowd of natives, half-castes, and lesser whites on the wharf, prepared to watch the steamer warp out into the fairway and get under way. Then Tahiti would be more or less normal until another mail day. I could no longer strut before the tourists with a knowing air, but as I leaned on the balcony and waved the departing ship off I felt as if I were one of the old islanders. Someone would ask me if I'd seen Turia; there was a moment's conversation with a planter I had not seen since last mail day; and on the way home I would know every bend and hill, every Chinese store; and the little cheerful Annamite road-workers with babes at their breasts would wave to me as I passed and smile with a betel-stained but friendly smile. It had come to be home, for a time at least.

"It was a source of never-ending interest to me to watch the comings and goings of the little island schooners, and the Tuamotu cutters, with their colourful cargoes of humans, cows, chickens, pigs, copra, pearl-shell, trade goods, and so on indefinitely—all mixed helter-skelter on a deck you'd swear would accommodate but a tenth of what it did.

"Native feasts occurred with surprising regularity, and I became fond of the exotic foods that burdened the tables in astounding profusion, and were prepared in the native oven of heated stones in the ground. The simplest of feasts would always have its raw fish with 'mitihaari' or coco-nut sauce, shellfish and several species of variously prepared fish, poi of bananas or paw-paw or some other fruit, taro, yams, native sweet potatoes, fei (the local plantain that must be cooked), pota well soaked in coco-nut sauce, fowl, sucking pig, and fruits.

"To the novice raw fish has a repulsive sound, but to the initiate there are few foods so delicious as this dish of cube-cut fish that has been well soaked in salt and lime-juice for several hours and is eaten with a generous bath of sauce. The pota, too, is a dish that once eaten is never forgotten. It is a species of greens —the tops of taro—and is cooked with bits of pork and chicken and perhaps onion, and develops a flavour that is peculiarly its own and delicious.

"The native dancing never lost its charm. I had plenty of it, for I happened to be there for the great festival that started on June 18th and lasted ten days, to be revived for another week on the French national holiday—July 14th.

"During this period, and for a month previous, when all the districts were practising for the competitive dancing, I lived to the accompaniment of drums and chanting, and spent the warm scented nights watching brown bodies sway beneath the palms by the light of the moon or perhaps a flaring smoky torch."

For the latter part of his cruise Robinson had a most remarkable little man as crew; a Polynesian native of Tahiti. He was a crew beyond price. He could steer, hand, reef, and cook in all weathers and conditions, and do everything well. He got drunk and was jailed in almost every port into which Robinson put, but it never seemed to matter. This is Robinson's account of how he came to join *Svaap*.

"Teriitehau a Tihone, more commonly known as Etera, appeared upon the scene the day before I was to sail. He would cast in his lot with me for as long as I wanted him. He was of uncertain age. Perhaps his estimate of forty-one years was somewhere near the correct figure but more likely not. Small for a Tahitian native—he boasts only five feet—Etera was the most singular-looking individual I had ever seen, and possessed a great bush of coal-black hair and a wrinkled-apple sort of face that was capable of the most extraordinary expressions imaginable. Looking more like a mixture of Gilbert Islander, Fijian, and perhaps a dash of Solomon blood, he claimed Tahitian ancestry of chiefly estate. I had mentally accepted him even before he told me the yarn of his life in the strange French of the Society Islands: black-birding or slave-running with the old pirates in the Solomons and New Hebrides, years of pearl-diving, and cooking on Frisco schooners.

"In reply to my query as to how long it would take him to get ready to go around the world with me, he said five minutes. Unwilling to let him out of sight, for fear I would lose him, I went along and supplied forty francs to get his possessions—all of them—out of hock in a Chinese laundry. That was all. No farewells or sentiment. On five minutes' notice he was ready to leave with me for a year, or five years, or perhaps the rest of his life. And so *Svaap* had her new crew."

Etera seemed to possess a magical charm over women:

"Etera's crowning achievement at Maupiti the night before we left was a personally conducted beauty contest of all the village beauties for my benefit. It was rather startling, for after the eliminations were over and the final judgment about to be awarded, I found that I was to be the prize. The problem was, fortunately or otherwise, solved by the arrival of the apologetic village mutoi, or native policeman, saying that after ten o'clock—and it was that time—all the lights should be out and everyone in bed, as it was Sunday evening. Thus have the missionaries accomplished in the far reaches of the Pacific! Etera took the three finalists home, and presumably concluded the contest himself, for he only returned in time to sail the next morning."

I mentioned earlier that Robinson was particularly outspoken about the government of some of the islands he called at. The following about the Cook islands is a typical passage:

"The Cook Islands, of which Rarotonga is the capital, and also the islands of British Samoa, are governed by New Zealand. This country has made the worst possible mess of governing its islands. The policy of restricting native activities and of sending second-rate men to administer the government has resulted in an unfortunate state of affairs. The natives are unsettled and restless, without faith in their white rulers.

"Several native chiefs, men with racial pride and dignity, voiced the same questions when I visited them.

" 'Why', they asked, 'did the high chief, who never visited the islands, insult them by sending men of a class fit to be their servants, to rule over them.'

"This is expressive of the mistaken policy which is so often followed by nations in governing their less advanced colonies. It is especially disastrous in dealing with a race of the intelligence of the Maoris who inhabit these islands.

"The Maoris were perhaps the finest of all the Polynesians, a people with a great deal of racial pride. Under the guidance of intelligent men, men of sympathy and understanding and tolerance, with a sincere interest in the welfare of their brown subjects, these Maoris would have undergone their inevitable readjustment in a spirit of co-operation, giving of their best.

"Instead of that they are given men of little or no accomplishment, without vision—petty politicians who could not make good at home. These men, commanding little respect in the beginning, lose even that through the example they set in their private lives, their intrigues, greediness and utter lack of understanding. Developing in the native a feeling of repression and dissatisfaction, they are soon confronted by problems with which their feeble abilities are unable to cope. Then we have affairs such as the entirely unwarranted massacre of natives in Apia when I was in that group a month later. Without any real provocation, the beloved and aged chief of Western Samoa and several of his followers were shot down by the police while walking unarmed through the streets."

He is equally outspoken about the missionaries he met:

"I cannot understand this bigotry that causes a certain class of men to consider it their God-given duty to thrust beliefs upon others, for, after all, the primitive peoples have as much right as we have to live their lives according to their own lights.

"It may seem ungrateful to write in this vein of the missionaries, after having accepted their hospitality in many parts of the world. Almost everywhere they were very kind—lavishing food, drink, and attention upon us. In several cases friendships developed which have been carried on by correspondence. These men will, I am sure, understand that this is not a personal attack.

"Occasionally the missionaries create an amusing situation. Just before *Svaap* came to the New Guinea coast a mission there had a grand idea. The natives were making their copra. They were told that they must make one sackful for Christ for each sack of their own. This would prove the sincerity of their religion and would help counteract their worldly sins, which might otherwise cause them to be tortured in Hell after death (Hell in this case was the live volcano, Manam, which steamed away a few miles off the coast). The mission would collect the copra later and see that it was safely delivered to its holy recipient.

"Life went on smoothly. A certain trader somehow got hold of the story. One day a schooner came to anchor just off the main village. A strange figure stood on deck in a flowing nightgown. He wore a beard and long hair. Unless you looked closely you would not have noticed that the hair was teased hemp, dyed. The stranger reminded one slightly of Anton Lang in the Passion Play.

"One or two of the native crew went ashore, and somehow the rumour sped far and wide that the stranger was Jesus Himself, come for His copra. There was tremendous excitement ashore and runners went to all the outlying hamlets with the news. All day the schooner lay there, and all day a procession of loaded canoes propelled by awed natives made its way along side. When the ship could hold no more copra the man that looked like Anton Lang offered thanks. Then the ship sailed off over the horizon, full of Christ's copra."

Robinson's world cruise differs from the classic circumnavigations of men like Slocum and Voss, and from more recent cruises like that of his fellow countryman, Harry Pidgeon, in that having sailed to the Southern Pacific islands he spent a great deal of time visiting many of these before sailing, not through the Torres Strait between Australia and New Guinea, but north of that island. Again he differed in shaping a course not to the Cape of Good Hope but north of Java and Sumatra to Penang, thence to Ceylon and Mangalore, before crossing the Arabian Sea to Makalla. (The chart will make this plain.)

Here is his description of part of his passage from Ceylon to India along the Malabar coast:

"We entered Colombo next morning and stayed a week.

"All in all I did not like what I saw of Ceylon. The man who wrote of it: 'Where every prospect pleases and only man is vile' came near the truth. It is a beautiful country, and its history and legends are enchanting. But to me—

Svaap in Tahiti

coming from worlds where begging is unknown—it was a disappointment to find its people nothing but a race of beggars whose persistency is so appalling that it ruins your visit. Had I gone there first—before knowing the South Seas—perhaps it would have been different.

"*Svaap* has been a most amazingly comfortable little ship. Many small boat voyages seem to consist largely of discomforts, accidents, and privations. I must confess that with two or three exceptions I have always been able to go below out of the worst weather to a welcome dry cabin. And that is one major explanation of the serenity and success of the entire voyage.

"The wettest exception to this happy condition was the run from Ceylon to India. Down out of the Bay of Bengal the north-east monsoon swooped upon us, funnelling between Ceylon and the land-mass of Southern India. Full upon our beam it came, driving a high sea before it. Under reduced canvas we carried on, staggering nearly to our beam ends with each sea. Cape Comorin, the southern-most tip of the Indian peninsula, tempted us on, proffering shelter.

"This whole Malabar Coast, as the west side of the peninsula of Southern India is called, is subject, even during the north-east monsoon, to a very heavy surf which makes it a dangerous shore. Most of the anchorages are merely open roadsteads, so caution is necessary. We found that we could progress along the coast quite successfully by working the land and sea breezes. During the south-west monsoon, however, this coast is practically closed to navigation.

"I should advise any yacht in this vicinity in the right season to spend quite a bit of time on the Malabar Coast. It is beautiful, backed by the impressive range of mountains, the Ghauts. The peninsula is aptly called the Garden of India and consists of several independent states under native rulers. All the towns along the Malabar Coast for a distance of two or three hundred miles are connected by a vast back-water system of canals and lagoons. I should think that one of the most interesting of all trips in India would be to do this inland waterway in a small boat of some sort, perhaps with an outboard motor. It is a pulsing artery of a most intensely interesting section of India, ruled by Maharajahs, abounding in magnificent old palaces, temples, walled cities, ancient Indian art and culture of all sorts."

One of the most entertaining passages in the Middle Eastern stage of Robinson's cruise is where he describes the adventure he had with a gang of Arabs:

"One evening after three days of nerve-racking navigation, we found our way through a winding passage into the inner anchorage of Lith. It was a great disappointment—merely a small settlement of squalid mud houses, instead of the populous town we had expected. As at Khor El Birk, the shore at once disgorged upon us a boatload of truculent Arabs, who tried to inveigle me ashore. This time I was not so easily caught, and they finally left. We were tired, and soon turned in for the night, sleeping on deck.

"Our ship's clock was just striking the eight bells of midnight. I awoke with a start, and thought for a moment that I was having a nightmare, for I looked into the muzzles of a motley assortment of firearms. A smoking oil lamp was held on high by a bulky, black-bearded giant with one eye. The flickering light fell on the wildest-looking gang of pirates I ever hope to see. There were more than a dozen of them, and more waiting in the boat which lay alongside. Every man of them was a walking arsenal, bearing rifle, revolver, and one or two knives or a sword.

"There was no temporizing with this crowd. I tried to joke it off, but instantly realised that these were not the polite captors of El Birk. They simply poked a gun in my ribs and took me along without even letting me dress, although I did slip on a bathrobe.

"Two stayed to guard Etera, who was speechless with fright. As we rowed off I shouted what I fully believed to be my last instructions to him; to try to escape on some passing dhow and tell the story to the first European he met. Somehow, I felt very melodramatic at that moment. I was certain that I would never see *Svaap* again, and I kept my eyes on her until she faded into the black night. This was the end, I thought.

"Three horses were waiting on shore, beautiful Arabian steeds, without saddles. I have always dreamed of riding a real Arab under the stars of Asia, but never in my wildest fancies did I imagine such a ride as I had that night as we galloped bareback over the rolling desert sands. In front of me rode the chief, his white mantle fluttering from his head like the wings of a phantom. Immediately behind me rode the guard, brandishing his old French musket towards the middle of my back. I quite expected a shot at any moment, and curiously enough, was quite calm about it, wondering what it would feel like when it came. I believed that I was being taken out in the desert to be killed where there would be no trace. Then they would go back and scuttle the poor *Svaap*. I learned that night what a condemned man feels like when he is being led out to the gallows.

"My predominant thought was that no one would ever know what had happened. This worried me very much. People would say 'I told you so, the boat was too small. It was a foolhardy thing to try to sail around the world in that boat.' I did so much want to complete the trip successfully, to demonstrate that it was not foolhardy, that a well-designed and built small boat could go anywhere safely if properly handled.

"On and on we galloped, over rolling desert dunes. The hot wind was oppressive. The stars shone overhead. My long bathrobe flew ridiculously in the wind, and I began to have painful reminders that I was unaccustomed to this form of violent exercise, not to mention the fact that I had never ridden bareback and stirrupless before. I longed to reach our destination, whatever it was.

"After a while we came to a lone, grotesquely dwarfed tree, where we stopped. The guard gave a peculiar cry, which was answered from somewhere in the dark. My heart beat rapidly, for I thought that this was to be the spot. But then a man appeared, examined us, and we moved on. Then we came to an oasis with a considerable settlement. There, grimly commanding its surroundings from a rise, stood a low, square, turreted fortress with round towers at the four corners.

"A few minutes later I took stock of my situation from a suffocating low cell in the fortress. There was no window or opening in the wall of any sort except the heavily barred door through which I had entered. There was not a single object in the room. The only break in the monotony of the four walls was a niche cut in the stone of one side, deep and long enough to form a sleeping shelf. A few rays of light filtered through a small aperture in the door, from a lamp hung outside. There was no possibility of escape.

"In this hopeless condition I languished for what seemed a week, unable to distinguish day from night. Occasionally some peculiar tough bread-like substance was passed in with foul water. Eventually some important Emir or Sheik arrived and examined me. We talked for hours, but as there was no interpreter I do not know what it was all about. As a matter of fact I have never, to this day, understood the whole affair. There was no effort to take *Svaap*. I was never even searched. No effort was made to get ransom. I believe they got cold feet for some reason or other.

"I was almost disappointed, eventually, that it all ended as tamely as it did. From a beginning that surely rivalled any 'Arabian Nights' tale, my adventure tapered off to an anti-climax."

In the Mediterranean Sea, Robinson visited the Grecian Islands, sailed through Messina Strait, to the Bay of Naples. At 7 p.m. on the 20th of July his log records taking on board, 15 miles off the mouth of the River Tiber ". . . the biggest sea . . . *Svaap* has ever had—whole forward part of ship under green water".

Ironically, it was here in the Mediterranean, and in a part of it associated with luxury yachting, and the kind of beautifully undressed yachtsmen and yachtswomen who seldom sail (or motor) far from shore, that *Svaap*, caught in a really bad gale on a lee shore, had the "fight of her life"!

"She was fighting for her very life, and what a glorious fight it was! Close astern lay the cruel black rocks—waiting. Once the jib, under immense strain, started to break away from the stay and we were at the crisis. If it went, we lost

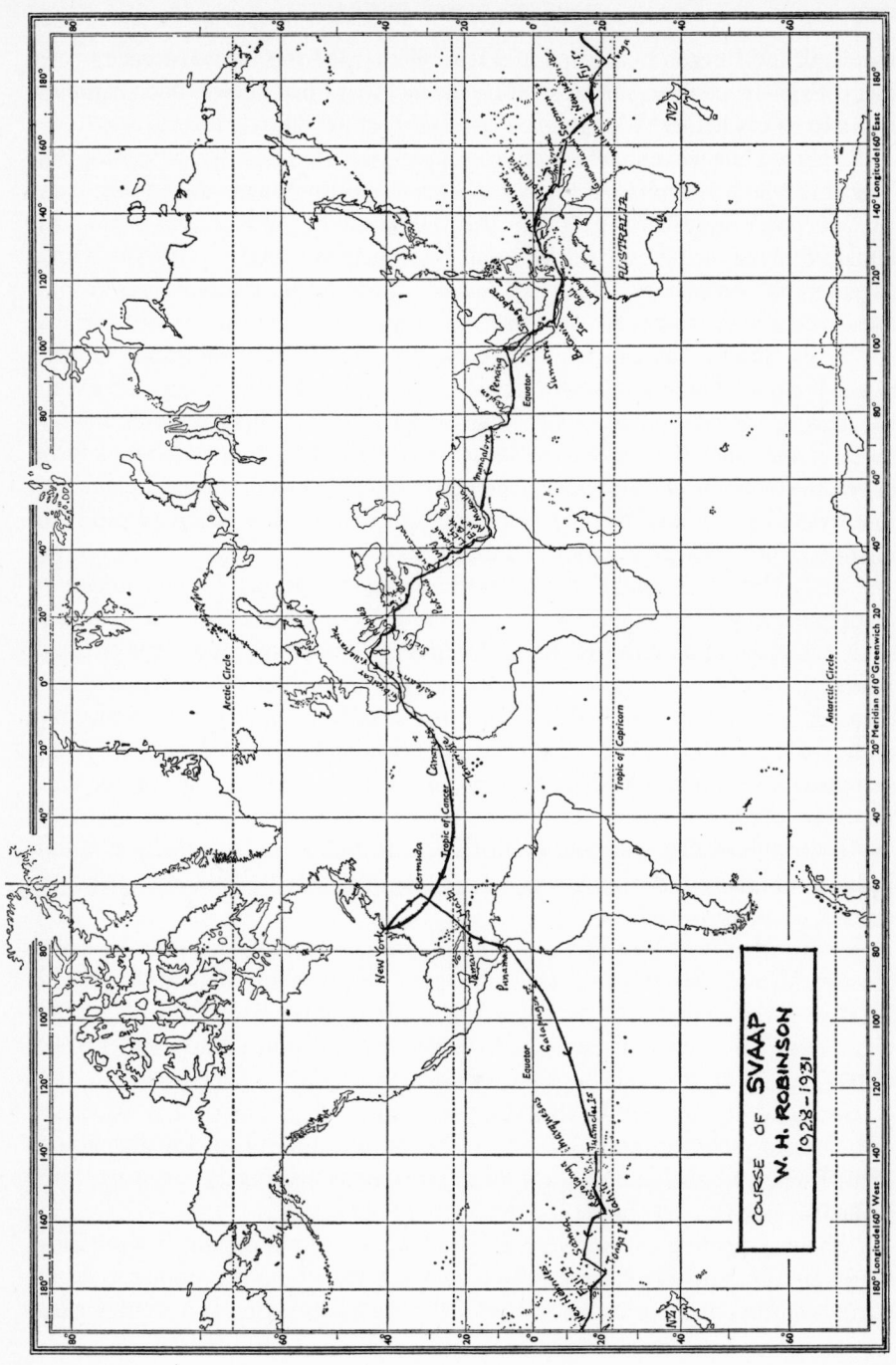

COURSE OF SVAAP
W. H. ROBINSON
1928-1931

our chance to fight. I spent ten minutes on the bowsprit, at the end of a rope, completely under water most of the time, coming up gasping for air between seas. But the sail was saved.

"During the height of the storm that night, when things were looking blackest, I gave the helm to Etera and tried to rest a little. I clung to my berth and watched the moon lurch past the porthole in sickening arcs as the ship groaned and tried to stand on end and beam at once. The gale shrieked in the rigging. Bilge water rushed about threateningly. An inch and an eighth of wood between us and Eternity!

"I was in one of my rare moods of doubt. Why should I choose such a life, I asked, and called myself every kind of a fool, while all the time I knew that I would yearn for it all again when I had been a little while on shore. Something makes me want to fight the elements, to endure hardships, to feel the great luxury of sailing into a strange and beautiful port when it is all over. I am always seeking beauty; in the storm itself, in the sunrise, in the scintillating sea and far places—always beauty and Nature. And so the ship strained on, the seas crashed overhead, and I lay there and knew that I loved it.

"The lights of Fiumara Grange shone out to us from shore. If they grew clearer, nearer, it would be only a question of time. The night wore away. At times the lights were closer. At times we seemed to hold our own.

"The very worst sea of all roared down upon us at dawn—a dirty green monster that broke just as it reached us. Pandemonium was let loose. I had turned the wheel over to Etera. He was lashed by a short length of rope to the mast, but I was free, doing something up forward. A single leap took me six feet into the rigging. For a moment I could see no boat at all, only swirling angry water with masts and rigging projecting. Then the cabin and deck emerged like a submarine rising from a dive, and *Svaap* freed herself from the deluge. Etera was gone. The wheel spun free. Then he, too, reappeared, sputtering in the water and grasping for the rail, still on the end of the rope. I pulled him back aboard.

"It had been the last threat of the storm. After that the heart seemed gone from it, and by noon the next day we were tearing past Monte Cristo with just a whole sail breeze, resting by turn from our ordeal of the night."

Robinson sailed close to the Cote d'Azur. On mooring for a short stay in Villefranche, he was surprised to find his grandmother waiting for him! He sailed from there to Gibraltar, via the Balearic Islands, and so came to the last leg of his voyage, the crossing of the Atlantic. In Teneriffe, in the Canary Islands, Etera got once again into trouble.

"I had to shanghai Etera away from Teneriffe, where he got into even more than the usual amount of trouble. He is the only man I have ever known with the ability to go anywhere in the world without a word of the local language, or a cent of money, and get unlimited liquor. On his first night out in Teneriffe he rolled aboard with a case of wine.

" 'But, Capitaine!' he protested with injured innocence next morning when I made him take it back, 'it is for sauce to cook fish in.'

"The next night he landed in jail. I think I have bailed him out of every jail this side of Tahiti. I got so that upon arrival in a port I usually notified police chiefs that they were about to have a customer, and to fine him as little as possible because I would have to pay it. Sometimes I would let them take care of him until I was ready to sail—then I would know where to look for him.

"In Teneriffe I got him out a day too soon. He escaped at the last minute, and for two days the police combed the town in vain for him while I tore my hair and delayed our departure at a time when every single day lost meant increased danger on the North Atlantic. The second night when he thought I was already sleep he came merrily aboard to get his favourite sun helmet. Perhaps he expected to captivate with it the little Canary Island charmers. I captured him and kept him aboard by force."

The Atlantic treated Robinson and Etera to a series of gales, but once off the American coast they ran into thick fog. For 90 miles they groped their way through it, creeping closer and closer to where Robinson thought the Cape Lookout shoals lay. He stopped the engine and listened for the buoy . . .

"And then, so close that we were startled, came the harsh clang of a heavy hammer striking metal. Twice more. Then the silence crept down.

"I laughed, a funny hollow laugh, and suddenly sat down where I was—not meaning to at all. It was then that I realised I was trembling like a leaf and running with perspiration although it was cold. The accumulated tension of the last magnificent voyage had snapped and was gone.

"We had come home at last."

The vessel in which Robinson rounded the globe was an interesting one. She was designed for offshore cruising by the well-known American naval architect John Alden of Boston. She measured 32 feet 6 inches overall, 27 feet 6 inches on the waterline, and her extreme beam was 9 feet 6 inches. It will thus be seen that her waterline length was approximately three times her beam— the normal proportion of a small cruising yacht. Her draught was 5 feet 6 inches.

Svaap was two-masted, and rigged as a ketch, so that not only was her mizzen-mast forward of the steering position but the two masts, and consequently the sails set from them, were not so very different in size. The ketch rig is useful when short-handed, because a fair amount of sail may be carried, but since the sail plan is divided into nearly equal areas, one man may hoist, lower or reef, without much bother.

Svaap's designed sail area was 660 square feet, but Robinson reduced this by 100 square feet. Her largest sail would therefore be well under 250 square feet, and this is an easily manageable size. Uffa Fox once said that no cruising vessel should carry any one sail of more than 500 square feet. Actually 500 square feet is quite a large area for a single man to handle in bad weather, but, knowing Uffa, I have no doubt that it presented no problem to him!

But it will be quite clear that *Svaap* had a rig that Robinson and his crew of one could handle with ease. Of course, in choosing the ketch rig there is an inevitable sacrifice of efficiency to windward, but on a cruise round the world the maximum efficiency on this point is not so important as, for example, in ocean racing. On the other hand, *Wanderer III*, the fine little vessel in which Eric and Susan Hiscock twice rounded the world, is rigged as a cutter, and this is the most efficient sail to windward. Her waterline length is 26 feet 6 inches, just 1 foot less than *Svaap*, and it would be hard to find a more able vessel than *Wanderer III* for her purpose.

When riding to a sea anchor a riding sail may be set on the mizzenmast of a ketch or yawl to help hold the bows to windward. This may well have been in Robinson's mind when he selected *Svaap*, but he was only 25 when he set off and was not experienced at all in offshore sailing, and it may be that he just liked the look of *Svaap*. Many a boat has been bought for such a reason, and he admits in the prologue of his book that he was anxious to see if *Svaap* should ". . . prove her worth as a sea-boat".

If one considers the rigs of a specimen selection of yachts which have made circumnavigations, one finds that many of them carried a small mizzenmast, and in the case of the first circumnavigator Joshua Slocum, his ship, the *Spray*, started as a sloop, but was converted to a yawl, by the addition of a small mizzenmast when the ship was in South American waters. On balance I would personally say that the yawl rig for a yacht designed for offshore is ideal, provided that her mainsail is not more than say, 450–500 square feet. If it is larger, it can be reduced again by turning the vessel into a ketch (like *Svaap*), moving the mizzenmast forward of the steering position and increasing the mizzensail proportionately. In a yacht of *Svaap*'s size it might seem that she carried a lot of top weight in her masts, and a glance at the sail plan which shows the original design might seem to indicate this. But *Svaap* had a good beam and draught and John Alden did not acquire his reputation by designing unbalanced ships. None the less for vessels going right off soundings it is better to be undermasted than over, and so it was wise of Robinson to lower the masts slightly and cut 100 square feet off the sail area.

One has only to remember the ill-fated *Tsu Hang* of the Smeetons described in their book, "Once is Enough". *Tsu Hang* was twice completely turned over in Southern Pacific waters. The reasons seem to have been the encountering of exceptional seas, but some might consider that she was overmasted. In point of fact, *Tsu Hang* had a fair beam, too, and there is no evidence that her capsizes were anything to do with top weight. John Guzzwell was a believer in carrying a mizzensail. It will be quite clear that the amount of top weight a vessel can carry depends on such factors as her draught and ballast and the general shape and design of her hull. *Trekka* was a light-displacement vessel by contrast to *Svaap* and *Tsu Hang*, and her mainmast was in consequence small by comparison, while the area of her mainsail was a mere 100 square feet.

A light-displacement boat, however, needs only a very moderate sail area to drive her, and many people today argue in favour of light displacement. My own boat is of this type, and although she measures 30 feet on the waterline (2 feet 6 inches longer than *Svaap*), she needs 40 square feet less of working sail to drive her at her best speed.

Trekka, measured only 20 feet 6 inches on the waterline and, one might think, was rather small for a yawl, and indeed in his own very excellent book "*Trekka* Round the World" John Guzzwell states (in an appendix) that he now prefers the cutter rig for its efficiency after all!

So there it is. One cannot arrive at the ideal ship, and it is probably just as well. The individual ideal "dream" ship is, of course, well known to every yachtsman—mainly in his dreams! But *Svaap* was as much a "dream" ship as any yacht, for she made Bill Robinson's own dream come true. She carried him to places and showed him things that most people, in the whole of their lives, never see. She gave him three and a half years of excitement and adventure almost beyond imagining, and all for £1,000. That £1,000 was all the money Bill Robinson had, but can anyone suggest a better investment?

16

THE HISCOCKS

Twice Round the World in "Wanderer III"

The double circumnavigation of Eric and Susan Hiscock I have kept to the last, perhaps as something of a treat for myself, as these two books are particular favourites of mine. The first book "Around the World in *Wanderer III*", was published in 1956, the second, "Beyond the West Horizon", in 1963, both by Oxford University Press. Both voyages were made in the same yacht.

Eric Hiscock and his wife have been sailing for many years, and both are expert in the handling of a small yacht at sea. The writers in this book have been selected, however, not only for the excellence of their seamanship but because they were also able to pass on their knowledge and experiences in an interesting and readable manner. Nowhere are these conditions fulfilled more completely than in these two books, for Hiscock is experienced as a writer and also as a photographer, and the colour plates in the second of these two volumes are mouth-watering beyond description. Indeed, anyone whose fate it is to catch the 8.15 train every morning of his life, save a fortnight in summer, had better be on his guard when he looks at these photographs, for they possess as insidious an appeal to the wanderbug in all of us as anything I have ever seen or heard. I looked at these and listened to the Hiscocks' recordings of Polynesian singing and playing on a cold, rainy winter's night in the Hiscocks' home in the Isle of Wight, and it made me grateful that there are people like Eric and Susan who have the guts to go out and face the hardships of such an undertaking as a world voyage in a small boat and can bring back with them so much of the magic of which they were made free, instead of leaving it behind them or remaining indifferent to it all, like the hardened steamship ocean traveller, as in the (paraphrased) words of Noel Coward, "China? Very large! Japan? Very small!"

It was William Robinson who wrote "one cannot know the sea from steamships". How right that is. The steamship traveller is protected from Nature deliberately. The very décor of the cabins and saloons of an ocean-going liner is designed to make the passenger *forget* that he is at sea. But in a small yacht, like *Wanderer III*, the sea is always very close. At times it is so close and so majestic as to be very frightening indeed, and maybe there are occasions, indeed I personally can think of several when the sight of wave-tops higher than the crosstrees makes one feel inclined to change places with those cosy passengers in the liner. But not for long—there is far too much on the credit side. No, one cannot know the sea from steamships.

It was in 1950 that Eric and Susan Hiscock made a voyage to the Azores (from the Isle of Wight) in the 24-foot cutter *Wanderer II*. So encouraged were they by the success of this venture that they decided on a world cruise. This meant selling *Wanderer II*, and other things as well, in order to find the money to do what every circumnavigator would like to do, build a boat specially for the job.

One can imagine the thrill of pleasure that must have been theirs many times over as their dream took shape. The selection of a designer, and the many discussions with that designer; the choice of builder, and the thrill of seeing the vessel taking shape before their impatient eyes to the accompaniment of an orchestra of shipwrights.

For a designer they went to Messrs Laurent Giles of Lymington, Hampshire, and for builder to Messrs William King of Burnham-on-Crouch, Essex. The cost of the yacht was £3,300, which, for an 8-tonner, judged by present-day prices, seems little short of miraculous. Work began in 1952. Although this book is not aimed specifically at the "yachting public", I have included in it some (moderately technical) descriptions of the various yachts—the "heroines" of the book—and I do not think anyone will disagree with my decision to devote a paragraph or two to describing this beautiful little ship, which, having been designed for a world voyage, carried her two owners twice round the globe, taking the weather in her stride so successfully.

Wanderer III measures 30 feet 3 inches overall, on the waterline she measures 26 feet 5 inches, her beam is 8 feet 5 inches, and her draught 5 feet. That actually was her designed draught, but in fact she drew about 5 feet 9 inches owing to the vast amount of food, water and equipment on board, and also, according to Hiscock himself, because of her "rather heavy construction". Her measurements give her a Thames tonnage of 8, and her displacement tonnage, which means the weight of the water she displaces when afloat and in sea-going trim, is about 9.

Her rig is that of a sloop, as can be seen from the drawing of her, and her sail area with mainsail and the big genoa jib set is 600 square feet. The genoa is her largest sail and measures 322 square feet; well within the Uffa Fox formula of 500 square feet.

Her mainsail measures 279 square feet, and it will be seen that this, too, is of an easily manageable size. The sails were made by Messrs Cranfield and Carter of Burnham-on-Crouch. The sails are made mostly of nylon and terylene. An interesting point about the mainsail is that although her seams were sewed by machine as strongly as one would expect from a first-class firm like Cranfield and

Carter, Hiscock had an additional row of hand-made stitches put in as an insurance against chafe (shades of Alain Gerbault and the *Firecrest*!).

Wanderer III possesses a small engine. It is an 8-horsepower Stuart Turner petrol-driven two-stroke, which gives a speed of something like 5 knots in smooth water.

Talking of water; the supply of fresh water for drinking, always a major problem for yachts that cruise well offshore, is assured by 60 gallons carried in three tanks able to be filled separately, so that contamination in one would not affect the others. Four water cans staved in the forepeak bring the total up to 70 gallons. Hiscock estimates that this will provide fresh water for two people for at least eighty days.

Wanderer III is planked with iroko, her frames, stem and stem post being of oak, as are her deck beams and carlines. The decks of western red cedar, canvas-covered and painted for maximum waterproofing. The deadwood and keel are of elm and the ballast keel is of lead. This weighs some 3 tons and there is no inside ballast, nor any need for it. The bolts holding the keel are of steel; the fastenings of the planking, etc., of copper. Other fastenings are of bronze or brass. The hull is sheathed with copper up to the waterline as a protection against worm or "marine borers" like the Teredo—a very necessary precaution.

If you are to be happy about your mast, you must have strong rigging, so placed and set up as to be able to hold the mast in position and take any strains that the force of wind and sea may impose. In *Wanderer III* this rigging (known as standing rigging to distinguish it from the "running" rigging which moves through blocks and controls the sails) is made of galvanized steel wire well soaked in boiled linseed oil. In his second book, however, Hiscock speaks of replacing this with stainless-steel wire—probably a wise, if expensive, move. The forestays are already of stainless steel, the running rigging is of terylene rope, except for the topping-lift (which supports the boom when the mainsail is lowered), which is of nylon.

Below decks *Wanderer* is a masterpiece of planning. Starting from aft, we find a large galley to port and an oilskin locker and ahead of that a chart table to starboard. The drawers below the chart table can contain up to 400 Admiralty charts. Then amidships comes the cabin, with two Dunlopillo settee-berths. The cabin sides contain bookshelves, and in the centre of the cabin stands a folding table on which fiddles can be fixed to keep plates, etc., in place in rough weather. Ahead of the two berths on each side are sideboards, and farther forward still lockers for clothes, photographic equipment, typewriter, etc. In the forepeak there are work benches to port and starboard and at the forward end the "Baby Blake" W.C. The water cans mentioned earlier stow under the benches. In the

WANDERER III

Length overall: 30 feet 3½ inches. Length water-line: 26 feet 4¾ inches
Beam: 8 feet 5 inches. Draught: 5 feet
Designed by Messrs. Laurent Giles of Lymington
Built by Messrs. William King of Burnham-on-Crouch, in 1951

eyes of the ship is stowage for sails, and this part of the vessel also houses the 45 fathoms (270 feet) of $\frac{5}{16}$-inch cable. Two anchors are carried, each of the C.Q.R. pattern and weighing 35 lb. apiece. For shore communication and as a lifeboat a dinghy is carried on deck bottom upwards. This is made of alloy and measures a little over 7 feet.

So it will be very clear that in *Wanderer III* we have as well fitted a little vessel in which to put a girdle round the earth as one could wish for, and all for £3,300. People familiar with the price of yachts at the Boat Show at Earl's Court will find this difficult to believe—but then in the late 1920s Bill Robinson not only bought *Svaap* but financed his whole circumnavigation, which lasted three and a half years, for £1,000!

Hiscock reckons that the all-in cost of his second voyage was £700 a year. What will it cost to sail a yacht round the world in 1984?

Let us now consider Hiscock's two voyages, and illustrate them with samples of his own, very descriptive writing. Before the first circumnavigation, they took *Wanderer III* on a trial cruise to Eire, but met with light airs, and when the time came for their start in July the ship was untested as far as bad weather was concerned. This was not to be so for long. In the Bay of Biscay *Wanderer III* had the pleasure of her first gale, making it necessary to heave-to. The course sailed by the Hiscocks in this early part of their first circumnavigation took them to Brest, across the "Bay" to Ferrol, where they spent a little time on that delightful part of the Spanish coast visiting Corcubion, Vigo and Bayona. Then southwards to Cascais in Portugal [where they had some unpleasant moments with the Portuguese (so-called "International") Police], and from there to Madeira, of which Hiscock writes ". . . had a perfect passage, the kind of sailing one dreams about, or even buys or builds a boat to get . . . All day long the sun shone from a clear blue sky and at night there was brilliant starlight and a blaze of phosphorescence in the disturbed water of our wake." From Madeira they sailed south again to La Palma in the Canary Islands.

In that passage from Yarmouth to Madeira and the Canary Islands we have a microcosm of offshore yacht cruising. The start down Channel, where they met with bad weather, and had to resort to Avomine pills to ward off seasickness—then, after a temporary rest in France, meeting far worse weather in the Bay of Biscay, when even the stoutest heart could be forgiven for wondering how many thousands of miles of such discomfort and worry lay ahead. The fear and apprehension of being on a lee shore in such conditions has to be experienced to be appreciated.

Then comes a friendly reception in Spain, some pleasant pottering under hotter skies, and the eating of different food and the drinking of native wine.

Wanderer III running under twin headsails at night on her second circumnavigation.

This is followed by a very slow passage down the "almost featureless coast of Portugal", and at the end of it a tiresome altercation with the International Police. And then the lyrical sail to Madeira, when the sun came out and the wind blew from the right quarter and all was optimism and joyful anticipation once again. In this cycle we have the magical distillation of good and bad, of worry and fear, and joy and excitement. A wine that Neptune offers to those with the courage to grab hold of the cup and drink. As Erskine Childers put it: it is "the purest . . . of vintages", and not "that bastard concoction . . . in the pseudo Bohemias of Soho".

With Soho a long way astern, the Hiscocks now had to face their first major test, the crossing of the Atlantic Ocean. They sailed on the 11th of October for Barbados in the West Indies, a distance of more than 2,650 miles, which was to keep them at sea for over twenty-six days. Now they had the chance to use their twin spinnakers, the classic rig of the modern trade-wind sailor. At first, with the two sails set, one each side of the mast, each on its own boom, the Hiscocks were delighted at the relief from continually being at the helm. They found that up to this time, working alternate watches of three hours at the helm and three below, they got very tired. The watch below has to use the three hours for cooking, eating, navigating and other tasks and there is not so much time remaining for sleep. But under the twin spinnakers all was changed and life became more leisurely. Hiscock writes of how his wife sang as she cooked more elaborate meals . . . but, there was a snag; the snag that all who have held this rig find sooner or later to a greater or lesser degree, depending on the size of the yacht. The snag was "rolling".

I cannot remember who it was but whoever wrote of "rolling down the path of the north-east trades" knew what he was talking about. The exhausting thing about it is that there is no let-up; the roll from side to side is unceasing. *Wanderer III* was no exception. She rolled 32 degrees each way, taking only two seconds for the roll.

But in spite of this Hiscock writes that they enjoyed themselves, and here let me quote from his book a passage that describes what it was like on that first Atlantic crossing of theirs—an experience shared by all who have made this crossing, but seldom has it been penned so vividly. "Each evening we sat together in the cockpit for what we called our twilight hour. Over a drink we discussed the doings of the day, and although those who have not made an ocean voyage under sail may consider it a dull business, I can assure them it is not, for there is always plenty to do. We admired the wide and empty ocean across which we sailed so effortlessly, and watched the sunset with its actual gathering of cumulus clouds piled up all round the horizon. If the sun set

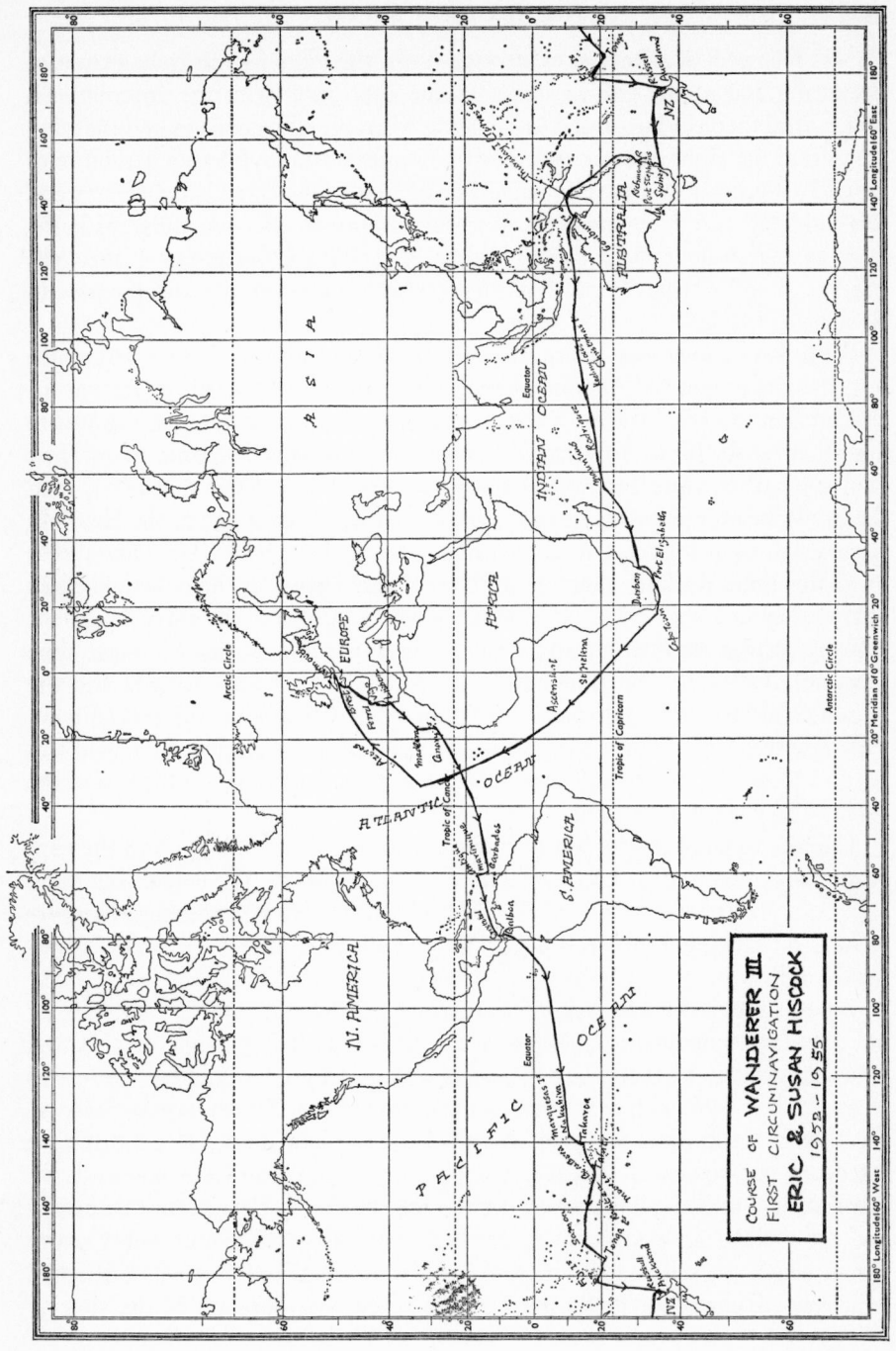

COURSE of **WANDERER III**
FIRST CIRCUMNAVIGATION
ERIC & SUSAN HISCOCK
1952—1955

clearly, as he sometimes did, we looked for the vivid, and so far as I know un-
explained, green flash which sometimes appeared just as he dropped below the
horizon. Then almost at once it was night. The planet Venus could then be seen
between the luffs of the twins, chasing the sun to bed, while Mars soon rose
astern. Most evenings, shortly after sundown, a black cloud approached from
astern bringing with it a shower of rain, then the sky cleared and most of the
night was fine, but there was often another small shower of rain at breakfast time.
Usually these showers brought with them a shift of wind, but that was only
temporary, and within half an hour or so the trade would be blowing from its
usual quarter again. While the rain lasted we had to close the hatches and ports,
but those were the only occasions during that Atlantic crossing when we did
have to close them. Once during the night I heard heavy rain beating on deck.
Then, much to Susan's surprise, for I am not normally of a spartan nature, I
rose from my bunk, took a cake of soap and had a thorough wash on deck; but
all the time I was fearful that the rain might stop before I had rinsed the suds
off, for not until we had passed the half-way point did we use any of our seventy
gallons of fresh water for washing purposes. This does not mean that we were
dirty, for although we never bathed at sea because of the risk of sharks, we often
used to sluice ourselves down on deck with buckets of sea water; also we discovered that we could get an excellent wash in salt water, using one of the modern
soapless shampoos, while for washing clothes and dishes we used a liquid
detergent.

"After supper we hung the riding light in the rigging and both turned into
our bunks. We considered the risk of collision to be negligible, for now that there
are no sailing ships, the trade wind routes are empty except for the occasional
yacht, and steamships generally keep to regular routes which are shown on
certain charts; when crossing those routes we always kept a lookout. So for the
most part we slept with easy minds. From our bunks it was possible to see
whether *Wanderer* was holding a steady course, for a small telltale compass was
fixed to the table leg between us, and we could easily reach to turn on its battery-
operated light and read it without getting up. But during the night one or other
of us usually had a look round several times to see that all was well. It was
fascinating to go on deck and find our little ship forging steadily on her way at
five knots, with a tumbling bow-wave and a broad hissing wake alight with pale
green phosphorescence. Looking up from the foredeck I could see the twins,
ghostly white, bellying out firm and round, pulling with silent power, while aft
the tiller was moved, mysteriously, it seemed, a little this way and a little that
way as the self-steering gear held the course. Perhaps I would give a touch of
grease to the foreguy and braces where they worked through the stemhead and

quarter blocks, a glance at the luminous compass and the star-filled sky, a slow and careful search of the horizon for lights, and then I went back to my comfortable bunk. By daybreak another fifty miles or so would be ticked off by the patent log.

"On the passage across the Atlantic we fed simply but adequately. For breakfast we had porridge, Macvita and marmalade, coffee and vitamin pills. During the early part of the trip lunch was always a cold meal, tinned meat or fish or cheese with biscuits and fresh tomatoes (they lasted for sixteen days with some wastage) and Portuguese wine. We abandoned afternoon tea as being a waste of time, for by then the heat of the day was declining and it was possible to work more comfortably on deck or down below. To begin with supper was a hot meal, the meat coming out of a tin, of course, but always with plenty of boiled, mashed, roast or fried potatoes (we had 40 lb. for that trip, and with an occasional picking over they lasted very well) and usually onions, of which we carried 8 lb., carrots, etc. Sometimes we had an egg dish, but we were short of eggs because many of those we had brought from England went bad owing to the lard with which they had been coated melting and running off them in the hot weather. All future supplies of eggs we greased with petroleum jelly, and they kept perfectly for as long as three months. As a sweet we often had a chocolate rice pudding, or mashed bananas with milk and sugar. Oranges and lemons wrapped separately and kept in tins lasted the whole voyage, so we were always able to have a fresh fruit drink during the forenoon. When night watches were kept, the helmsman had chocolate and biscuits within his reach and perhaps a cup of cocoa at the change of watch."

They reached Barbados at noon on their twenty-sixth day at sea, and it was a tremendous thrill to see the "low, green island" appear where Hiscock had predicted (and as he writes ". . . secretly prayed") that it would be. A successful landfall after a long passage never loses its thrill.

While in the West Indies *Wanderer III* cruised up to Antigua Island, calling in at each of the islands on the way. In St Lucia they found an ideal anchorage in Vigie Cove. Of this paradise, Hiscock writes: "Can you imagine a tiny, land-locked pool from which not so much as a distant glimpse of the sea can be had; so small that you can, and we often did, swim right across it from one grassy bank to the other; surrounded by green foliage, palms, and brilliant flowers, and with hardly a ripple on the surface?"

Wanderer lay in this paradise for one peaceful week before continuing north-wards to Martinique, Dominica, Isles des Saintes, Guadaloupe, and Antigua. While between the Isles des Saintes and Dominica, the weather turned on them and produced a Force 7 wind with heavy rain; but only for a day, and on the following day the sun returned, leaving the islands . . . "fresh and rain-washed, sparkling like jewels in their setting of dark blue sea".

The Hiscocks are the sort of people who make friends wherever they go and this emerges as one of the most pleasing characteristics of the two books. In the first book we are introduced to a lot of people who we meet again on the second time round.

The chart of the first voyage will show that from the West Indies the Hiscocks sailed to the Panama Canal. Passing through the Canal presented considerably less trouble for them than some of the other circumnavigators in this book. After listening to a barrage of advice as how best to hold *Wanderer* safely in the locks, they decided on their own methods, which surely cannot be beaten? They planned to keep the yacht in the very centre of the lock by using four lines, two from the bows and two from the two quarters. Their method was approved by the despatcher, but they were told they would require lines of at least 120 feet in length and that each one would have to have a separate person to handle it. This was done with the assistance of two Swedish friends, Sten and Brita Holmdahl, who in their ship *Viking* were making a similar voyage to that of *Wanderer III.*

From Panama the Hiscocks, unlike many of their predecessors, did not sail to the Galapágos Islands, but elected to make the tremendously long passage direct to the Marquesas—a distance of just under 4,000 miles (Hiscock logged it as 3,972). Compared with this, the Atlantic crossing was nothing; as Hiscock puts it, "There is a lot of blank white space on the chart between the Galapágos and the Marquesas . . ."

Here again in the Pacific the problem was lack of sleep. Time and time again Hiscock found himself, and his wife, too, nodding off to sleep. This, apart from being obviously undesirable, had another disadvantage, and Hiscock explodes one of the myths about such sailing when he writes: "The sad thing about our lack of sleep was that it left us in no fit condition to enjoy to the full the wonderful experience of making such a voyage. We could not properly appreciate the satisfying sensation of steady progress as the trade wind hummed a tune in the taut rigging, and the bow wave flashed and chuckled."

The passage from Balboa to the Marquesas took 36 days 22 hours. After such a length of time at sea, in so small a boat, on the immense Pacific, which dwarfs the largest of liners, small wonder that the first sight of their first Poly-nesian Island gave them a thrill which, they admit, is unlikely to be repeated. "It was at 10.30 p.m.", Hiscock writes, "on our thirty-sixth day at sea that the newly risen moon showed us the silver-grey lump of Ua Huka island fine on the starboard bow." What a moment to remember on a drizzly day in England in January! Their first actual Polynesian anchorage was in Nukahiva, some

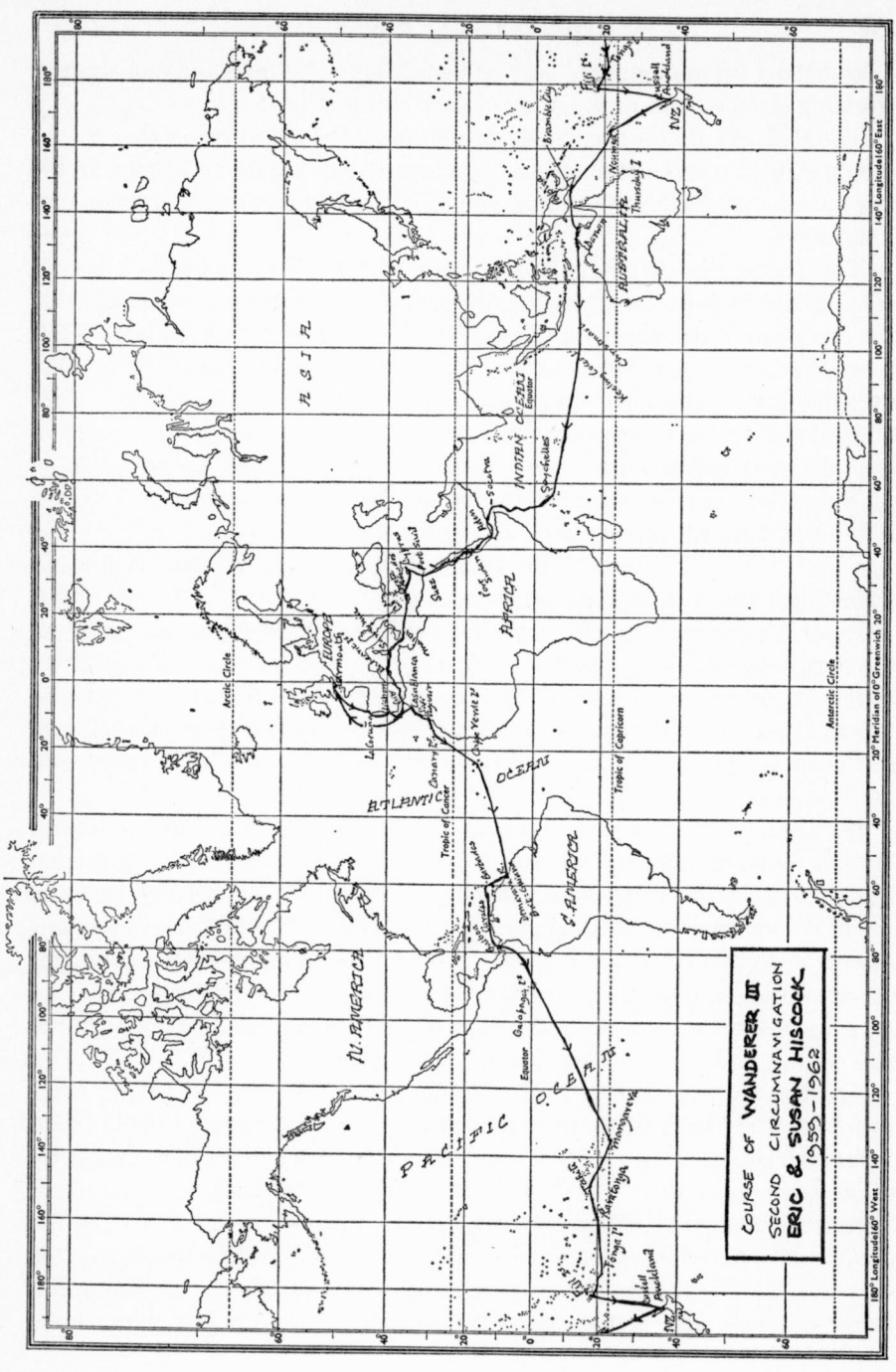

COURSE OF WANDERER III
SECOND CIRCUMNAVIGATION
ERIC & SUSAN HISCOCK
1959 – 1962

24 miles to the westward, and there, "at breakfast time", at the head of Taiohae
Bay in 2 fathoms of water, after a passage of close on 4,000 miles.

From here the course of *Wanderer III* follows that of many of the circumnavigators, as may be seen from the chart. Tahiti (perhaps inevitably) they
visited, and on both voyages. We have had descriptions of this enchanted cross-
roads island elsewhere in this book, and although Hiscock's own account is as
entertaining as one would expect, yet it is in the descriptions of being at sea that
Hiscock excels, and so I am confining most of my quotations to these.

A comparison of the two charts of the voyages of *Wanderer III* will show two
main differences. On their first time round the Hiscocks visited Australia, sailing
up through the barrier reef to Torres Strait and so into the Indian Ocean. They
then sailed across that ocean west and south-west to round the Cape of Good
Hope. On the second time round, although they visited New Zealand (they had
made many good friends there) they did not visit Australia, and this time they
sailed home via the Red Sea and the Mediterranean.

Both voyages were carried out with the minimum of fuss. Hiscock writes how
in Sydney reporters who crowded the deck of *Wanderer III* when she newly
arrived in the harbour rapidly lost interest when they found no stories of un-
manageable hurricanes, broken masts and spars and sails torn to shreds. One
does not go to these two books for the more obvious forms of excitement, but for
a subtler deeper thrill that comes from this feeling of being there with Eric and
Susan in that small ship. In the second book there is a passage describing the
loneliness of being becalmed 800 miles from land in the empty space of the
Pacific. I quote:

"The futility of man's attempts to tie nature down to a set of rules, or to show
that she arranges things in percentages or obeys the law of averages, was
impressed once more upon us during this long passage. When we had reached a
point midway between Galapágos and Mangareva, with the nearest land, Easter
Island, 800 miles away to the south, and were in a five degree square where the
pilot chart showed 52 per cent of south-east wind and 48 per cent of east wind,
and no calms, the wind fell lighter and lighter; the bow wave, which had roared
day and night without a pause for the past 1,500 miles, dropped to a chuckle as
our speed slackened, and finally died away as *Wanderer*, quite becalmed, stood
upright above her own reflection. The sea changed from wind-ruffled dark blue
to a colour so matching the sky that one could scarcely see the boundary between
them, and the stationary clouds were mirrored in it. Apart from the listless
flapping of the idle nylon spinnakers, the silence was profound. There was some
swell, of course, for the open oceans are never quite free from that, but it was
longer and lower than usual, a gentle undulation; so we were able to launch the

dinghy in order that I might row away to see what our small ship looked like becalmed in an empty ocean, something neither of us had ever done before.

"At sea I do not think either of us is normally conscious of the smallness of our ship, or suffers from a feeling of loneliness. There is nothing to scale her by; she is sturdy and compact, the centre of our universe for the time being; we have each other for company, and our time is fully occupied. But when I had rowed a hundred yards or so away from *Wanderer*, I began to realize how small she was; she looked curiously frail and vulnerable, and very beautiful, out there on the silent, slowly heaving ocean beneath an immensity of sky. Her smallness was emphasized by the length of time her hull was hidden from my view by the intervening swell, and the peculiar angles she assumed when she did come into sight, for there was no straight or steady line anywhere on which to fix my eye. Having taken my photographs, I remembered that the sea on which I was float-ing in my cockleshell dinghy was more than two miles deep, and although one can drown just as easily in six feet of water as in two miles of it, I suddenly felt scared of I don't know what, and rowed back to *Wanderer* rather faster than I had rowed away. As Susan grabbed the dinghy painter she said:

" 'I'm glad you are back. We don't seem to have been so far away from one another since we left home.' "

These two books, no less than the others in this book, make fascinating read-ing, and I hope I have said enough to give a general impression of them. So I will conclude with two more quotations, both from the second book. The first describes the taking of *Wanderer* through the Suez Canal. The second, appro-priately, I feel, for the last British circumnavigator in this book, describes the run up the English Channel at the end of the voyage.

Let us join *Wanderer*, then, lying at anchor off the monument at the southern entrance to the Canal.

"Having heard that Egypt is a difficult country for a visiting yacht, and that the formalities and paper work in connexion with a transit of the canal are formidable, we had in advance engaged the services of shipping agents—the first time that we had done so, although in the past some had, unasked, kindly given us assistance. The British firm of Messrs Hull, Blyth & Co. did every possible thing to smooth our transit, and looked after us with fatherly care at both ends of the canal and refused to make any charge.

"There are one north-bound and two south-bound convoys each day. A yacht starts her transit at the tail end of a convoy, normally taking two days and stopping for a night at Ismailia on Lake Timsah, about half-way through, for even if she could maintain convoy speed ($7\frac{1}{2}$ knots) she would be unable to carry the huge searchlight which is compulsory for night movement in the canal. But as the convoys were still running late when we left Suez, we had to make two stops instead of one, the first being at El Kabret, where the Great and Little Bitter Lakes merge, and the second at Ismailia. That, incidentally, was the place at which we had planned to stay for a month or more to allow the worst part of the winter to pass before we emerged into the Mediterranean, for the anchorage there is clean and safe and the place is quiet. I had in advance asked for permission to do this, and so had our agents; but permission was refused, and I was advised that the only places at which we might linger were Suez or Port Said.

"We had looked forward to the transit with some misgivings, for we had heard frightening stories of the awful things that could happen to little ships when meeting big ones in the canal. It was during the morning of the second day that we met our first south-bound convoy, and this was the moment Susan and I had been dreading. The leading ship, a big Frenchman, appeared to be pushing a considerable amount of water ahead of herself, and seemed from a distance almost to fill the canal. We edged in towards the western bank, steering inside the small buoys which mark the edge of the deep channel. Up we rose on the advancing wave reaching its summit just before the ship's great flaring bow came abeam, then sank gently into the trough which followed, where the water was sucked away from the canal's steep bank. A breaker followed the trough along the shore, and then came the quarter-wave to lift us up again, but not so high as the bow-wave had done. There appeared to be no tendency for *Wanderer* to be sucked or slewed in any direction, and within a few moments the high steel wall of the ship had slid harmlessly past, and our attention was directed to the next ship of the convoy, a huge Dutch tanker flying light. The disturbance she made was even more alarming as we saw it approaching, but it proved to be no more difficult to negotiate than had been that of the Frenchman, and as she slid past a voice from high up on her bridge hailed us: 'Good luck! Be careful.' A tanker of that size when going the other way laden can pay as much as £11,000 in canal dues. Ship after ship—different shapes and sizes, different colour schemes, different flags—went by in procession at five-minute intervals, and the last to go was President Nasser's graceful steam yacht—there are some advantages in being a dictator.

"No dues are charged for small vessels using the canal, and although pilotage is compulsory—one pilot goes only as far as Ismailia, another one taking over there for the run to Port Said—no charge is made for that. Both our pilots were Egyptian; they spoke little English, but seemed to know their business. Although the 87-mile canal cuts for most of its length through flat, desert country, we found much to interest us: ships, dredgers, signal stations, the one and only swing bridge, and even some fishing dinghies and up-river racing fours. For much of the way we had a breeze well forward of the beam, and were able to keep our sails full to assist the motor."

Like William Robinson, the Hiscocks found that the Mediterranean lived up to its reputation and produced a couple of gales. They were given real V.I.P. treatment at Malta, and spent some time indulging in "real Mediterranean yachting" of the drinking wine through the afternoon and evening type. However, in spite of such pleasant interludes Hiscock writes ". . . with either a lot too much wind or not enough, and frequently with a tiresome, steep swell, we did not find more than five days of enjoyable sailing in the whole 2,500 miles of that long sea".

While in Gibraltar (which they found "a very dull place"!) the Hiscocks lay alongside a cutter called *Alano* belonging to Fred and Joan Georgeson, who were on their way back to England with a friend as crew. The evening before leaving they were entertained by the Hiscocks aboard *Wanderer* and treated to an evening of tape-recordings of South Sea Island magic. The next morning Georgeson announced that they were now not going back to England. On passing through Gibraltar Strait, they intended to turn "left" instead of "right", and keep going for the West Indies and Tahiti. The Pacific Island music had made another conquest.

The Hiscocks, however, turned right and stood out into the North Atlantic in light airs to try to pick up a westerly slant to take them to Ushant and the English Channel. And so they eventually arrived off the South Cornish coast in heavy rain, and wind that freshened right up to Force 8—a real English welcome! It was August Bank Holiday as they approached the Eddystone light, and the wind blew and the rain rained all day, until in the evening it stopped miraculously, and here let us join them.

"In the evening the rain stopped, and there, clear-cut against the background of Devonshire hills, stood the thin, grey pencil of the Eddystone lighthouse only a few miles away. The wind by then had moderated a little, and as there was no future in remaining hove-to, and slowly fore-reaching towards the shore, for the forecast promised more gales to come, we bore away for the Start and the run up Channel.

"Night was falling as we hurried past Bolt Head, black and sinister, and as we passed the Salcombe entrance, clear above the noise of wind and sea came the double explosion of the life-boat maroons. A few minutes later, when we had brought the Prawle abeam, I saw what I took to be the lights of the Salcombe life-boat coming out; they passed astern and vanished seaward in the rain which had started to fall again.

"Off the Start the wind resumed gale force, but as it was blowing obliquely off the land the sea was not too heavy, and throughout the night we ran fast on our way to clear Portland Bill by seven miles. The rain continued all night, but it did not much reduce visibility, and as we were just inside the shipping lane we had nothing to worry about. At breakfast time, with the tide against us, we had the Bill bearing north, the wind had dropped a little, and soon dropped more, and at noon when we beat into Studland Bay there was only a gentle breeze, and soon there was a little sunshine to help dry our wet things. We had put in there for a rest and a tidy-up after being at sea for twenty-one days, and we had a wonderfully silent, smooth, and sleep-filled night. The passage home had certainly been a slow one, for we had made good only 1,130 miles in those three weeks.

"Next morning, 8 August, we found a moderate west wind with showers and some sunshine as we ran under full sail across Poole Bay towards the Needles. How jolly the English scene looked; the land was green, the sea was green, and all around were yachts, the first we had seen for many a day.

"In the early afternoon *Wanderer* entered Yarmouth, her home port, with the ensigns of the seventeen countries she had visited flying in a colourful string from her starboard upper crosstree. News of her approach had, apparently, been sent ahead from the Needles, for some of the yachts in the little harbour were dressed overall and blew their sirens as she entered. Charlie Attrill, the harbourmaster, met us and led us to our berth, where he took our lines and soon we were secure. Everyone was so very kind that our eyes were a little damp."

I will end this chapter with Hiscock's description of how he and his wife came to make their second world voyage. Its message is plain: ". . . there's really nothing to stop you . . ."

". . . often as we travelled on the ferry between the mainland and the Isle of Wight, where we live, we looked out through Hurst Narrows and beyond the Needles lighthouse to the western horizon, knowing that we had only to slip out through those narrows in *Wanderer III* and keep going in a south-westerly direction to reach in time the area where the warm trade winds blow: they could carry us on over the blue and rolling sea until one day a landfall with a strange-sounding name—perhaps some colourful island with gleaming beaches, leaning palms, and haunting music (here our thoughts dwelt particularly on the South Pacific)—lifted out of the sea ahead. The salt water that washes the shores of the Isle of Wight could also break on the barrier reef of Tahiti.

"On our earlier voyage we had made a chain of friends around the world; what a pleasure it would be for us to visit them again, and what a surprise for them! But we must not keep too closely to our earlier track; there were many, many places we could not touch at then, but would wish to visit now, and this time, maybe, we would have to accept (chiefly for reasons of self-respect) the challenge of the Red Sea, instead of taking the earlier, and easier, way home round the Cape of Good Hope. But the Panama Canal would have to see us again, as it is the only reasonable way for a small sailing vessel to reach the Pacific.

"A hundred yards or so up the creek above the bridge at Yarmouth *Wanderer* lay idly, and perhaps impatiently, swinging on her mooring to the tide, and although a fair amount of work was needed to make her in all respects ready for sea again, much of it could be done with our own hands. It should not be difficult to find a tenant to look after our house and garden. I could not write and illustrate any more books until I had something fresh to write about and photograph (this time, we said, we would also try our hands at movie making and tape recording), and the books I had written were at the time bringing in royalties enough at least to enable us to start the trip, after which I must earn by writing articles. Indeed, we thought of every possible reason and excuse for doing what in our hearts we longed to do. The difficulties, the dangers, and the discomforts —the problems of pilotage among coral reefs, the handling of the ship in bad weather, the long, dark nights when it hurts to keep awake and steer a careful compass course, the heat, the flies, the mosquitoes, and the officials of the ports —seemed just then of no great importance. In short, we were getting itchy feet.

"That disease might have taken longer to develop properly had it not been for the women of Rochdale. Our agents had engaged us to give a show to the Rochdale Women's Luncheon Club in the town hall. For the past ten days we had been travelling in the Midlands and the North, giving one and sometimes two shows a day, so perhaps we were a little jaded and easily upset; but it did seem thoughtless of the Rochdale ladies to have failed to black out the room in which we were to show our slides, particularly as the screen had been placed between two bright and inaccessible windows (the curtains, they said, had been sent away to be cleaned), and in loud voices to discuss one another's hats throughout the talk.

"That evening we had to change trains at Todmorden railway station, and while we waited we discussed the women of Rochdale, the children in Burnley library (who throw things), and the Rothwell Teachers' and Parents' Association (who fidget and rattle coffee-cups), forgetting for the moment our wonderful reception in the Caird Hall, Dundee, where they turned out 1,800 strong and applauded every slide, and the grand affair in Church House, Westminster, to which a distinguished and appreciative company came.

"For a little while there was silence between us, and I wondered idly what new discomforts our hotel would produce that night. A fire burned red in the huge bogie stove, the smoke-grimed posters looked yellow in the light from a single hissing gas mantle; our fellow travellers stamped their feet on the dirty floor and whistled tunelessly, and from the foggy night outside came the mournful hoot of a locomotive and the clatter of shunting goods wagons.

" 'Well,' said Susan presently, 'I think we ought to make another voyage in *Wanderer* while we can. There's really nothing to stop us.' "

It would be hard to find a better description of that sudden urge to "close the door behind you and go sea voyaging", and it is a fitting ending for the circumnavigations and cruises in this book.

I have added an appendix on sailing in bad weather which will, I hope, be of interest, to some maybe of help, but the very last words of the book, expressing so well what it is all about, I have, in all humility, left to Kenneth Grahame's "Seafaring Rat".

APPENDIX I

Some remarks on Sailing small boats in bad weather

The new-comer to sailing often makes the discovery that steering a boat seems to be much easier than he had imagined. Sitting blithely at the helm, he thinks this is easy! It is probable, however, that some other vessels of similar shape and size overtake him, sailing the same course. Try as he will, these other boats seem to be able to sail much faster than he can. Our new-comer has just had his first lesson in helmsmanship. He begins to realize the extent of his ignorance.

As he progresses he will enter his boat for races, or if cruising is his aim he will become ambitious and venture offshore. Whatever he chooses one thing is quite certain, and that is that he will meet sooner or later with bad weather.

The handling of a small boat in bad weather is something which can really only be acquired through experience and practice, and once acquired gives a wonderful feeling of confidence. However, those who have written down their experiences and theories about handling small ships in bad weather have left us a basic code of behaviour which, once learnt, can then be adapted to the circumstances at the time. Handling a boat in bad weather falls into three categories. The first is when you can keep sailing your course, although reefed, the second is when you are forced to run before the wind, and the third is when you have to heave-to or lie-to under a sea anchor. Let us consider these three stages in that order.

We are sailing to windward on the port tack and the wind, which has been freshening, has reached a strength where we have considered it necessary to put a reef in the mainsail and maybe also set a smaller jib.

Most boats can be steered easily enough in smooth water. It is when freshening winds and steeper seas create strains that steering becomes harder, in more ways than one. If you are sailing to windward, the stronger winds will cause your boat to heel. This means that she will carry "weather helm" and will try to come up into the wind. The more she heels the greater the lack of balance. The good helmsman will so steer his boat that she will not luff up too much and starve herself of wind, nor sail too freely (off the wind) and consequently heel too much. When it comes to the point when this essential balance can no longer be achieved by the helm alone, then the sails must be reefed to reduce the pressure and strains.

Another obstacle when sailing to windward in a strong wind is provided by waves. It is a golden rule that one must always keep the boat moving, because if you allow her to lose way or be stopped she will be at the mercy of the wind and sea. The question of the best way to deal with large on-coming seas when sailing to windward is a good debating subject round the yacht-club fire or in the cabin of your boat. There are, like most things in sailing, conflicting views. For example, there are many who hold that an approaching wave with foaming crest should be met head-on. If this can be done and way kept upon the boat, there is no danger. It only becomes dangerous when your vessel has stopped and is at the mercy of the elements.

There are many, however, who hold that it is better to twist and turn in the seas so as to avoid the worst without losing way. When the seas are big the helmsman bears away a little so as to take the force of them sideways rather than bows-on. Taking them bows-on tends to stop the boat, because the whole force of the sea and its steep foreside is pitched directly against her, while her own speed merely adds to the blow. By bearing away and taking the sea on the beam you reduce these forces and are able to keep way on, so that it is a matter of a moment to bear up on your course again as soon as the big wave has passed harmlessly beneath you.

There are so many factors to be taken into consideration. The shape, buoyancy and manoeuvrability of the boat, the size and type of sea, height and length of the waves, that it is impossible to lay down hard and fast rules, apart from the golden one already mentioned, "Keep the boat moving".

Let us now imagine that the wind instead of being ahead is well abaft the beam. This point of sailing, the "broad reach", is the fastest for most boats, but when the seas are big it can also be the most difficult. This is because the seas are coming at you on the after quarter of your ship nearest the wind (the weather quarter), and the result is that she is lifted up aft. She will want to bury her bows in the trough of the wave ahead as the next succeeding wave lifts her stern. This tends to make the boat turn up into the wind or "gripe", and the experienced helmsman, aware of the dangers of this in such conditions, will correct this tendency with the helm in good time. If he were to apply correcting helm too late, he could find it wellnigh impossible to stop his boat shooting into the wind. If this does happen, the sails lose the wind and start to shake violently and the boat stops. Under conditions of very strong winds this would place the boat in a position of danger, since, having no way on her, she would fall off and lie in the trough of the seas, temporarily helpless until way could be got upon her. It will therefore be very clear that on this point of sailing great care and judgement are called for.

Supposing now that we have had to put our vessel before the gale and "run for it". If sailing with a quartering wind is the most difficult, sailing with a wind of gale force aft is certainly the most dangerous. There are three dangers. The first is when your vessel's weight aft so disturbs the following seas that they break heavily on board; often sweeping the boat from stern to bow. This is called being "pooped". The second danger is when your boat, rushing down the face of a wave, tends at the hollow to turn so as to bring both wind and sea on the beam. The yacht, being heeled, will dip her boom in the water, which may start to pull the boat over. With the boom in the water, the rudder is useless. This manoeuvre, which obviously if allowed to occur puts the vessel in danger, is called "broaching-to". The third danger, of which more later, is that of an accidental gybe.

The question arises, therefore, how can these dangers be avoided. As far as the first two are concerned, the largest seas can usually be dealt with by steering so that the boat presents her stern to the sea. If the seas are so great that you cannot sufficiently control your boat's movements with the tiller, you should not be running, but should heave-to. The third danger, that of gybing, should not arise, if you are careful to keep the wind slightly on the quarter rather than directly astern. However, in bringing the stern towards the seas in the way we have described, you will, of course, also be bringing the wind more directly aft, and indeed you may well at times have the wind blowing from the lee side—that is on the same side of the yacht as the mainsail.

When sailing downwind you will also probably be rolling, and it is when the roll of the ship lifts the main boom and the wind happens to be on the lee side that it can whip the mainsail violently across. This can under certain conditions get you into real difficulties. The boom, swinging over with great force, will take up hard against the running backstay and may part it or snap off the boom or even endanger the mast. So that of the things to avoid in heavy weather, an accidental gybe is certainly one!

The answer lies in very careful watching of the wind's direction. Keep it over the quarter opposite to the mainsail, and if you have to bring the boat's stern to a large sea, put her back on a safe course as soon as you possibly can. I mentioned that an accidental gybe is often made more likely by rolling. Rolling is one of the bugbears of sailing downwind. Boats which have a broad beam roll more than narrow boats when running. If the yacht has a centreboard, lowering it will help, and so will hauling in the mainsheet a little. It is a good idea to top the boom up with the topping lift, so that it will keep out of the water when the boat rolls.

Providing that she keeps in deep water and well clear of the land, any normal, well–balanced yacht will be quite safe, as long as she is sensibly handled. When the seas get too big for her and too much water is coming aboard it will be necessary to heave-to. This consists in trimming the reefed mainsail and helm as if to sail to windward while the small jib is hauled a'weather. The yacht then lies comparatively quietly. Heaving-to when running needs cool judgement. For one thing, it is very easy to underestimate the force of the wind. When a yacht is running her own speed reduces that of the wind as felt by those on board. Consequently it is a commonly made mistake to put off heaving-to for too long. When running it is good practice to bring the wind on to the beam from time to time, so as to check how much it is increasing. The appearance of the sea, however, will usually be a guide. As a gale increases the seas appear steeper and more threatening, especially those directly astern. When you decide to heave-to you should wait for a comparatively calm patch. There is an old superstition that every seventh wave is larger than its six predecessors. Be that as it may, a particularly large wave is usually followed by a succession of smaller waves, and that gives you your chance to put the helm hard down and round into the wind and heave her to before the next big sea.

Most boats, when hove-to, tend to range about, pointing towards the wind, so that the mainsail flaps, until the backed headsail pushes the bows off once more. Some yachts heave-to a great deal better than others. Some are very bad at it, and are better off lying to a sea anchor like that used by Captain Voss with *Tilikum* during her world cruise. Very light-displacement yachts do not as a rule heave-to well, but this does not mean they are not suitable for cruising offshore. Indeed, a long slim yacht will be able to run for longer than her shorter, heavier sister, for she will leave a smaller wake to disturb the following seas and cause them to break. Some fine cruises have been made in light craft; converted six metres and in Dragons, for example. The whole principle of heaving-to, or lying-to a sea anchor is to reduce the speed of the vessel to a minimum while retaining control of her. Once the boat's movement through the water has been so reduced, the danger from breaking seas is greatly minimized.

The usual sea anchor consists of a conical canvas bag, open at both ends. The larger end is kept open by an iron ring or by diagonal cross bars. To use it, the ship is brought to the wind with headsail stowed and the sea anchor paid out over the weather bow. It is a good plan to have a short length of chain in the way of the fairlead to prevent chafe. The mainsail is then stowed. If the vessel is two-masted, a small riding sail may be set aft, and is very effective. A small tripping-line on the smaller end of the sea anchor enables it to be hauled in easily by that end when the weather moderates. A sea anchor can also be used to check a vessel's speed. It acts as a brake when towed with the large end forward.

Some yachtsmen advocate the use of a trysail, a small heavy sail of triangular shape that may be set in place of the mainsail, but there is also a powerful school of thought which holds that the cruising yacht should have a sufficiently tough mainsail to stand up to very hard winds when well reefed. Then, when the weather gets too bad, so that the vessel will not heave-to safely, hand the jib, stream the sea anchor and stow the mainsail.

Another method which can be used to assist a boat in gale weather is the use of oil bags. Oil is allowed to drip from bags over the bows on each side, and has a calming effect on the sea. I have never personally used it, and the only yachtsman I met who had was more impressed with the appalling oily mess he got himself into than other features. But "pouring oil upon troubled waters" would not have become so firmly fixed in our vocabulary were it not in reasonably common and effective usage, though, I suspect, in older times.

When one is overtaken by bad weather at sea it is of tremendous value to have had some experience, for then you have the confidence which will not only help you to handle your boat in a seamanlike manner, but will also be felt by and greatly encourage your crew. The best helmsmen are good seamen and understand all the interacting and complex ways of a ship at sea. And the more knowledge we have, the fuller is our enjoyment of the "best of all sports".

APPENDIX II

The "Call" by the "Seafaring Rat"

"There, sooner or later, the ships of all seafaring nations arrive; and there, at its destined hour, the ship of my choice will let go her anchor. I shall take my time, I shall tarry and bide, till at last the right one lies waiting for me, warped out into midstream, loaded low, her bowsprit pointing down harbour. I shall slip on board, by boat or along hawser; and then one morning I shall wake to the song and tramp of the sailors, the clink of the capstan, and the rattle of the anchor-chain coming merrily in. We shall break out the jib and foresail, the white houses on the harbour side will glide slowly past us as she gathers steerage-way and the voyage will have begun! As she forges towards the headland she will clothe herself with canvas; and then, once outside, the sounding slap of great green seas as she heels to the wind, pointing South!

"And you, you will come too, young brother; for the days pass, and never return, and the South still waits for you. Take the Adventure, heed the call, now ere the irrevocable moment passes! 'Tis but a banging of the door behind you, a blithesome step forward, and you are out of the old life and into the new! Then some day, some day long hence, jog home here if you will, when the cup has been drained and the play has been played, and sit down by your quiet river with a store of goodly memories for company. You can easily overtake me on the road, for you are young, and I am ageing and go softly. I will linger, and look back; and at last I will surely see you coming, eager and light-hearted, with all the South in your face!"

[From "The Wind in the Willows"—Kenneth Grahame]